British History in Perspective

General Editor: Jeremy Black

PUBLISHED TITLES

(List continued overleaf)

Please note that a sister series, *Social History in Perspective*, is available.
It covers the key topics in social, cultural and religious history.

British History in Perspective
Series Standing Order
ISBN 0–333–71356–7 hardcover
ISBN 0–333–69331–0 paperback
(outside North America only)

You can receive future titles in this series as they are published by placing a standing order. Please contact your bookseller or, in case of difficulty, write to us at the address below with your name and address, the title of the series and the ISBN quoted above.

Customer Services Department, Macmillan Distribution Ltd
Houndmills, Basingstoke, Hampshire RG21 6XS, England

SCOTTISH NATIONALITY

MURRAY G. H. PITTOCK

palgrave

First published 2001 by
PALGRAVE
Houndmills, Basingstoke, Hampshire RG21 6XS and
175 Fifth Avenue, New York, N. Y. 10010
Companies and representatives throughout the world

PALGRAVE is the new global academic imprint of
St. Martin's Press LLC Scholarly and Reference Division and
Palgrave Publishers Ltd (formerly Macmillan Press Ltd).

ISBN 0–333–72663–4 hardback
ISBN 0–333–72664–2 paperback

This book is printed on paper suitable for recycling and
made from fully managed and sustained forest sources.

A catalogue record for this book is available
from the British Library.

Library of Congress Cataloging-in-Publication Data
Pittock, Murray.
    Scottish nationality / Murray G. H. Pittock.
        p. cm. — (British history in perspective)
    Includes bibliographical references (p.) and index.
    ISBN 0–333–72663–4
      1. Scotland—Politics and government. 2. National
    characteristics, Scottish. 3. Nationalism—Scotland–
    –History. 4. Scotland—Relations—England. 5. England–
    –Relations—Scotland. 6. Home rule—Scotland. I. Title.
    II. British history in perspective (Palgrave (Firm))
    DA765 .P58 2001
    941.1—dc21
                                              2001019442

10   9   8   7   6   5   4   3   2   1
10   09 08 07 06 05 04 03 02 01

Printed in China

For Jeremy Black

CONTENTS

PREFATORY REMARKS

This book is a brief and condensed study of the phenomenon of Scottish nationality, patriotism and identity over the whole history of the country: its purpose is to provide a general overview which will enable the interested reader to turn to more specialist studies as appropriate. *Scottish Nationality* is a complement to books such as Norman Davies's *The Isles* (1999), in its reading of the particular issues of Scottishness and the nature of what is now Scotland's dialogue with the rest of these Isles throughout the last two millennia. Incomplete as a survey which covers so much ground will necessarily be, it is the aim of the author that the student who reads this book should emerge with a broad understanding of the history, significance and current state of Scottish nationality. In particular, its later chapters deal with the long debate in Scotland on Home Rule, a debate which, although it was often overlooked elsewhere, has had a significant impact on the nature of constitutional change since 1997. This book, then, aims to fulfil the brief of the *British History in Perspective* series by placing an account of the experience of Scottish nationality, stated in broad terms, before a wider readership, rather than by trying to subsume it under an all-encompassing narrative of the Isles, better done elsewhere.

In a work of this kind, I am naturally indebted not only to the writings of many scholars, but also to their conversation. Figures such as Alexander Broadie, Ted Cowan, Cairns Craig, Tom Devine, Owen Dudley Edwards, Richard Finlay, Colin Kidd, Michael Lynch, David McCrone, Allan Macinnes and Lindsay Paterson have transformed the study of Scottish culture in the last twenty years. The launch by Edwin Morgan of the joint Glasgow–Strathclyde School of Scottish Studies in Glasgow in November 1999, which created the largest school of Scottish Studies in the world, is one of the latest chapters in this process, of which I am proud to have been a part. In addition, the particular symbiosis in

Scottish society between scholars, opinion-formers and politicians has been a very important resource. Here I am grateful to Colin Bell, Allan Burnett, Pat Kane, Joan McAlpine, Neil MacCormick, George Rosie, Paul Scott, Cameron Simpson, David Stenhouse and many others.

External perspectives are in some ways the most necessary thing of all to have in discussing nationality, so easy is it to slide into parochialism or to trumpet as unique achievements and processes common in other countries. In this area I have benefited enormously from the work and conversation of Jeremy Black, Jonathan Clark, Howard Erskine-Hill, Brean Hammond, Tom Keymer, Joep Leersens, Mícheál MacCraith, Frank McLynn and Claude Rawson. Closer to home, my wife, Anne, has provided me again and again with valuable perspectives which have altered my approach. I am grateful to her, and to my daughters Lexie and Davina, for their good nature and patience.

A broad spread of authorities have been leant on in the construction of this book. In particular I am indebted to the work of Geoffrey Barrow, Archie Duncan, Richard Finlay, Bruce Lenman, Michael Lynch, James Mitchell and Lindsay Paterson. The faults that follow are my own.

Bearsden, May 2000

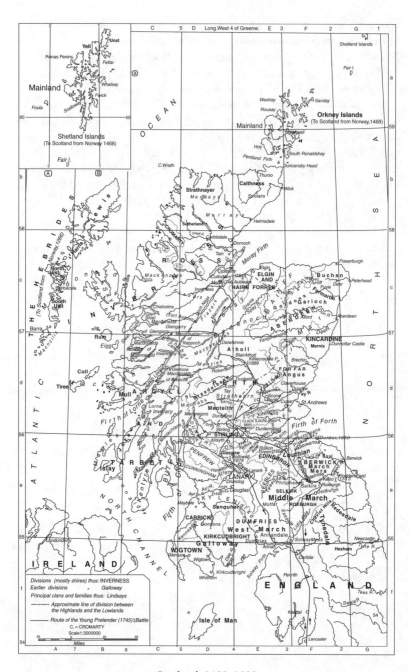

Scotland, 1488–1688

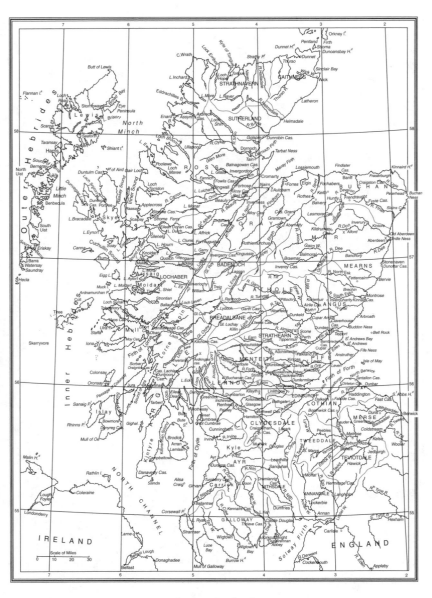

Ancient Scotland

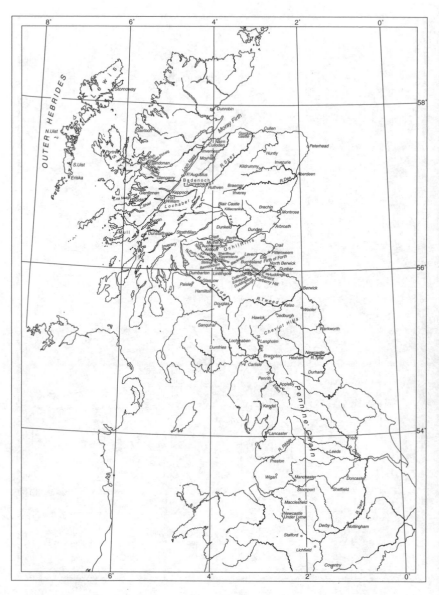

Scotland and Northern England: The Jacobite Campaigns

INTRODUCTION

Whoever – whatever man – be he black, white, red, or yellow,
the moment he identifies with the institutions of Scotland,
that moment he became a member of the Scottish nation . . .
Patrick Dove (1853)[1]

The subject of this book is Scottish nationality, defined in the broadest
sense in terms of the external, objectifiable ways in which ideas or feel-
ings of Scottish difference are and have been articulated or displayed. In
this Introduction, I shall outline the major issues surrounding Scottish
identity today, before going on to examine the historical development of
the Scottish nation and the cultural and political manifestations of Scottish
distinctiveness which have accompanied it through time. In doing so,
a brief summary of what seem the salient and contributive points of
Scottish history will be provided: insofar as the interpretation of these is
controversial, this controversy is most often itself a function of Scottish
nationality and the debate over what it means. History is produced and
consumed on at least three levels: the professional, the popular and the
sociocultural. Academics, popular historians and the cultural interpretation
of certain historic moments (e.g. William Wallace, the Rising of 1745) in
Scottish society at large, are more or less open to controversy in direct
proportion to the event's importance to the present. Where there is little
of this in history at large (as in certain aspects of the political history of
Greece and Rome) enduring textbooks are frequently reissued with
upgraded contents, sometimes over as long as a century; where controversy is fierce, there can be a hail of books and articles with widely varying
interpretations. Sometimes (as in revisionist accounts of the reign of
Mary Tudor) this is a mainly academic debate; sometimes (as in the case

1

of the Rising of 1745) it is conducted at every level of historical writing and through the manner of its social consumption. The consciousness of Scottish nationality itself depends on the interpretation of such events as the Wars of Independence, the Reformation, and so on, as well as on the social contexts and processes which surrounded them. Any controversy this book may inspire will thus endorse its central subject: the nature of the historic genesis of Scottish nationality and its results today.

Considerations of space will constrain me from spending too much time on theories of nationalism: these are dealt with in greater detail in my *Celtic Identity and the British Image* (1999). Suffice it for present purposes to say that the present author has more sympathy with the historical position of nations as mediaeval realities espoused by Susan Reynolds, John Cannon, Adrian Hastings (*The Construction of Nationhood* (1997)) and others than with the over-determined Anderson/Gellner view which sees them as products of the late eighteenth and early nineteenth centuries: in this context, Benedict Anderson's articulation of the 'imagined community' as 'explaining how we can claim common cause and common attachment to people we have never met' reaches back much further than the early modern means of communication and dissemination which he regards as crucially important.[2] Gellner's similar view that 'Nationalism . . . is sociologically rooted in modernity' likewise lays too much weight on theoretical socio-economic transitions, and too little on the histrical evidence. 'Nation' is a much older word than its derivatives such as 'nationalist' (1715) and 'nationality' (1691). On the field of Bannockburn, Robert Bruce told his army that 'Saint Andrew and the martyr Saint Thomas shall fight today with the saints of Scotland for the honour of their country and their nation' – and even if this report was inaccurate, it is mediaeval.[3] As Adrian Hastings argues, Gellner ignores 'medieval and early modern use of the term nation in a recognizably modern sense, not least in the Bible'.[4] It is thus, as Geoffrey Barrow tells us, 'no accident [that] Barbour puts into King Robert's mouth on the eve of Bannockburn the very words of Judas Maccabeus'.[5] Undoubtedly Anderson and Gellner are right insofar as a mass public culture gives a different emphasis to nationhood in the post-Enlightenment period: but this is only one of the five points of nationality identified by Anthony Smith in 1991 (a historic territory and homeland; common myths and memories; common mass culture; common legal rights and a common economy).[6] As Graeme Morton argues, following the Anderson/Gellner methodology suggests that Scotland had no nineteenth-century nationalism, unlike Smith's more flexible measure of 'any concept of the nation' as 'wholly dependent on how the cultural attributes of that nation are shaped and mobilised'. Colin Kidd's view that nationality in the earlier periods was the product of a network of non-national loyalties, often dynastic, has much to commend it (is it not still sometimes partly true – many think Britishness closely linked to the Royal Family): but although the mediaevals had no equivalent to the current obsession with identity politics, there are certainly signs of a sense of collective nationality in times of stress. Judas Maccabeus fought to defend the holy places; but he was nonetheless a Jewish patriot.[7]

Moreover, the concept of 'imagining' the nation (Anderson, 1983, 1991) lies dangerously close to the debunking potential of 'inventing' it (Hobsbawm and Ranger, 1983), with its concomitant idea that a mass of people can accept a fraud perpetrated by a publicist or creative artist as part of their own identity. This is still a woefully common view: for example, in the idea that Sir Walter Scott tricked the Scottish Lowland public into imagining that the kilt was their national dress, a view so emplaced as now to be a *canard* of the history of Scottish culture, and especially potent when combined with the assertion that the kilt itself is a recent 'invention'.[8] Such a view continues to have a powerful popular presence, from the depiction of the Jacobite Risings to exhibitions such as *O Caledonia! Sir Walter Scott and the Creation of Scotland* (Scottish National Portrait Gallery, 1999). Yet not only are there continental images and accounts of similar dress worn by Scots dating back to the mediaeval period: there is also longstanding evidence of tartan and the kilt being used as a sign of traditional, authentic Scottishness from at least 1596, and especially evident in the Jacobite century. As Michael Lynch observes, 'a cult of "tartanry" at the royal court [in Holyrood] briefly flowered in the 1680s'.[9] Useful as the concepts of 'imagining' or 'inventing' the nation may be, adopting them without interrogation places too much power in the hands of creative writers and the impact of created narratives (did Yeats 'invent' Ireland, for example, as some would claim?), and too little on the lived experience and shared traditions of national communities: the invention of Scotland or Britain draws on these lived traditions, but it alters them, and requires critical questioning rather than explicatory acceptance.[10] There is ample evidence that the concept of a 'nation' in the Middle Ages was not purely an elite construct: when Blin Hary (1440–93) wrote in *The Wallace* that 'brave true ancient Scots' do not wish to see 'the Saxon blood in Scotland reign',[11] he was putting a gloss on a popular reaction which can be found at every level: from continental commentators remarking on Scottish anti-Englishness to the instructions of the Aberdeen authorities to the townsfolk in 1511 to release an Englishman who 'has only come to Town to perform his pilgrimage to St. Ninian'.[12] What Homi Bhabha calls 'the narcissism of self-generation' in national narratives is an idea meaningless to those who lived before 1900, probably 1945, and they do not deserve to have it foisted on them.[13] When Robert Bruce in 1296 opined that 'no man holds his own flesh and blood in hatred' and that he must return to fight with 'my own people and the nation in which I was born' he was making a statement accessible then and now: if it was a 'narrative' it was so in no more than the sense in which as individuals have biographies, nations have histories. Likewise, Baldred Bisset's plea to Rome on behalf of Scottish nationality in 1301 may have played down the Pictish contribution, but if it was a lawyer's case, it was one based on what Scots believed to be their own history, one of antiquity of national rights acquired long before the Saxon invaders entered southern Britain.[14] If we entirely invent ourselves, then we can be said to invent our nation: but this sense of total existential freedom from our family and wider environments is illusory. Contemporary theorists of nationalism often implicitly deplore the Sartrian 'bad faith' of unselfconscious patriotism: but these intellectual tools are themselves a product of the environment of our own century, and there is little reason but novelty why we should prefer them to others: 'Of Ingland the nacion Es Inglis man thar in commun' was well said in 1300.[15]

What, then, underlies the popularity of this stress on choosing identities, so popular since the 1970s? It is part of the same trend as terms like 'virtual reality': the acknowledgement of shallow political, cultural and moral opinions moulded, manipulated and bombarded by an exponentially expanding electronic media. It is in a different disciplinary field a commonplace of our age that political radicalism (as opposed to single-issue protest) is in decline, and there is plenty of evidence to support this. Terms such as 'compassion overload' describe the inability to respond to real human suffering in the face of so many images of it, so few of which touch the viewer. It is from this world that the notion of identity as an existential choice derives. Oscar Wilde wisely commented that criticism is a form of autobiography, and the 'nation' as a 'virtual reality' is the autobiography of our own age.[16] Neither Scott nor Yeats, Bruce nor Wallace, Garibaldi nor Parnell had the means to influence a consumerist audience to acquire or shed beliefs at will. In this the Victorians and Edwardians knew themselves better than we. As Richard Jenkyns shows in *The Victorians and Ancient Greece* (1980), many in the British Establishment in the late nineteenth and early twentieth centuries strongly aligned themselves with Greek concepts of self-identity, based on a tradition by no means then alien to those who understood it. In Simonides' fifth-century-BC epitaph for the dead at Thermopylae ('Go tell the Spartans, passer-by/That here obedient to their laws we lie'), three elements of Smith's 1991 definition of nationalism are present: territory, community and shared laws. The Spartans defended their nation, their homes and their altars, not their narratives. It is on this basis that I propose to examine Scottish nationality, and to show 'tantae molis erat Romanam condere gentem' ('So massive was the effort to found the Roman nation'), for in the past lie the roots of all things.[17]

What is a nation? Much has been written since Ernest Renan asked the same question 140 years ago, but relatively little of it improves on his answer:

> The nation, even as the individual, is the end product of a long period of work, sacrifice and devotion . . . our ancestors have made us what we are . . . To have common glories in the past, a common will in the present; to have accomplished great things together, to wish to do so again, that is the essential condition for being a nation. A nation is a grand solidarity constituted by the sentiment of sacrifices . . .
> 'Qu'est-ce qu'une nation?'[18]

One can note that Renan does not lay great stress on ethnicity, and this is appropriate, as Scotland has never been an ethnically homogenous nation (are there many such?), which makes attempts to prove that it isn't a nation on these grounds somewhat circular and pointless. However as William Ferguson notes in his groundbreaking *The Identity of the Scottish Nation* (1998), there is a dominant influence at work: 'there can be no doubt . . . that the national identity of the Scots sprang from an earlier Gaelic tribal root that first flourished in Ireland'.[19]

If Scottish nationhood is questioned under the terms of Renan's definition, it is often on the grounds of 'common will' and 'solidarity': Scottish disagreement and ideological division have been seen by many commentators as fissures in nationality. If identity, as Edward Said and others argue, is defined by opposition, the Scottish habit of opposing each other rather than the common foe can be seen as compromising the development of a consistent sense of nationality. In the Wars of Independence (an ideological and relatively recent title for the wars of 1296–1328 and the 1330s), Scottish magnates took the English side; in the later Middle Ages, the Lords of the Isles did the same thing; from

the 1640s to the 1740s, Scotland was riven by religious and dynastic conflict, which cut across the issue of political independence, and in the end
secured its destruction. Conflict within Scotland between Scots was only
ended by the Union on this reading; and even so, the country's imagina-
tive literature continued to provide image after image of the 'divided
self' as a source for the theme of the irreconcilability of personal and
political dualities. Edwin Muir (1887–1959), one of the most sensitive
twentieth-century commentators on Scotland, wrote in *Scottish Journey*
(1935) of an Austrian mountain scene where he had witnessed 'green
snakes struggling in a death battle', commenting that

> The comparison was too swift and dramatic, I told myself, for the stubborn anger
> that burns through Scottish history; but nevertheless it would have been as
> impossible to put a stop to that at any of the disastrous turns of Scottish history...

Muir's vision is one of 'the intestine dissensions' which had continued to
'rend' Scotland throughout its history, with Scots 'fighting one another
and flying from their enemy' towards a 'final betrayal of Scotland which
made it no longer a nation'.[20] Many cultural commentators have at least to
some extent endorsed Muir's conclusion, though not always with his over-
tone of fatalism – more recently, there has been a slight but growing tendency to valorize Muir's position by glorying in perceived diversity as
normative.

In emphasizing Scottish divisions, however, four important details are
commonly neglected. First, there is a tendency not to compare Scotland
with other countries who have faced similar situations and who have
reacted fissiparously, with no 'common will': the United States both in
the war of independence and the Civil War; India; and, overwhelmingly, Ireland. Greece facing Xerxes' Persia was more divided than
Scotland ever was, and yet the issue of nationality and the Other,
Hellene and Barbarian, has been a clear-cut cultural premiss of the
West for hundreds of years. Scotland, in other words, is not necessarily
different from other countries under pressure from a stronger power
with many allurements of its own to offer. Secondly, the divisions
adduced are nearly always those of an earlier stage of history before
many modern states had securely formed; thirdly, there is a concentration on that which divides more than that which unites, with its underlying presumption of favour towards the status quo.

The fourth measure of division to an extent encompasses all the other
three. It is the quality of invention and construction, often generated

externally, which exists either to polarize internal Scottish experience or to set it in opposition to that of the rest of Britain. On one level, it can be seen in the Romantic and Victorian *Gemeinschaft/Gesellschaft* (Ferdinand Tönnies's terms) split between a rural idyll (the Highlands) and the urban, cosmopolite, impersonal world of Central Belt and English Britain.[21] Although the rural idyll was also used as an idealization of England ('the cottage small/Beside a field of grain'), its historical message of Primitivist essentialism (what Scotland truly 'is' is prehistoric, out of time, beyond the reach of world events, an Ossianic dream) is most powerfully emplaced in a Scottish context. Tourists and expatriates were and are its main consumers, in the sense that the Highlands became a playground in which their fantasies could sport. The traditional feminized characterization of the Scottish nation is subdued, and becomes a passive *Kulturnation* to be explored at leisure by the Anglo-Saxon *Staatsnation* which struts the world stage at the head of the British Empire. In the late eighteenth and nineteenth centuries, Scots living outwith the Highlands increasingly identified themselves with the Teutonic world destiny of Anglo-Saxonism and intensified the constructed images of bifurcation and division between themselves and the inhabitants of Romantic Scotland.[22]

This emphasis on polarities and division is at the heart of most accounts of Scottish nationality. Even to the extent that it reflects an underlying reality, it is easily misunderstood. To some nationalists, the Scottish National War Memorial in Edinburgh is a monument to the 'cheated dead' who suffered disproportionate casualties in England's wars;[23] to unionist Scots, it 'is a grand solidarity constituted by the sentiment of sacrifices', in Renan's terms. Yet although that solidarity may ultimately be with Britain and the wider world, it is 'national' none the less: the horrific casualty rates which show to some Scots a national betrayal, to others display how Scottish troops took a disproportionate share in winning and defending the British Empire. Both are proud of 'Scotland', nor does one think of it as a synonym for a locality merely: it is a nation with national traditions, in partnership on the international stage.[24] This view, once ubiquitous, is in decline, and there must be some doubt as to how far patriot unionism (as it will be called) can survive in a Britain without its own international, imperial dimension: this shows its irreconcilability to a merely Anglocentric Britishness.

It is thus often stated, and with some plausibility, that the rise of modern Scottish nationalism is in symbiotic relationship with the decline of the British Empire. This position is more often adopted than explored: where the underlying relationship is examined, it can be concluded that the decline of empire deprived Scots of international career opportunities which they had hitherto enjoyed, a fact of peculiar importance to a country with a 400-year history of exporting talent. Sometimes it is argued that the European Union (EU), and the concept of 'Independence in Europe' fathered on the Scottish National Party (SNP) by Jim Sillars in the 1980s, represents an alternative future in which Scottish internationalism (and, romantically, its pre-Union 'Europeanism') can be reconstituted. This is an influential view, and one which has some historical (though more limited contemporary) evidence in its support: but there are also significant coun-tervailing indicators. A single European market has brought very little change to the limited numbers of Scottish graduates seeking employment in the continental EU, while in the schools the number of pupils with a Higher grade foreign language has sunk since the 1970s. Europe is, like Gaelic bilingual signposting, a chic designer accessory to contemporary Scottish cultural nationalism not altogether sustained in society at large. Nonetheless, as in the case of Britishness, there is intermittent evidence of a Scottish wish to differentiate their identity by putting it in European terms: in a 1994 poll, 26 per cent of Conservative, 27 per cent of Liberal Demo-crat, 53 per cent of Labour and no fewer than 64 per cent of SNP support-ers in Scotland were willing to identify themselves as to some degree Scottish and European, although it is true that other findings have put the degree of indifference to Europeanism in Scotland at far higher levels.[25]

There are two other aspects to the 'decline of Empire' thesis which are, however, neglected: and both are to do with the space occupied by 'Britishness'. This important dimension of the imperial ideal is often overlooked: it is the reason why Scots were, in a manner now puzzling to their descendants, long prepared to describe themselves as 'English'. Britishness was international in scope: its cultural and political symbols belonged to New Zealander, Canadian and Scot (if not quite African) alike: in this context, to be 'British' was to be part of an international family of politics and manners, headed by England perhaps, but none-theless diverse. Sir John Seeley's effort to develop a 'Greater British' history encompassing the Britains beyond the seas was the historic counterpart to this now lost mindset, which once placed Britishness as a concept occupying the whole world, a universal space of the best in human values.[26] The Gordon Highlanders might have an 'English heart', but so too could 'The Guides at Cabul, 1879':

> SONS of the Island Race, wherever ye dwell,
>   Who speak of your fathers' battles with lips that burn,

> The deed of an alien legion hear me tell,
>   And think not shame from the hearts ye tamed to learn . . .
> To fight with a joyful courage, a passionate pride,
> To die at the last as the Guides at Cabul died.

Here even the wild native hearts, 'tamed' by Britishness, have a lesson for that very nationality, 'the Island Race', whom they 'an alien legion', have, by virtue of their heroism, now joined. Britishness is international ('wherever ye dwell') but its achievements (here at Cabul) occupy a particular part of the total space it claims as its own.[27] It was under such a cultural rubric that John Buchan was able to claim that he supported 'Scottish Nationalism' *for the sake of Britain and the Empire*', a statement almost semantically incomprehensible today.[28]

The major exhibitions of the Victorian and Georgian period sought to make this very point, both visually and in the dynamics of their organization: 'a conservative pride in local colour and tradition went well with the grand design', as Tom Nairn remarks.[29] Britishness thus then subsumed a multitude of local patriotisms, of which Scotland's was one, and an important one by virtue of its 'junior partner' status in Empire; but after the decline of the 'Britains over the seas', Scotland stood (and stands) increasingly alone in a shrinking sphere where the abstract, idealized qualities of Britishness are coming under pressure everywhere due both to the centripetal collapse of the global British ideal and a general Western increase in relativism. At the same time, British society, with no further need of an ideology of local patriotism spread throughout the Empire, became more monolithic, its dependence on key features of English class culture and the political establishment more apparent than ever: the 'new kind of patriotism' called for by Enoch Powell in 1963 did not materialize,[30] and Powell himself eventually retreated to Ulster Unionism, one of the oldest kinds of all, and a brand strongly associated with ethno-religious hatred. If this seems a surprising statement in the light of our contemporary multiculturalism, it must be noted that this too has rested on assumptions of monolithic homogeneity in 'British' society. The extent to which noted sociologists and cultural critics have subscribed to this has also been a marked tendency since the 1960s. Richard Hoggart, one of the most noteworthy commentators in these areas, began a lecture at Aberdeen in 1989 with the words 'When you go into your local branch of W. H. Smiths', apparently oblivious that there were at that time none in Scotland, while his *The Way We Live Now* (1995), though careful to formally exclude comment on

Scotland in its introduction, still in its overarching 'We' pushed an avowedly 'English' cultural agenda into every part of the British market: if Jock isn't 'We', well then he must be 'them'.[31] As Gwynfor Evans irritatedly put it in 1981:

> What is Britishness? The first thing to realise is that it is another word for Englishness ... If one asks what s the difference between English culture and British culture one realises that there is no difference. They are the same. The British language is the English language. British education is English education. British television is English television. The British press is the English press. The British Crown is the English Crown, and the Queen of Britain is the Queen of England.[32]

Evans's objections mattered less when the 'social style' of Britishness was a world civilization with international presence.[33] Once again, he is responding to the shrinkage of British space, which without an empire is all too clearly English and has no room nor need for the localism in which Wales and Scotland, together with New Zealand and Natal, could once rejoice. Both Welsh and Scotsmen played their part in designing British identity when it was international in scope: shrunk to an island, both find reasons to object to it.

This is a newer phenomenon than we think, and this brings us to the second issue relating to Britishness and space: that the development of post-imperial Britain since 1945 has hemmed Scottish institutions in by provincializing them. Lindsay Paterson's interesting conclusion in *The Autonomy of Modern Scotland* (1994) (substantively reiterated in Graeme Morton's study of nineteenth-century *Unionist-Nationalism* (1999)) was that those who lamented Scotland's lost nationhood had overlooked the fact that a good deal of the fabric of Scottish civic society had been preserved since the Union by distinctively Scottish institutions, staffed and led by Scots. This position was largely preserved throughout most of this century, but the collapse of empire combined with trends towards increasing social and personal mobility has led to greater numbers of non-Scots operating Scottish institutions: it was anxiety concerning this in the 1980s and 1990s which led to public agitation over the so-called 'Englishing' of Scotland. As a by-product of globalization it is unremarkable: but combined with the already limiting new parameters of Britishness, it appears a threat. Moreover, it is compounded by the declining influence not only of Scottish heavy industry, but also of the Scottish elites outwith Scotland. If Oxford, Cambridge and the English public schools led the way in providing the old British elite, the products of

Glasgow, Edinburgh, the merchant company and burgh grammar schools were not impossibly far behind, in an era when the big English provincial universities were newly formed or hardly existed. In the eighteenth century, for example, of 2500 entries in the *Dictionary of National Biography* who attended university, 65 per cent went to Oxbridge, over 20 per cent to Scotland (14 per cent Edinburgh) and only 15 per cent to Ireland, which had two and a half times Scotland's population. Of the 680 scientists in the period, 19 per cent went to Cambridge, 17 per cent to Oxford and 13 per cent to Edinburgh.[34] Given that the new and revised *DNB* aims to increase coverage of those from the 'peripheries', these are already impressive figures. They represent a silver-medallist, junior-partner position which can be seen elsewhere (e.g. in cabinet posts, administrative civil service appointments and even in the teaching of Scottish literature and history in English schools, both commonplace before the war) and which has been lost. The development of Scotland as a province of Britain rather than a junior partner in empire has unsurprisingly led to a rise in hostility to the British core at all but the very highest levels of Scottish society. In 1974, a poll taken on the importance of moving power away from London found 66 per cent of Scots in favour, but only 20 per cent in Yorkshire and 36 per cent in Wales. Scotland was the only one of eleven 'regions' with a majority in favour:[35] and that word 'region', seldom if ever used about Scotland before 1945 but now commonplace, itself expresses the degrading of the country within Britain and Britishness. Twenty years later, polling evidence from the 1990s mirrored these earlier findings, with 28 per cent of English regarding themselves as more English than British; 48 per cent in Wales more Welsh, and 64 per cent in Scotland more Scottish.[36] Within those claiming Scottish rather than British identity, 'Catholics are somewhat more likely than Protestants to claim Scottish national identity'.[37] In 1999, the figures are even more marked, with 77 per cent of Scots-domiciled adults backing Scottishness and only 17 per cent Britishness when faced with an 'either/or' question concerning their identity.[38]

Is the British state then in crisis, as magazine articles and newspaper reports have been intermittently stating or prophesying since the end of the 1980s? There can, of course, be no firm and fixed answer to such a question: all that can be done is to measure it by various criteria. Yves Meny, for example, argues that there are five types of crisis in the state: crises of identity, participation, distribution, penetration and legitimacy.[39] By these tokens, it is arguable that, in the post-imperial period, British identity is diminishing, although to a fluctuating extent, as is evident in times of war or national emergency or in defence of particular British institutions, such as the National Health Service (NHS) and other aspects of the newer British identity of post-war welfarism. Scotland participates in the British polity and is reasonably prosperous within it, so (leaving aside issues such as oil revenues), the second and third criteria do not operate in such a way as to provoke crisis. Arguably, penetration and legitimacy were major issues when the Conservatives governed Scotland with a rump of Scottish seats, but are so no longer, though this may only be true up to a point in the case of the penetrative power of Britishness. However, it can be argued that Scottish distinctiveness within the Union has always limited the penetrative power of British identity north of the Border, at least in certain areas. In other words, by Meny's measure, the British state is only significantly threatened in Scotland by the growing strength of 'Scottishness': but the weakness of this distinctive identity is borne witness to in the fact that it seldom manifests itself against the common British interest in foreign affairs or issues of economic power (e.g. control of oil revenues, NHS funding). In other words, restored to the international stage which was once its proper purview, Scottish pride in Britishness remains. Wolfe Tone's mantra that 'England's war is Ireland's opportunity' never did have much of a following in post-Jacobite Scotland: its absence is probably the reason both for the deeply peaceable nature of Scottish nationalism, and also its ambivalent relationship to traditional symbols of Britishness (it was the SNP who supported the 'save our Scottish Regiments' campaign in the 1990s, for example). Whether or not Scottish inferiorism is the result of external political control,[40] emergence from it into modern 'Scottishness' seldom involves any marked level of oppositionalism to the British polity, its interests and institutions. If identity is strengthened through opposition, these are not signs of great strength. Scottish Britishness is a stronger and more enduring beast than some excitable journalism gives it credit for.

Michael Hechter's 1975 study, *Internal Colonialism*, made a powerful if occasionally historically flawed case for the internal colonization of the British Isles, with the Scottish/Welsh periphery being dominated and exploited by London. Hechter's view stressed the malleability of local elites, particularly in the Scottish context: 'Because the rulers of the Scottish state were themselves culturally anglicised, their English counterparts felt it unnecessary to insist upon the total control of Scottish cultural institutions.'[41] Hechter's ideas are suggestive in the context of the Highland Clearances, and in their notion of a common 'Celtic' experience of the opposed colonizing 'other' in the histories of Scotland, Wales and Ireland.[42]

In cultural terms, Scottish national feeling at the end of the millennium is both passionate and unfocused. Sophisticated commentators are able to explain away the lack of branding and imaging (well known elsewhere in the EU) in public buildings and social space as a mature ease with postmodern cultural flux; more evident, however, is a lack of interest in historical precedent and an unwillingness to aspire to its creative reinterpretation at the highest levels. The arguments over the cost of the Scottish Parliament building (and whether it should even be built!) in 1999–2000 could only have taken place in a society which is unwilling to make its own image the centre of attention for itself or anyone else; similarly, the 1999 Museum of Scotland's twentieth-century section shies away from cultural interpretation to give pride of place to a meaningless populism. A jumble of contemporary items chosen by celebrities (including a Saab convertible!) do not symbolize 'Scotland' any more or less than they would 'Coventry': and if there is no 'Scotland' to imagine or interpret, why have an iconic 'museum' of this non-existent 'it' at all? Poor levels of cultural intellectualization and a lack of confidence in Scotland the brand are, if not ubiquitous, still widely evident north of the Border.

1

FREEDOM IS A NOBLE THING: SCOTTISH NATIONHOOD TO 1707

The Making of Scotland

The perceived division in Scotland between Highland and Lowland dates from the fifteenth century, and was exacerbated by the Reformation of 1560. For many writers and authorities on Scotland, it has appeared a *donnée*, a given certainty about the country. Some of the figures of the Scottish Enlightenment, John Pinkerton (1758–1826) most notably among them, compounded this perceived alienation between Highlander and Lowlander by suggesting that Lowland Scotland was ethnically Teutonic and Saxon, as opposed to the 'Celtic' Highlands.[1] This opposition fed into all kinds of stereotypes and assumptions about the 'Celtic' character of the Highlands, which in their turn re-emphasized existing views of the wildness, savagery and uncivilized indolence of the Highlander. Laziness and lack of industry were qualities associated in the Protestant mind with Catholicism (particularly Irish Catholicism), and so the Highlands were, from the seventeenth century on, often categorized as 'Catholic', and their language from even earlier as 'Erse', Irish. The idea of Protestant industriousness and the perception of Highland indolence would have appeared what they were, self-contradictory, had the extent of adherence to the Reformed confessions in the Highlands been admitted.

There are several issues concealed within the inherited paradigm of Highland/Lowland distinctions in Scotland, two of which stand out: the ethnic and the geographical. Are Highlanders racially distinct? and is

Scotland historically divided along cultural, social and at times political lines along the so-called Highland Line, the mountainous curve sweeping up the country from Aberfoyle to Dunkeld, and from Dunkeld to Ballater, before it turns back towards the west?

The answer to both questions is much more doubtful and complex than is sometimes assumed. As I shall show in the brief résumé of Scotland's early history which follows, Anglian penetration into the country never reached for long or far beyond the Forth–Clyde line, and evidence for longer-term settlement is largely confined to parts of Lothian and the eastern Borders. Elsewhere, Britons (Welsh-speaking) could be found south of Forth–Clyde, and latterly in the south-west, though there are Welsh-derived place names such as 'Aberdeen' (cf. 'Aberystwyth', 'Aberdare') in other Scottish locations. North of Forth–Clyde lay the northern and southern Picts, whom tradition continues to associate with the culture of north-east Scotland, that part of the country perhaps least affected by elite population shifts in the mediaeval period.[2] The Scots themselves came from Ireland, founded the kingdom of Dal Ríata in Kintyre in the fifth century, and after intermittent dynastic alliances, had united their kingdom with that of the Picts by the ninth century (traditionally under Kenneth MacAlpin (841–58)). Immigration from conquered Anglo-Saxon England under Malcolm Cean Mór (1058–93) and from Norman adventurers under David I (1124–53), as well as of Flemings and others, has not been held by Scottish historians in general to have been accompanied by large movements of people, although it had a major cultural impact on Scotland's elite. Traditionally, these movements have been supposed to signal the end of Scotland as a 'Celtic' kingdom, and its beginning to be a 'Saxon–Norman' one. Such a view not only ignores the 'going native' practised by Norman knights turned clan chiefs such as the Frasers, but also tends to attribute 'Norman-ness' to Scots nobles living hundreds of years later. By such tokens, William Rufus would be a Viking and George VI a German. As Michael Lynch observes, what in fact happened was that Celtic traditions of localism were adopted by the Norman colonists, which may have reinforced regional and linguistic differences in Scotland, but had nothing to do with ethnic identity.[3] Indeed, there is evidence from the Wars of Independence which suggests the recrudescence of a fundamentally Celticist nationalism. As Colin Kidd informs us:

a thirteenth-century Celtic antiquarian revival is now believed to have contributed significantly to the strong sense of collective identity which enabled an

ethnically-diverse Scottish political nation in the late thirteenth and early fourteenth centuries to preserve an independent kingdom of Scotland in the
face of Plantagenet imperialist ambitions.... From the fourteenth to the
eighteenth century Scottish political identity was essentially Gaelic.[4]

The idea of distinctive 'Celtic' and 'Norman' Scotlands is an example
of the conflation of ethnic and cultural realities, aided and abetted by the
growth of the vernacular at the expense of Latin in the language of trade
and government in the later Middle Ages. The decline of Gaelic was
slow, but the coastal towns, economically influenced by England (as is
evident in many ways, not least in the preponderance of English coins
in Scottish coin hoards), early spoke a form of northern Anglic speech,
called at first 'Inglis' and later 'Scots'. In England, when the vernacular
began to displace Latin and Norman French towards the close of
the fourteenth century, the dominant dialects were those of the East
Midlands and South, which over the next hundred years became the
written standard throughout England's elite, even in Northumbria: in the
process, many new words were borrowed from Latin and French to better
fit the newcomer's task of replacing them. In Scotland, a similar process
took place, but here it was 'Inglis', the tongue of the east coast and the
major burghs, which prevailed, likewise borrowing new words for itself
from Latin and French. The different vocabulary borrowed, and the
distinctiveness of the constructions under which it was incorporated
constitute some of Scots' major claims (together with its relations with
Norwegian and Dutch) to be a language, not a dialect. International in
origin, like English, it was nonetheless not English.[5]

It was perhaps unfortunate (though any connection is admittedly
speculative) that the rise of the vernacular coincided with disruption
in the north of Scotland caused by magnate rivalries, which led to two
major disturbances on the border of the Highland Line: the sacking of
Elgin Cathedral by the Wolf of Badenoch in 1390 and the Battle of Harlaw in 1411. Both (especially the latter) have been long portrayed as
quintessential Highland–Lowland conflicts. The distrust they helped to
generate between northern Scots who still spoke Gaelic (as did many in
south-west and central Scotland) and the Scots speakers of the burghs may
have contributed to a Highland–Lowland split along linguistic lines.
Cultural differences came to be more greatly stressed, though at first
these were not linked to locality: Highlanders are viewed as 'obedient
enough and ready to respect the law' in thirteenth- and fourteenth-century chronicles.[6] By contrast, in these days when cultural criticism of the
Highlands is almost exhausted, the continuing strength of the linguistic

paradigm is borne witness to in the continuing conflation of the Gaeltachd (the Gaelic-speaking area) with 'Celtic' Scotland, as if a farmer in mainland Argyll called MacCormick whose father spoke Gaelic automatically became Anglo-Saxon when the tongue retreated to the islands, or as if the massive Highland emigration to Glasgow, visible today in as simple a witness as the telephone directory, involved some subtle transmutation into Teutonism.[7] As D. E. R. Watt points out:

> It is well known that the customary modern distinction between Lowlands and Highlands was not one which was in use in the earlier centuries of the Middle Ages; and when from the late fourteenth century onwards we do find Lowland writers beginning to make the distinction, it is expressed either in terms of difference in vernacular language . . . or . . . in terms of a general contrast between those who were domesticated, cultured, trustworthy, law-abiding and devout, and those who were wild and untamed, rough and unbending, if handsome and easy-going. We cannot, however, attach any specific geographical area to contemporary definitions of this kind.[8]

Similarly, R. W. Munro points out that the very term 'clan system' is a concept only two centuries old, and John Macinnes, writing in the context of the term 'Alba''s shift from being descriptive of the whole of Britain to identifying only the Gaelic-speaking area of it, can nonetheless state that 'a Lowlander is unequivocally an Albannach' among those who use the name of Alba. Moreover, Alasdair MacMhaigstir Alasdair, the great Gaelic poet and patriot, argued in *The Resurrection of the Ancient Scottish Language* (1751) that both Highlander and Lowlander were 'a small but precious remnant' of 'the Celtic nation'.[9] As the Highlander Sir James MacDonald put it, 'my Race has bene tenne hundreth yeeris kyndlie Scottis men under the Kingis of Scotland'.[10]

The idea of a cultural and ethnic Highland/Lowland divide, then, is one which is both more complex and more compromised than it has popularly appeared. As Allan Macinnes points out, 'emergent clans were Anglian, Anglo-Norman and Flemish as well as Celtic and Norse-Gaelic in origin. Clanship was by no means confined to the Highlands of Scotland'.[11] Any purely ethnic definition is misleading, while the presence of a cultural schism is much more plausibly linked to particular historical circumstances (circumstances which still lead the Gaelic contribution to Anglophone Scotland to be underestimated) than to any aboriginal distinction. The 'early Gaelic tribal root' of which Ferguson writes had many manifestations, often unacknowledged, in the culture of Anglophone Scotland, then and now.[12]

Social distinctions likewise prove more friable and uncertain than they are popularly held to be. The idea of the Highlands as populated by lawless clans whose livelihood was maintained by raids on the prosperous, civilized Lowlands, still beloved by popular history and the tourist industry, is untenable as a general rule. As Allan Macinnes has shown, such raiding as did exist was often carried out by broken and landless men, themselves pushed to the edge of Highland society, while a study of the Atholl estates by Leah Leneman points up the lack of differentiation in 'Lowland' and 'Highland' parishes: 'the estate records make no distinction between Highlanders and Lowlanders', while approaches to crime and justice are the same.[13] The distinction between the Highland chief, the Borders family such as Armstrong or Elliot and the 'chief of the name' of Erskine, the Earl of Mar, is one of circumstance and degree at best, rather than of kind.[14] Even in the mediaeval period, as Geoffrey Barrow points out, 'there is absolutely no suggestion . . . that grants and infeftments of landed estates in the Highlands or in the Isles differed in any fundamental respect from those made by the Crown elsewhere in the realm'.[15] It is to no inconsiderable degree an accident of the heritage and tourist industries that the 'wild Borderer' of the southern uplands has barely any profile beside that of the Highland cateran, who turns the history of towns like Crieff into frontier heritage, a 'kind of Dodge City in the rain', as George Rosie has caustically remarked.[16]

I have paid this degree of initial attention to the Highland/Lowland divide in Scottish history not only because it has the capacity to distort our understanding of the development of Scotland and Scottish nationality and identity across time, but also because it focuses our attention away from what is arguably a more important geographical barrier: the moss of the Forth with its 'brooch' at Stirling (the geographical feature of the Great Glen, while significant, has never been claimed to have had a major socio-political impact).[17] Until the land round Stirling was drained almost a century after the Union, central Scotland could only be passed through via Stirling itself, which for this reason was long one of Scotland's key points of fortification and conflict:

> the wide marshes between the Firth of Forth and the highlands of Dunbartonshire formed an all-but-impenetrable barrier between north and south, other than across the fords and bridge near Stirling.[18]

On this reading it is the division between Scotland north (Scotia) and south of Forth which is more crucial over more of Scotland's history than the split at the Highland Line. Even though the Mounth running west of Aberdeen also formed a barrier,[19] it was a secondary one: the establishment of sustained control of Scotland depended on Stirling. Indeed, one of the ironies of categorization of Scotland as 'Highland' and 'Lowland' is that sometimes uncertain accounts describe as 'Highland' events that took place simply north of Forth: in other words, the two geographical barriers are confusingly conflated. Not only is this true in the Jacobite period, when in 1745 the so-called 'Highland Army' was more properly speaking a 'north-of-Forth' army; such an essential confusion can also be found in more modern accounts, such as Brendan Bradshaw and John Morrill's collection, *The British Problem* (1996):

> Both England and Scotland for centuries consisted of an Anglo-Norman core with a bare and fluctuating control over the mountainous wholly Gaelic-speaking borderlands to the North and West, and the Norse speaking fastnesses beyond those borderlands.[20]

This account of Scotland is erroneous in several respects (e.g. we may doubt that the Battle of Largs against Norway in 1263 took place in a remote fastness, being only 25 miles from Glasgow, itself in earlier days a Scandinavian cutural centre), but for our purposes here it serves to note that it presumes a dominance by Central Belt Scotland which did not exist until the eighteenth century, and describes as 'Gaelic-speaking borderlands' all that lay beyond this core to the north and west. Yet Aberdeen, with two universities, was almost as far from Edinburgh as York from London; while Gaelic was spoken within 50 miles of Edinburgh until the eighteenth century. What Morrill is doing here is conflating the Forth–Clyde line with the Highland Line, apparently ignoring the vast swathe of eastern Scotland from Dornoch to Kirkcaldy, which was neither 'core' Scotland nor 'mountainous...borderlands'. How borderline the borderlands were is in any case highly doubtful: as Michael Lynch points out, 'the occurrence of two sets of placenames, in Gaelic and Scots, in many parishes in the foothills of the Grampians indicates a bilingual population and a flexible linguistic frontier'.[21]

It is important therefore to be careful when assessing the undoubted significance of geographical factors and early historical development to the identity of Scotland and the growth of the Scottish state. Dark Age historians suggest that the coalescence of a Scottish state north of Forth in the ninth century was made possible by the disruption of Northumbrian power by the Danes and hence the easing of Anglian pressure on Scotland south of Forth, where the Scots' original kingdom of Dal Ríata was located.

If this was the second significant development which enabled the emergence of a distinct polity to the north of Saxon England, the first was surely the victory over Ecgfrith by Brudei at Dunnichen Moss or Nechtansmere near Forfar in 685, which effectively ended Anglian attempts to penetrate beyond Forth. Nechtansmere in its turn can be seen as the closing phase of a history of unsettled peoples and boundaries from Humber to Forth which goes back to Roman times. Hadrian's Wall, guarding as it does against attack from both north and south, remains an eloquent architectural symbol of the onset of this period, when Rome, pushing into northern Britain, found the worth of their *foederati* transient, and the value of subduing them doubtful. Agricola's battle against the Caledonian tribes at Mons Graupius (possibly Bennachie in Aberdeenshire, though several other sites between Angus and the Moray Firth have been suggested) in AD 84 was, like Nechtansmere, the climax of an attempt to make inroads into Scotland north of Forth by the east-coast route. Unlike Nechtansmere, it ended in victory for the invader: nevertheless, in the longer term, and despite its clever plugging of the eastern glens by fortified outposts, Rome found it burdensome to endeavour to hold Scotland north of Forth. In 87, their great fortress at Inchtuthil was abandoned, with one million nails buried to deny them to the Caledonians, while shortly after 105, a swathe of forts from central Scotland to Corbridge was burnt to the ground.[22] The fears expressed in Calgacus' speech at Mons Graupius, as voiced in the 'noble barbarian' rhetoric of Tacitus, were not to be realized:

> There are no lands behind us, and even on the sea we are menaced by the Roman fleet.... Pillagers of the world they have exhausted the land by their indiscriminate plunder, and now they ransack the sea. A rich enemy excites their cupidity; a poor one, their lust for power.... To robbery, butchery, and rapine, they give the lying name of 'government': they create a desolation and call it peace.[23]

Solitudinem faciunt, Pacem appellant. The first Scottish patriotic sentiments which have come down to us are those of a Roman patrician with an eye to the reputation of his father-in-law, which nonetheless provide a subsequently influential image of the Caledonian warband as 'hidden away' in the 'secret places' of Britain's mountains, hardy and freedom-loving.[24] Whatever the truth of Tacitus' characterization, it matched the subsequent image of the Highland warrior too well to be overlooked, even if the Roman's view of the Caledonian tribes as Germanic was more problematic for the ethnic projections of the Scottish Enlightenment, concerned as they often were to contrast German virtue with Celtic indolence.[25]

In the end, the 'cowards' who had pleaded with Agricola for a '"strategic retreat" behind the Forth' had their way.[26] The Antonine Wall (AD 142) was built to mark the limit of established Roman power, and even then was only intermittently occupied, Hadrian's Wall remaining the more consistent frontier, although between the Tyne and the Forth Rome long maintained an uneasy sway, which continued to require campaigns which brought three Roman emperors north in the third and fourth centuries.[27] The striking thing about Roman power in Caledonia between 80 and 400 is the extent to which it geographically foreshadows the pattern of Northumbrian control between 650 and 1000: intermittent and ultimately unsuccessful forays north of Forth, with the Lothians and Borders uneasily but more consistently controlled. Even if the Forth could be passed, the east-coast route was vulnerable to descent from the glens and higher ground: and where it narrowed at Stonehaven, a fortress, later the great castle of Dunottar, was built at an early date.

It has been argued that the Romans saw the Caledonians as a 'single ethnic group', the inhabitants of a single country. Whatever the truth of this, by the end of the second century 'it is possible that the first steps were ... taken towards the creation of a single Pictish kingdom uniting the peoples south of the Mounth under one war-lord'.[28] The title 'Pict', from the Roman identification of them as 'Picti', 'painted',[29] is one which is applied to the Caledonian kingdoms which developed at this period. Later Romano-British influence between Clyde and Cumbria may have led to the establishing of 'territorial bishops' south of Forth–Clyde by the fourth century (including at Whithorn in Galloway where Magnus Maximus, a claimant to the purple, may have 'established a line of [local] kings'), but north of Forth the Pictish kingdoms retained their integrity at this period, although the southern Picts in Fife and Angus were Christianized by St Ninian in around AD 400.[30]

In the fifth century, south-west Scotland was, like many other parts of Britain, disrupted not only by Roman withdrawal, but also through the movement of peoples, in this case the Scots, who had established their kingdom of Dal Ríata by AD 500. Despite the continuation of Pictish-controlled kinglets in Argyll and the persistence of a strong British kingdom at Dumbarton, the long-term trend slowly began to turn towards Scottish expansion. In this, the fact that the Scots were remote from the main centres of Anglian intrusion in the east helped, since these confined and distracted the military attentions of the Picts and Britons. The *Gododdin*, the earliest major piece of Scottish (or Welsh, according to taste) literature extant, records the unsuccessful attempt of a British warband from Dun Eidyn (Edinburgh) to attack the Northumbrians at Catraeth (Catterick) in *c*.550–600. Half a century later, the Gododdin had been displaced from Lothian by the Angles, and by the middle of the seventh century, Northumbrian forces were beginning to occupy the southern territories of the Picts, including the south coast of Fife. Thus far, the expansion of Northumbria was proceeding along much the same lines as Anglo-Saxon power elsewhere in Britain, which was forcing the British tribes and polities back behind the Tamar and the Severn. By *c*.650, the Northumbrians 'had reached the Solway and isolated Strathclyde from Wales',[31] shortly after their southern neighbours had split Wales from Cornwall at the Bristol Channel. A Northumbrian bishop was installed at Abercorn in *c*.681, and the Northumbrian warband pushed beyond Forth.[32]

Then came Nechtansmere, by tradition the decisive battle: and this is also the view of Scotland's leading Dark-Age historian, who sees no good reason to suppose that this defeat did not halt Anglic colonization. Brudei Mac Bili, who led the victorious Picts and Britons at Nechtansmere,[33] had links to both the royal houses of Pictland and the British kingdom of Strathclyde, and so may have been able to unite their warbands. In any event, he drove Northumbria back to the Forth, and sent the bishop of Abercorn in flight to Whitby.[34] Subsequent battles in 698 and 711 resulted in one victory apiece to Picts and Northumbrians, and may have led to the settlement of a frontier at the Pentland Hills.[35] The loss of any hold on Fife, with its rich agricultural land which offered 'a secure base to the would-be conqueror', was a major disaster for the Northumbrians.[36] Brudei's Pictish successor, Oengus MacFergus (729–61), was even more successful, being the first to reduce 'all Scotia, Scotland north of the Forth, to his authority', and thus to foreshadow a future united Scottish kingdom. Dal Ríata itself, meanwhile, was under Pictish overlordship, victory over the Northumbrians having alleviated Pictish difficulties in extending a sphere of influence into the south-west.[37]

It was perhaps fresh pressure from Norse immigration and attacks in the west which helped to drive Scottish ambitions east and led to Kenneth MacAlpin's successful opposition to Pictish overlordship and eventual rule (843–47) over at least southern Pictland:[38] developments which make him by tradition the first king of Scotland. The Picts were indeed excluded from the genesis of the nation in the mediaeval period.[39] The Norse assault began in the west in 794, and the following year the Vikings devastated Skye and Iona: the latter's sanctuary was to be attacked twice more by 806.[40] Constantine MacFergus and Oengus MacFergus founded major ecclesiastical developments at Dunkeld and St Andrews, distant from the vulnerable west. By the ninth century there was also heavy Scandinavian settlement in the north.

Strathclyde continued to be an independent kingdom, but it was now under pressure not only from the Northumbrians in the east (who set up a bishopric in Whithorn in 731 (and conquered the plain of Kyle in 752), but also from the Norse in the west. The Britons had retreated from West and Mid Lothian (where 70 per cent and 35 per cent of place names respectively show their influence) to a west-coast heartland which itself suffered a decisive blow when Dumbarton, the capital, was taken by the Vikings in 871. Thereafter, Strathclyde was dependent on Scandinavian power and the kingdom of the Scots for its continued political existence.[41] When Donald II attacked in 889, Strathclyde's nobility fled to Gwynedd. By the tenth century, it was effectively absorbed into the Scottish polity.[42]

The Norse also displaced the northern Picts from Orkney and Shetland after 800, so completely that 99 per cent of place names there (to which should be added a good number in Caithness, Sutherland and the west Highlands) are of Scandinavian origin:[43] a form of Norse, Norn, survived in Shetland until the nineteenth century. By 850, Norsemen were also established in Lewis and Skye.[44] Elsewhere, Gaelic place names are predominant, except for strongholds of Scandinavian names in the north and west Highlands and Anglian ones in Lothian and Berwickshire. Outwith these areas, Anglian place names are scarce.[45] Norse power continued into the western isles and Man until the thirteenth century; the last mainland raid was made (on Aberdeen) in 1151.[46]

If the Norse invasions caused problems for Scotland in the north and west, their fellow-Vikings caused greater problems for the emerging state of England. From the first raid at Lindisfarne in 793, Northumbria was under threat from the Danes, a threat which culminated in the establishment of a Danish kingdom at York after 870. As a result, Northumbrian power weakened considerably, and under Constantine II (900–43), Scotland was able to push south of the Forth for the first time, into Lothian and possibly as far as Tweed.[47] The long battle with Northumbria for the land between Forth and Tweed was about to move to its climax; it was to be followed by three more centuries in which Scottish kings made intermittent efforts to gain control over the whole of Northumbrian territory, an aim which was ultimately to prove over-ambitious, and which contributed to an uneasy relationship with the English Crown.

Constantine's forays coincided with those of Edward the Elder (899–924) in the south. Edward was recovering vast swathes of Saxon territory from Danish control. Constantine and his ally the King of Strathclyde were no match for Edward, and acknowledged him as 'father and lord' to get themselves off the hook.[48] This formula, often repeated subsequently, was a relatively painless way of agreeing a peace with a superior power which ceded nothing except a nebulous claim to suzerainty, and usually a personal suzerainty at that, not one yielded in perpetuity. Nonetheless, this frequent Scottish escape route from military overcommitment was later to be built up in English eyes into an acceptance of overlordship.

How little it practically was so is demonstrated by Athelstan's (924–46) need to raid Scotland as far as Dunottar in 934 to keep Constantine in bounds: Constantine yielded him his son as hostage.[49] His fate is obscure, but is unlikely to have been pleasant, given that Constantine, together with the Strathclyde warband and support from Man, Dublin and York, invaded England in 937 and was defeated in a colossal battle at Brunanburgh, the site of which is unknown: the Wirral has been suggested.

Despite this setback, Scotland remained stable enough for Constantine to retire to an abbey in 943, to be succeeded by Malcolm I. Just as Scotland had benefited from the weakening of Northumbria by Danish power, so the centring of the emerging united kingdom of England in southern Wessex distanced the Scots from the heartland of their likely adversary, thus increasing the likelihood that Scotland could pick territory at the margins of England's far-flung borders in the north. In the long run, the centring of the English state on Winchester (later London) made it invulnerable to Scottish attack; in the short run it provided easier pickings in the North, where in 945 King Edmund ceded 'Cumbria' (possibly remaining Northumbrian territory in south-west Scotland rather than Cumberland) to King Malcolm, 'on condition that he be his helper both on sea and land'.[50] This was a fairly meaningless condition, being agreed as it was in an atmosphere of rapidly developing Scottish control over Anglo-Saxon territory: in 948 Malcolm plundered 'the English as far as the Tees'.[51] In 954, the Earl of Northumbria abandoned Edinburgh to King Indulf, while Lothian was ceded by Edgar the Peaceable (959–75) to Kenneth II (971–95) in 973.[52] The extent to which this act was accompanied by Scottish 'homage' remained a bone of contention right into the debates on Anglo-Scottish Union at the turn of the eighteenth century: the story that Edgar had been rowed on the Dee at Chester by eight subordinate kings including the King of Scots being cited in pro-English pamphlets as justification for English overlordship of Scotland.[53] Similarly, the pro-Scottish publications of the period countered that the story was 'the vain whim of *Edgars* being row'd over *Dee* . . . devised by the Monks'.[54] Whatever was the case, Lothian's good farmland was back in Northumbrian hands by AD 1000: but this was for the last time. Malcolm II (1005–34) devoted himself to winning back what is now south-east Scotland on a permanent basis, and his siege of Durham was succeeded in 1018 by the decisive victory at Carham, which set Scotland's eastern frontier firmly on the Tweed. By the end of Malcolm's reign, the client kingdom of Strathclyde was fully incorporated into the realm, though Galloway retained a distinct and quasi-autonomous identity for at least two centuries more.[55]

From now on, the kings of Scots aimed no longer at securing Lothian and the Southern Uplands, but rather England's northernmost counties, the incorporation of which (whether or not by means of holding the earldom of Northumbria) remained a clear strategic aim until the thirteenth century. Malcolm II's attempts on Cumberland and Westmorland were driven back by Cnut (1016–35), and the Scots king was forced to submit when the Anglo-Danish emperor reached the Tay in 1031. However, though the King of England's arm was long, his reach was slow, and a pattern began to be set whereby as soon as English backs were turned, Scottish armies or raiding parties poured across the frontier: indeed, in some form this cast of events endured all the way to Flodden in 1513. Scotland effectively controlled Cumberland and Westmorland for about half of the eleventh and twelfth centuries.[56]

Malcolm III Cean Mór (1054/7–93) became one of the most pertinaciously persistent raiders of the northern English counties in the history of these islands. William the Conqueror could subsequently cow Malcolm, but not stop him, even though his marriage to Margaret, heiress of the House of Wessex, would no doubt have made this a desirable end. Indeed, any attempt to provide an account of Anglo-Scottish relations in this period from the point of view of English 'overlordship' and Scottish 'homage' cannot withstand the comparators it invites. Both Saxon and Norman kings destroyed or put to flight 'overmighty subjects' who irritated or threatened them, even those with major power bases: Gruffydd ap Llywelyn in 1063, Earl Morcar in 1071 and the House of Rollo in Normandy in 1106 being three examples. The King of

Scots' case was otherwise: he could be intimidated and temporarily subdued, either by negotiation from strength or through a pitched battle,
yet he could always return to the fray.

   Attempts to enforce political will through the ecclesiastical claims of
York to be metropolitan of Scotland (1072) were unsuccessful, and when
in 1094 William II Rufus (1087–1100) had the power to place Duncan II
on the throne, the 'Scots rose against him' and replaced him with Donald
Ban, Malcolm's brother. Though a second attempt by Rufus succeeded
in establishing Edgar in 1097, there was some temporary success in quieting
the Scots, but Alexander I (1107–24) moved away from the implications
of a client relationship with England, revolting against ecclesiastical
obedience to York. Whereas Edgar may have allowed 'further English
settlement in Lothian', Alexander moved the core of the Scots kingdom
'north to Scone and Gowrie, the heart of Celtic Alba'. David I (1124–53)
confirmed such moves towards Scottish distinctiveness by importing
minor-league Anglo-Norman adventurers to Scotland to develop it
along lines which could compete more directly with England. By his
marriage to Maud, the daughter of the Earl of Northumbria, in 1114,
David gained not only title to the coveted earldom but also other English
lands including 'the honour of Huntingdon'.[57] These gains were, however,
a two-edged sword, for the duty of homage owed by the Scottish king for
his English lands (the English king at this stage owed a similar duty
for his lands in France) was easily conflated by English monarchical
propaganda with a duty it claimed was owed for Scotland itself. Thus,
although David was the most territorially successful of Scottish kings,
controlling Northumbria 50 miles south of Newcastle in addition to
holding the honour of Lancaster and his other lands,[58] the nature of his
relationship to England ultimately made it easier for English regimes
to claim overlordship of Scotland. That such a claim was more spin
than substance is shown by England's imposition of overlordship on the
captured William the Lion (1165–1214) by the 1174 Treaty of Falaise
(cancelled 17 years later by the Quitclaim of Canterbury): why insist on
a treaty to impose conditions to which an acknowledged right is already
possessed? Scotland's position was internationally recognized to the
extent that Pope Alexander III denounced as 'lay interference'
Henry II's demand of an 'oath of obedience' to the English Church by
the Scottish bishops. Questions of 'obedience' were further vexed by the
'homage to Alexander' given by the Northumbrian lords in 1215, which
acknowledged (in the context of John's declining regime) Scottish
claims to the northern counties, a claim further reinforced by the

homage given to the king by the Yorkshire barons at Melrose in 1216 Alexander II (1214–49) marched south to Dover, doing homage in his turn for the northern counties to the King of France. Although this house of cards collapsed very quickly, it illustrates the complex medi-aeval realities which undermine any attempt to view Anglo-Scottish rela-tions in terms of simple and direct suzerainty. Indeed, the comparative stability of the Anglo-Scottish border in European terms is indicative of the coalescence of two polities within stable boundaries. Within Scotland itself, Alexander II had no real control over the western islands. Attempts to buy them from the Norse in 1244 failed. Nonetheless, by Alexander's death, his jurisdiction covered the whole of what is now main-land Scotland. His successor was to add all the islands (including Man) save the Outer Hebrides following the Battle of Largs in 1263,[59] and the final incorporation of Scandinavian territory into Scotland followed in 1468–72, when as part of a marriage settlement (the payment for which was never completed), the 'earldom of Orkney and the lordship of Shetland were annexed to the Scottish crown'.[60]

Nonetheless, English governments continued to use the issue of homage to place additional pressure on the Scottish monarchy, even after the effective end of Scottish claims to Northumbria by the Treaty of York in 1237, when Alexander quitclaimed Northumberland, Westmorland and Cumberland.[61] On 6 April 1251, the Pope rejected 'an English petition that the Scottish king might not be crowned or anointed without consent of Henry III',[62] and when Alexander III (1249–86) came to London to do homage for his English lands in 1278, pressure was placed on him to conform to greater demands:

> At Westminster, Alexander, king of Scotland, did homage to the Lord Edward, king of England, son of king Henry, in these words: 'I become your man for the lands which I hold of you in the kingdom of England for which I owe homage to you, saving my kingdom'. Then said the Bishop of Norwich: 'And saving to the king of England, if he has right to your homage for the kingdom'. To whom at once and openly the king replied, saying: 'To homage for my kingdom of Scotland, no one has a right save God alone, nor do I hold it save of God alone'.[63]

In the uncertainty following Alexander's death in 1286, compounded by the death of his successor, the Maid of Norway, before she reached Scotland in 1290, Edward I (1272–1307) took the opportunity to press his claims to overlordship by stating that only on that condition would he judge between the various claimants to the crown. His choice,

John Baliol (1292–96), became effectively Edward's subordinate, an insupportable position which he was under great pressure from many of his nobles to bring to an end. In 1295, Scotland and France made a treaty of mutual support, continuing their links under William the Lion: this date is often taken as marking the formal beginnings of the Auld Alliance, which for many years in the early modern period would lead to a Scots entitlement to become citizens of France. Such a treaty with a threatening foreign power was insupportable to England, and in 1296 Edward invaded. The result was a ferocious war, which, with interludes, continued for 40 years. In it, William Wallace was 'a true champion of the kingdom for the independence of its people',[64] fighting for Baliol, and Robert Bruce was that even rarer thing, a military success against English arms. As Geoffrey Barrow comments of the first Rising of 1297, 'Bruce ... joined the Scots because he was a Scotsman.' He certainly told the 'knights of Annandale' that 'I must join my own people and the nation in which I was born.' 'The concept of Scottish nationality' was real, and its reality obtruded to the extent that the country, far from being abandoned by its nobility, in what Barrow has called 'one of the hardest-dying half-truths of Scottish history', provided a real obstacle to English ambition, while the concept of that nationality was further developed in the case for a distinctive Scottish nationality put on the Continent and to the papacy by lawyers like Baldred Bisset.[65] Scotland was no diversionary sideshow for English power. In the Falkirk campaign of 1298, England arguably raised the second largest army it ever put into the field before the Union of the Crowns, drawing on Gascon, Welsh and Irish manpower to subdue the soldiery of one small and divided nation. After Bannockburn in 1314, Robert I (1306–29) attempted and nearly succeeded in undermining these sources of manpower by attacking Ireland and threatening Wales in the Scottish interest. As a result, 'the spectre of a pan-Celtic international' became a concern of English policymakers.[66]

Whatever Scotland had been before, the ringing tones of the Declaration of Arbroath (1320), a remonstrance to John XXII on the status of the Scottish nation, effectively became a statement of completed nationality that were subsequently to prove influential on later claims for Scottish sovereignty, and (as has been argued) on Enlightenment thought and the cause of American independence.[67] Its relative sophistication was the fruit both of the constitutional wrangles of the 1290s and of the arguments developed over many years to make Scotland's case heard in Europe. The Declaration praised the king, but made clear the priority accorded to the nation:

our most serene prince, king, and lord Robert, who, for the delivering of his people and his own rightful inheritance from the enemy's hand, did, like another Joshua or Maccabeus, most cheerfully undergo all manner of toil, fatigue, hardship, and hazard.... But after all, if this prince shall leave these principles he hath so nobly pursued, and consent that we or our kingdom be subjected to the king or people of England, we will immediately endeavour to expel him, as our enemy and as the subverter both of his own and our rights, and we will make another king, who will defend our liberties: For so long as there shall but one hundred of us remain alive we will never give consent to subject ourselves to the dominion of the English. For it is not glory, it is not riches, neither is it honours, but it is liberty alone that we fight and contend for, which no honest man will lose but with his life... admonish and exhort the king of England (who may well rest satisfied with his own possessions...) to suffer us to live at peace in that narrow spot of Scotland beyond which we have no habitation, since we desire nothing but our own.[68]

The Declaration would at any time have been a remarkable document; dating as it does from the early fourteenth century, it is an astounding one. Those who reject a pre-eighteenth-century nationalism should apply the test of the razor developed by an English contemporary, William of Occam: not to multiply entities beyond necessity. If it looks like nationalism, sounds like nationalism and smells like nationalism, then that is what it is: we do not deserve to be deprived of our empirical senses by postmodern semantics. The use of Judas Maccabeus clearly indicates the identification of the nation with the chosen group which is so profound a part of Old Testament consciousness, and which, like Simonides' Sparta alluded to above, the mediaevals knew how to interpret much better than we.

Even given the formative nature of the Declaration, one of the questions that remains is – Was Scotland a 'nation' before this, in the eleventh, twelfth and thirteenth centuries? Certainly it had 'well-formed and independent political institutions', with 'a tradition of submission to one king': a Scottish 'Parliament' first sat in 1235, with representatives of the commons from 1326. Scots and Picts in the north, Britons in the west and Angles in the east showed little sign of ethnic conflict, as Archie Duncan has pointed out, despite their differences in culture and inheritance. In 1100, Gaelic was, 'except in Lothian', the general language of the country,[69] and by the time its position had altered significantly, other factors were reinforcing a sense of distinct Scottish identity, particularly the development of a unitary kingship,[70] further extended by David I's Normanization. But this was in all probability simply the development of a process which had earlier origins. It is a modern view that the Picts themselves 'enjoyed cultural unity and attempted to maintain political unity' for three centuries before the establishment of a united monarchy,[71] and this legacy appears to have made it easier to establish a coherent and relatively stable core polity reaching as a minimum from the Great Glen to the Forth–Clyde line. The earliest laws of Scotland had been promulgated at Forteviot by Donald I (858–62), and by the thirteenth century the Galwegian legal system, last of the provincial survivals of different laws (with the exception of Norse Law in Orkney and Shetland, not abolished until 1611[72]), began to yield 'to the processes of royal justice'.[73] It is arguable, however, that the Galwegian cry *Albani, Albani* at the Battle of the Standard in 1138 betokened some kind of emergent national consciousness of themselves as Scots, and Barrow describes Galloway as 'in its own way intensely Scottish' at the end of the thirteenth century.[74] Even in 918, the staff of St Columba had been carried at the Battle of Corbridge as a consequence of his status as 'apostle' of the 'men of Scotland'. As such, it 'allowed a mixed army of Picts and Scots to fight together . . . as *Albanaich* against a common enemy'.[75] The recognition of different ethnic groups within the polity does not appear to have militated against its construction: it is thus important to realize that Scotland was never a 'people-nation', and that 'ethnic' nationalism was, from the very beginning of the Scottish polity, a contradiction in terms. Edgar (1097–1107) addressed his subjects as 'Scots and English', while later royal charters are addressed to 'French and English, Scots and Galwegians', who are all regarded as the *'probi homines'* ('worthy men') of the king.[76] There was a further development at the turn of the thirteenth century: as William Ferguson notes, 'before William's reign ended in 1214' his subjects were being described without reference to their ethnic origin, shortly after Henry II (1154–89) had addressed his subjects as 'English'.[77] Although there were revolts against incomers in Galloway and a flight of British nobility from Strathclyde to Gwynedd,[78] there is little evidence of sustained ethnic conflict even in the early period, although this was certainly posited by Enlightenment historians. Their view of Highland history, with its story of aboriginal retreat in the face of Scoto-Saxon advance, is still widespread at a popular level: powerfully and inaccurately conflating linguistic and ethnic identity, it appears oblivious both to agricultural and to urban immigration from the Highlands into Lowland Scotland.

If the monarchy was important, so was the role of the Church. Although the struggle for freedom from the metropolitan control of York was not finally won in the case of Galloway until 1355,[79] in the rest of Scotland it had long and largely successfully been resisted. A 'Scottish Church' can be identified in the ninth century; by 1192, all but one of the Scottish dioceses had formally been declared free of English episcopal control, and the national Church, lacking as it did a metropolitan, became a 'special daughter' of the papacy. In 1225, a 'national provincial council' of the Scottish Church was set up; in 1250, the canonization of Queen Margaret consolidated the Scottish Church's status:[80] St Margaret remained an icon of Scottish nationality into the eighteenth century, and tenuously even later. Even before 1296, the Church's significant role in the Wars of Independence was foreshadowed in clear signs of the development of a national cultus:

> By 1279, the seal of the Bishop of St Andrews bore the image of St Andrew cru-cified, and in 1286 it also appeared on the seal of the Guardians of the Kingdom, accompanied by the legend, 'Andrew be leader of the compatriot Scots'. By 1318, when St Andrews Cathedral was consecrated in a service of national thanksgiving 'for the notable victory granted to the Scottish people by blessed Andrew, protector of the realm' four years earlier at Bannockburn, the identi-fication of saint and nation was complete.[81]

St Andrew was also used as a focus of multi-ethnic unity, being pre-sented as suzerain 'over all the peoples of Scotland, "the Picts, Scots, Danes and Norwegians"'. In the Wars of Independence themselves, the Scottish bishops in general strongly backed the national cause: the diocesans of Glasgow and Moray even 'likened resistance against Edward I to a Crusade against the infidel' (this of course was part of the implication of Bruce as Judas Maccabeus, with his heroic resistance to a pagan invader and overwhelming odds). Subsequently, native saints and continental ones were also influential in the development of local cults, and 'nationalist' interest in them was a force in 'anti-English patriotism'. In 1472, St Andrews was elevated to an archbishopric; in 1492 Glasgow followed.[82]

The role of the Scottish bishops in the Wars of Independence has long been acknowledged, and they had their own territorial ambitions in England too: in the historic Scottish territories in Cumbria 'the bishops of Glasgow claimed ecclesiastical jurisdiction ... as late as the 1260s'. The 'full rites of anointing and coronation' were at last recognized in the fourteenth century by the wider Church as a legitimate endorsement of the Scottish king's status:[83] they also endorsed the national Church's status, and possibly underlie the statements of sovereignty made by the depiction of the closed crown of imperium in later mediaeval Scottish architecture.

There is no space here to embark upon an exploration of the extent to which Scottish social, legal, military, cultural and landholding customs and institutions diverged from English ones, even after the adoption of Norman practices, but nonetheless this was early realized to be an important indicator of Scottish distinctiveness and difference. Patterns of 'lordship' found elsewhere in mediaeval Europe were grafted on to an underlying Celtic aristocracy by Flemish and Norman servants of the monarchy: some of them, such as the Frasers, becoming almost indistinguishable from their predecessors. In addition, 'many of the old features [of the landholding system] and even their names remained well into the medieval period . . . the majority of rural place-names can be traced to the period before 1250'. By the 1150s, most of the land colonists in Scotland's newly monetized economy were showing signs that 'their first loyalty lay with the King of Scots'. Monetization in its turn undermined the nature of serfdom.[84] Distinctive qualities in these developments may have lent varied nuance to the originally feudal idea of the 'community of the realm' and its 'guardians' so ably explored by Barrow for their role in promoting a 'wholly new and remarkable' political environment during the Wars of Independence, when 'the conservative community of the Scottish realm stands out in advance of the age'.[85]

Many features of mediaeval Scottish culture continued to have an impact on the nation's identity deep into the modern period. The 'runrig' strip system of land, for example, survived from possibly as early as the twelfth into the eighteenth century;[86] in the Chanonry in Old Aberdeen, the professors succeeded the canons, and remained there until the 1980s; in the lineaments of eighteenth-century Scottish philosophy its mediaeval tradition can still be discerned.[87] It is tempting to think that the flexibility and innovation of the Scottish banking system in the eighteenth century has its roots in a mediaeval culture accustomed both to a depreciating monetary standard and currency arbitrage;[88] a sense of grim and gargoyle humour extends across half a millennium of Scottish literature[89] – and of course, no matter how strong the similarity of Scottish to English civilization and Scots to English people might be, the passion to differentiate is one with a long pedigree.

The monarchical foundation-myth was one of the key areas where Scotland and England diverged, and where that divergence underlined national difference. The English version, codified by Geoffrey of Monmouth in his *Historia Regum Britanniae* (1136), was designed to give 'a precedent for the dominions and ambitions of the Norman kings'.[90] It stated that Brutus, the great-grandson of Aeneas, legendary founder of Rome, had come to Britain, which was subsequently divided between his three sons, Locrinus (England), Kamber (Wales) and Albanactus (Scotland). Locrinus, the eldest, had, by right of primogeniture, authority over the other two: there was, however, an alternative form of the legend in which Brutus and Albanus were brothers, and where Scotland was thus posited as England's equal.[91] Unsurprisingly, English rulers preferred the first version. In 1301, the Brut legend was invoked by Edward I, in 1401 by Edward IV; in 1457, John Hardyng the historian urged Henry VI (who had other things on his mind at the time) to act on the English claim, and in 1542 Henry VIII made claims to suzerainty on the same grounds. It was perhaps from the primogeniture version of the Brut/Britain myth that the use of 'England' as a synonym for 'Britain' derives. As early as the fourteenth century, John of Fordun 'like many Scots since ... was outraged by the way in which the English used the term "Britain" itself and applied it indiscriminately to mean either England or the whole island'. John Mair's concept of 'Greater Britain', the ancestor of our 'Great Britain', was a response to this which allowed for Scotland's inclusion.[92] Mair himself was unusual for a sixteenth-century Scot in his desire for union between the kingdoms.

The Scots, Picts and Irish appear in the Monmouth Brut genealogy as treacherous enemies of King Arthur, descendant of Brutus: indeed, they ally with the traitor Mordred in the last battle at Camlann. The Scots themselves are 'depicted as a mongrel race begot of Picts and Hibernians'.[93] Naturally, the Scots declined to accept this view, and instead a Scoto-Irish form developed where 'Gathelus ... the *eponymus* of the Gael, marries Scota the daughter of Pharaoh'.[94] Valuable recent work by Dauvit Broun has established that the Scottish kings were long conscious of their Irish past. Even though the last public recitation of Irish royal descent appears to have taken place at the coronation of Alexander III in 1249,[95] Irish monarchical ancestry continued to be cited, and in Ireland itself this proved a useful support for Stuart legitimism in the eighteenth century: indeed, even in 1903, W. P. Ryan noted the continuing prevalence of the view that the Irish were descended from Scota. The Stone of Scone, returned to Scotland in 1996, had once been at Tara: this, perhaps, was the reason that Michael Collins had attempted to take it while in London.[96]

The historic cultural and literary links between Scotland and Ireland, which date from this period, have long been underestimated, possibly for essentially sectarian reasons. It has proved possible for historians to altogether overlook the deep-seated presence of legends of the Fianna in both countries in their condemnations of the supposed fabrications of James Macpherson's *Ossian* poetry, and the connection of many sites in

Scotland to Irish stories is neglected in both countries. Cuchulain, for example, by tradition trained in Skye, Naoise fled to Scotland with Deirdre and several place names in Scotland are associated with Usnach's sons.[97] Similarly, the Fianna are located among other places in Glen Lyon, which perhaps lay along the boundary between northern and southern Pictland: an interesting conflation of legend and political reality.[98] The place where Ossian was held prisoner by Niamh is supposed by Scottish accounts to be on the banks of the Spey.[99] Among historical figures, Robert I (1306–29) is heir to the 'sleeping king' tradition of Fionn and Arthur in a manner which displays both Scottish and Irish characteristics, for 'in the tradition of Rathlin (the Gaelic of which is Scottish rather than Irish) he is the Sleeping Warrior, the Saviour King'.[100] Bruce of course famously termed the Scots and Irish, even in 1320, as a single nation (*'nostra nacio'*), although the undifferentiated term 'Scoti', once applied to both indiscriminately, had begun to fall out of official use more than a century before.[101] Its earlier use can be sometimes startling: the quintessentially Irish hero Brian Boru, for example, being described as *imperator Scotorum* ('Ruler of the Scots') in 1004. After Bruce, as Ferguson remarks, 'from the late Middle Ages onwards different historical developments destroyed the original essential identity of Irish and Scots'.[102] Fittingly, one document at least of Bruce's reign describes him as 'by God's grace king of Scotland and Ireland'. Though his brother's attempt to make the Bruces the latter was unsuccessful, King Robert's reign saw an interesting attempt to conjoin the two country's fortunes: nor was this the last occasion on which it was suggested.[103]

Enemies and Relations

Meanwhile, troubles continued for the Scottish Crown, albeit at a lower level of intensity. In 1322, an English force was 'routed at Byland in Yorkshire'.[104] The Treaty of Northampton folowed in 1328, which, but for the pride of the young Edward III (1327–77), should have heralded a period of peace and the recognition of Scotland's independence. Instead there were renewed attempts to put a Baliol vassal on the Scottish throne in the 1330s. After victory at Dupplin on 12 September 1332, Edward Baliol (John's son) was crowned at Scone, subsequently giving homage to the English king and ceding 'most of southern Scotland' to Edward III. David II (1329–71) was forced to flee to France in 1334, but his supporters continued to hold the north and west. In 1335 Andrew Moray, son of the Moray who had raised the standard in 1296, defeated Baliol forces near Ballater, and over the next two years steadily recovered most of Scotland outside the Baliol lands. David returned, but after his capture at Neville's Cross in 1346, Baliol made a last effort. It was doomed: by this time Edward III, busy in France, had in any case realized that supporting an unpopular pretender was more expensive and less rewarding than 'the prospect of a lucrative ransom' for the rightful king. The Baliol candidacy had reached the end of the road.[105]

In 1363, 'tentative proposals' for Anglo-Scottish regnal union were 'formulated'. Under the proposal there would be one king, to be styled 'King of England and of Scotland', who would be crowned in both countries. As well as a preserved share of offices, Scotland would also retain its political independence:

> The name and title of the realm of Scotland shall be preserved and maintained with honour and with due distinction, without union or annexation to the realm of England.

Despite this commitment, the lack of ability to maintain a separate foreign policy in an era when war was very much the king's prerogative would have severely limited Scotland's ability to function on its own, and the Scottish Parliament rejected these proposals in March 1364.[106] Nonetheless, they reinforced the future Unionist lore that Robert the Bruce's victories had won for Scotland the right to be negotiated with on equal terms, and that after Bannockburn, the prospect of Union loomed larger than the possibility of conquest. It was long an attractive theory, but the evidence of Scotland's history over the intervening centuries does not altogether bear it out. One of the ways in which the new British history is too like the old is the manner in which it presumes that the primary relationships of the countries of the British Isles have been with each other, a view which is arguably an extension of English insularity. Thus Keith Robbins in his *Great Britain* (1998) argues that John Mair 'demonstrated that there were no fundamental barriers of communication which stood in the way of a single kingdom' and that London in the sixteenth century attracted 'visitors from all over Britain' (in earnest, one presumes, of its role as a future metropolis of Empire).[107] In fact, 200 years after Mair, it could take four weeks to travel from Edinburgh to London, far longer than a voyage to the Continent, while in the mid-sixteenth century there were only 50 Scots in London, but hundreds of

Frenchmen in Edinburgh.[108] Scotland's core relations until the seven-teenth century were with continental Europe, however much the new British history would like to project the M6 back into the Middle Ages.

Relations with France continued to be important after the signing of the original treaty in 1295. As the Hundred Years War drew to its climax in the early fifteenth century, significant Scottish military support sus-tained the French war effort, notably at Baugé (1421), where the Planta-genet army was defeated by 10 000 largely Scottish troops. As a reward for their services, the Earl of Douglas was created lieutenant-general of France and Duke of Touraine and the Earl of Buchan made Constable of France. Many Scots continued to fight, serving under St Joan in 1429–30; the Scots Guard continued to speak Scots in France into the 1500s.[109] They were not always popular, being 'collectively condemned by their French allies as mutton guzzlers and wine bags'. Certainly, there was a longstanding fondness for claret in Scotland, not replaced by the Anglo-Portuguese port until the eighteenth century. Three hundred years earlier, 'Edinburgh merchants were despatching their children to Bordeaux, specifically for the purposes of learning a foreign language and gaining proficiency in business'.[110]

Trade and military links with the Low Countries, Scandinavia and the Baltic were extensive, particularly via the east-coast ports. In the fifteenth century, Aberdeen was importing goods from the Low Countries, the Rhineland and France.[111] Local settlements of Flemings kept their own laws in the burgh for a time, while in the early fourteenth century, both Flemish and German pirates maintained agents in Aberdeen to sell cap-tured English spoils to the inhabitants.[112] On the Continent, pedlars were so commonly Scots that eventually the words became synonymous.[113] In 1700, there were 1000 Scots in the port of Rotterdam alone,[114] while Scot-tish merchant colonies, sometimes composed of ex-officers, remained influential long after the Union: into the nineteenth century in Gothen-burg, for example. Swedish Scots such as the manufacturer William Gibson (1783–1857) and the engineer Alexander Keiller (1804–74) made a major impact on the economic well-being of their host country.[115] Domestic religious observance also had its place abroad, for 'Scottish altars...were maintained at churches in Danzig, Elsinore, Copenhagen, Bruges, Ber-gen-op-Zoom, Regensberg and elsewhere.' Scottish national saints such as St Ninian and St Andrew were celebrated by their dedications; the cross of St Andrew, Scotland's national symbol, was also shared by Burgundy.[116]

Scotland's military contributions to France continued to the Revolu-tion, but were proportionately greatest in the mediaeval and early

Renaissance periods. After the Reformation, it was Sweden and Russia who received the greatest influx of Scottish military support. In the seventeenth century, Gustavus Adolphus could boast 84 Scottish battalion and regimental commanders, and was 'said to have made over 60 Scotsmen governors of castles and towns in the conquered provinces of Germany'. When Frankfurt fell in 1632, 'Lumsden's Regiment alone captured nine stands of colours from the enemy.' At Leipzig, the Scots Brigade were in the van. Men like Alexander Erskine were President of the War Council of Sweden; while 'as late as 1857, the Marshal of the Kingdom . . . was a Hamilton'.[117] In Russia, Henry Farquharson, a don on the staff of Marischal College, Aberdeen in the 1690s, was recruited by Peter the Great to help found Russia's first naval academy. Later he 'supervised the building of a highway' from Moscow to St Petersburg, 'published the first Tables of Logarithms in Russian', surveyed the Caspian, published textbooks and became a Russian brigadier. Generals such as Sir Tam Dalyell (1615–85), Gordon of Auchintoul (1669–1752) and Robert Armstrong (1791–1865) (leaving aside the Scots ancestry of Barclay de Tolly) made an impact on the Russian army, while Thomas Gordon (1662–1741) did much to develop the Russian naval service. Businessmen, agriculturalists and diplomats were all supplied to Russia by a Scottish diaspora which continued into the nineteenth century.[118]

If Scotland maintained wide-ranging trade and military links with northern Europe, it was nonetheless the case that for many continental observers the country was regarded as either poor or almost impossibly remote: '*in finibus orbi*', as the Milanese ambassador to the French court put it in 1474. If it was famous for anything apart from being far away, Scotland was known 'for its hostility to England', both at home and through 'the involvement of Scottish soldiers in battles against the English in fifteenth-century France'. The future Pius II, visiting Scotland in 1435, 'noted that the Scots liked nothing better than to hear abuse of the English'.[119] This attitude, perhaps crystallized in the Wars of Independence, is repeated again and again in the evidence of the mediaeval period: it clearly indicates the presence of a strong national cohesiveness based on defensive solidarity against a powerful neighbour. Regnal unity might be important for this, but the identity expressed so frequently in this manner was set deeper in the social fabric than any question of allegiance alone could have placed it. In this as elsewhere, it is important not to take explanations of Scottish nationality under any single heading as comprehensive.[120]

Anglophobia may also have been an important measure of self-definition because Scots abroad were often confused with other nations, at first

the Irish (until '*Scoti*' as a generic term for Scots-Irish fell out of use in
the later mediaeval period) and later (as Inglis/Scots grew more predominant in Scotland) the English. This confusion was surely perpetuated
both by the similarity of some Scots to northern English speech,[121] and
by the Scots' description of their own tongue as 'Inglis', one which
endured to 1400. In 1326, at least one Scotsman (from debatable Berwick)
was interned along with English nationals in France, and thereafter
'harassed by French officials' as English; in 1350, four Scots were killed
in France on the mistaken assumption that they *were* English. At universities such as Paris, Scots were included under the umbrella of 'the
English-German nation'. Scots nonetheless often appeared in different
dress from the English: 'in the twelfth century a monk from Cambrai
recorded that many Scots wore no drawers but covered themselves with
garments which were left open underneath and at the sides'. This was
'the dress of... western Scotland' rather than those of the knights or
burghers, whose clothes appear gradually to have (by the mid-fifteenth
century) conformed to a western European norm. Naturalization
among Scots abroad was widespread, but there also remained discrete
Scottish communities gathered together at locations ranging from Durham
to Bergen-op-Zoom,[122] while continental universities, particularly those
at Paris and Leiden, were major magnets for Scottish students as late
as the eighteenth century. Following improvement of the harbours on
the east coast, overseas travel became commonplace among moneyed
and educated Scots. After the papacy moved to Avignon in 1309, Scots
tended to be drawn increasingly to universities in France and the
Empire rather than Oxford or Cambridge.[123]

Despite these markedly cosmopolitan elements, however, Scotland
was developing a strongly autonomous culture of its own. Under David
I, the first separate Scottish coinage was issued. The teaching of Duns
Scotus (1266–1308) began a long tradition in Scottish philosophy, with
Scotus himself not only being influential on Catholic thinking, but also
on the philosophy of such figures as Thomas Reid and Martin Heidegger;
indeed, it has been recently argued that Scotus' emphasis on freedom
is linked to the contemporary national struggle of his own homeland.
In historiography, the arguments concerning Scottish nationality from
the Wars of Independence helped feed the work of John of Fordun
(1320–84) and Walter Bower (1385–1449), while the music of Inchma-
home Priory and later Robert Carver's (1486–1568) masses marked a
path towards a high point in the 'slee' polyphonic culture of late
mediaeval Scotland.[124] In 1375–77, Archdeacon John Barbour com-

bined historiography and contemporary literary genres in producing his poem *The Bruce*. It was to be part of a cultural continuum of Scottish writing 'which linked late medieval and early modern Scotland across the seeming fissure of the Reformation of 1560'.[125]

Barbour's poem is both an epic and a romance, emphasizing the qualities of 'chewalry', 'leaute', 'pite' and 'curtesy' as the 'high' virtues of the Scottish knights, Bruce himself above them all. This reinforces the epic scale of their achievement, for, speaking in the voice of great genres recognizable in Europe for their prestige and universality, the poem forestalls any English attributions of disloyalty, treachery, meanness or simple good fortune to the success of Scottish arms: *The Bruce* claims Scotland's place in the ranks of fitting subjects for elevated literary treatment on a European scale. At the same time, Barbour hints that the 'high' qualities of chivalry and courtesy are not the sole preserves of the Scottish nobility, for in war the 'symple yumanry' can be as good as a knight. For Barbour, his story is reinforced as an exemplar by its 'suthfast' quality, the 'doubill plesance' of it being no idle romance, but the truth that he is telling. That truth is the struggle for national freedom, as expressed in Barbour's famous apostrophe, put on the lips of William Wallace in the 1995 film, *Braveheart*:

> A, fredome is a noble thing,
> Fredome mays man to haiff liking,
> Fredome all solace to man giffis,
> He levys at es that frely levys.

Given the considerable role played by the Church in Bruce's cause, it was fitting that a priest should write the king's patriot epic, and frame its nationalism in eschatological terms: 'he that [deis] for his cuntre/Sall herbryit [received] in-till hewyn be'.[126]

In education, the development of the burgh grammar schools, closely linked to the cathedral, was early evident at centres such as Glasgow (1124) and Aberdeen (the thirteenth century). The first steps to extend access to education at these schools were taken before the end of the mediaeval period: indeed, recent research suggests that Scotland had up to 1000 schoolmasters by the time of the Reformation.[127] By this stage, Scotland had three universities: King's College at Aberdeen (1495), St Andrews (1410; St Salvator's (1450)) and Glasgow (1451), located at the heart of what were probably the three wealthiest dioceses in Scotland. Clerical lawyers, many educated in France or Italy, returned to the appointments opening up in such centres. At Aberdeen, Bishop Elphinstone developed a Scots liturgy, the '*Breviarum Aberdoniense*', published in 1509–10.[128] At a lower level, the 'Education Act' of 1496, the first example of an attempt to develop universal education among the sons of freeholders, may be taken as a sign of rising demand for educated administrators from the state apparatus.[129] There are even the first hints of equality of opportunity. At one point in the fifteenth century, almost 90 per cent of brewers in the town of Aberdeen were female,[130] while women were admitted as simple burgesses and even (as at Inverurie in 1536) voted.[131]

Despite these achievements, the Scottish polity remained under stress. In 1462, the Lords of the Isles 'bound themselves and their subjects and followers to become vassals of England' by the Treaty of Ardtornish; nor was this the only occasion when Scotland's most powerful because inaccessible nobles would attempt to detach themselves from the kingdom.[132] It is important, however, not to overemphasize the importance of such developments, and still less is it appropriate to conflate them with some kind of broader projected *Gaeltachd* sentiment. English nobles such as Percy had threatened to split the kingdom in pursuit of his own aims (with Owain Glyn Dwr before the battle of Shrewsbury in 1402), while a Gaelic poem written before Flodden calls for common purpose for Scotland against 'Saxons... Let us after the pattern of the Gael of Ireland watch over our fatherland', in a display of 'remarkable patriotism'.[133] Scotland was settling down to its current borders, with the final absorption of the 'earldom of Orkney and the lordship of Shetland' by the Scottish Crown in 1472, following James III's (1460–88) marriage settlement with Norway. The English capture of Berwick in 1483 finalized the bounds of modern Scotland. Some on the fringes of the twentieth-century nationalist movement have suggested the return of Berwick (still an ambivalent town in that its county lies in Scotland and its football team plays there), but otherwise no significant remaining territorial dispute continued to exist after the fifteenth century. One of the matters to be remarked on, indeed in the history of both nations, is the longstanding near-stability of their frontiers over almost a millennium.

The enduring if intermittent alliance with France was linked to two of the great cataclysms which struck sixteenth-century Scotland and in the end permanently changed its political orientation: the battle of Flodden in 1513 and the regime of Mary of Guise during the minority of Mary Queen of Scots. The developments in Scottish military technology under James II (1437–60) and still more James IV (1488–1513) appear indicative of a growing overconfidence, almost amounting to hubris, in later Stewart Scotland. James III 'had planned an invasion of Brittany in 1472' while James V 'toyed with the offer made to him in 1538 of the kingship of Ireland', both possibilities requiring resources far beyond those available to the King of Scots. Neither of these had serious consequences, unlike Flodden, where up to half of James IV's 20 000-strong army died, including the king himself; 'nine of the twelve earls present were killed in the battle'.[134] This was not a Scottish expeditionary force, but a vast host, possibly the largest army ever raised in Scotland before the Reformation, sent over the border in support of Louis XII of France. Scotland was not equal to the task, and from the Treaty of Rouen in 1521, French troops in numbers, together with sophisticated fortifications, began to appear in Scotland on an intermittent basis to protect it from Henry VIII (1509–47), who was steadily developing a pro-English party in Scotland, which would become much more visible after the English Reformation.

Following James V's death in 1542, the military crisis intensified. English demands for a marriage between Edward (the future Edward VI) and Mary were accompanied by an unwillingness to see Scotland maintain its treaties with France and 'demands that the Queen should be sent to England for her education'. After initial agreement, these requirements were 'rejected by the Scottish parliament', and in 1544 the Earl of Hertford invaded. Old English suzerainty claims were 'revived', and 'English military pressure' led to numbers of 'assured Scots' in the east-coast counties being forced into a pro-English stance. The patriot Cardinal Beaton was murdered by Reformers in 1546. After 1547, 'increasingly ... Protestantism was made the litmus test of English favour'. The seeds of a Protestant Britain were already being sown. Nonetheless, they did not yet bear fruit. Mary left for France in 1548: in return for her agreement, French troops came to counter English power, and fought England to a standstill and peace in 1550–51.[135]

Reforming the Kingdoms

Traditionally, and with some root in fact, the earliest signs of Protestantism in Scotland made themselves manifest in fifteenth-century Ayrshire Lollardy:[136] certainly the south-west of Scotland was subsequently the heartland of the country's most radical Protestants. In the east-coast ports, it was Lutheranism rather than Calvinism that brought the Reformation to Scotland. Papal authority was being attacked in north-east Scotland as early as the 1520s in admittedly isolated incidents.[137] Although there were fewer than a dozen martyrs in the 1530s, the martyrdoms of Patrick Hamilton (1528), George Wishart (1546) and Walter Myln (1558) were symbolic catalysts. By the 1540s, the east coast south of Aberdeen and Ayrshire in the west were showing markedly Reformed sympathies. The marriage of Mary to the Dauphin in 1558 quickened the increasingly pro-English Protestant nobility into action; what was once (and to some nationalist Jacobites much later remained) a glorious alliance with France had now become conflated with a Catholic threat. In 1559, the Congregation nobles, 'lairds and burgesses..."purged" a series of towns in central Scotland'. Mary of Guise was driven from her regency, and alliance with England made in early 1560. By the Treaty of Edinburgh the same year, French troops were removed from Scotland. The Protestant Reformation had become the first herald of future Union. Scottish linguistic forms began to disappear from the growing publishing industry under the influence of sympathy with the English Reformation and its vernacular. For the first time, Scotland as a nation looked politically to English power, 'offering it support in a conquest of Ireland'.[138] After her return to Scotland in 1561, Mary's situation gradually became untenable, and she fled to England in 1568 with the political astuteness for which her dynasty was famed: she was in Elizabeth's toils, and there she remained until she was judicially murdered nearly twenty years later. In vain the Catholic apologists protested on behalf of the old Church, the old alliance and the Scots tongue: 'Gif ye, throw curiositie of novations', wrote Ninian Winzet, 'hes foryet our auld plane Scottis, quhilk your mother lerit you, in tymes coming I sall wrytt to yow my mind in Latin, for I am nocht acquyntit with your Southron.' Such protests were of no use: before 1560, English forms do not appear in Scottish printing; by 1560–80, 18 per cent of books have them; by 1580–90, 57 per cent, 1590–1600, 68 per cent, 1600–10, 78 per cent and 1610–25, 93 per cent. Scots was disappearing from the printed realm of high culture.[139]

During the conflagration, some towns and cities had the Reformation imported into them from outside: in the case of Aberdeen, a mob of Reformers from Angus and Mearns pushed their way into the burgh, casting the great statue of Our Lady at the north-east end of the Brig o Dee into the water, whence it was conveyed to Ostend and thence to Brussels.[140] The Cathedral in Old Aberdeen had 50 kg of ornamental silver alone: it was ransacked (though the Earl of Huntly's protection saved it from the worst) and the monasteries despoiled.[141] Aberdeen in general and the Aulton (Old Town) in particular, remained sceptically disposed towards a Calvinist Kirk of Scotland for many years. In the Aulton, the image of Our Lady on the cross by the Town House in the High Street was not removed until the 1790s, while the 'portrait of our Blessed Virgin Mary and her dear Son Baby Jesus in her arms' at the Bishop's Palace did not disappear until 1640.[142] The north-east produced a good number of conservative figures who were to underpin the continuation of a traditional, Church and King sense of Scottish nationality. After 1707 these figures were commonly anti-Unionist Jacobites; indeed, it can be argued that the preservation of traditionalist concepts of Scottish nationality in the region did not die out until the nineteenth century – though even that may be too cautious a speculation, for the north-east has been the core Lowland heartland of the SNP for many years.

The kind of cultural outlook present and preserved in the north-east after the Reformation has been variously described. There are certain consistent features: a greater attachment to Royalist Episcopalianism than found in the rest of Scotland, combined with a strong Catholicism in the rural areas, defended by the Gordon family (up to 50 per cent of Scottish Catholics lived in Aberdeenshire and Banffshire in the seventeenth and eighteenth centuries); a 'Scoto-Latin' tradition in writing friendly both to Latin and Scots, and exalting Scotland's traditional values and alliances (e.g. with France), and a strong folk culture. Isolated by river and distance from much of Scotland in an era of poor transport, the north-east nonetheless possessed a university, a powerful regional centre in Aberdeen and much rich farmland. Episcopalian conservatism (one estimate from 1708 is that around 50 per cent of the population was Episcopalian in Aberdeen, Banff, Moray and Ross,[143] an area which stretches for almost 200 miles) was itself succoured by the examples of prominent recusant nobles, such as the Earls of Huntly and Erroll, as well as the longstanding influence of a powerful group of Catholic burgesses, centring on the family of Menzies of Pitfodels.[144] In the first General Assembly of the Church of Scotland after the final establishment of Presbyterianism in 1690, the 180 who attended were 'all from south of the Tay...a partition church of southern Scotland'.[145] The fragmentation of Scottish national identity along clerical lines had finally appeared, for it was the bulk of this southern Church which accepted the terms of the Union, while for 40 years afterwards it was Scotland north of the Tay, the 'conservative north', in Gordon Donaldson's memorable phrase, which was at the forefront of armed Risings designed once again to secure Scotland's vanished independence.[146]

After the Reformation, this continuing tradition in the 'conservative north' was exemplified in figures such as Patrick Forbes of Corse, bishop of Aberdeen from 1618 to 1635, who developed the study of ecclesiastical history at King's and revived the old pre-Reformation links between the staff and the Church; William Forbes (1585–1634), bishop of Edinburgh, who held that 'many of the differences between the Church of Rome and the Protestants were merely superficial' and that 'Purgatory, Praying for the Dead, the Intercession and Invocation of Angels and Saints' were all practices which could be derived from Scripture',[147] George Conn (1598–1640), the Papal Nuncio to the Court of St James, St John Ogilvie (1579–1615), martyred at Glasgow Cross, and James Sharp of Banff (1618–79), archbishop of St Andrews, murdered at Magus Muir in 1679. Among writers and thinkers there are men like the Latinist Jacobite Thomas Ruddiman (1684–1757), Fr Thomas Innes of Aboyne (1662–1744), James Burnett, Lord Monboddo (1714–99) and the great philosopher Thomas Reid (1710–96), whose Common Sense approach owed much to the mediaeval philosophical tradition.[148] Both Sir Thomas Urquhart (1611–60) and George Dalgarno (1626–87) attempted to develop a 'universal language'.[149] Later, some of the most famous poets of eighteenth-century Scotland, such as James Macpherson (1736/8–96), Robert Fergusson (1750–74), and even (by descent) Robert Burns (1759–96) himself, all came from north-eastern Scotland. There were also important original Latin writers, such as Dr Arthur Johnston (1577–1641), Professor of Logic and Metaphysic at Sedan, Latin Secretary to James VI, and a patriotic Episcopalian, and James Philp of Almerieclose (1655/6–1714/25), standard-bearer to Viscount Dundee in the Jacobite Rising of 1689 and author of the last attempt to write a Latin epic in Britain, *The Grameid*. George Jamesone (1588/90–1644) was Scotland's first portrait painter; his great-grandson John (1686–1766) and great-great-grandson Cosmo Alexander (1724–72) were both considerable artists and Jacobites; James Gibbs (1682–1754), one of the most prominent architects of his generation in England or Scotland, shared their political views. Dr Patrick Abercromby (1656–1718) was Physician to James VII (as Arthur Johnston had been to Charles I), wrote *Martial Achievements of the Scottish Nation*, and supported the Jacobite Rising of 1715; Dr John Arbuthnot (1667–1735), Pope's friend, was likewise physician to Queen Anne: his brother was a Jacobite agent. Alexander, 4th Lord Forbes of Pitsligo (1678–1762), set up an ecumenical religious retreat at Rosehearty in the early eighteenth century which was indicative of the rapprochement which could exist between Episcopalians and Catholics in the 'conservative north'.[150] Chevalier Andrew Ramsay, later tutor to Charles Edward Stuart ('Bonnie Prince Charlie'), was among the early enthusiasts for this community Pitsligo himself fought in both the Jacobite Risings of 1715 and 1745, in the latter as General of Horse.

In the period 1603–1745, after the Court had left Edinburgh and before the last Jacobite Rising, many of these men preserved what has been called a 'castle culture' with a distinctive, patriotic outlook on the whole unmoved by the growing appeal of London. It was associated both with the preservation of Scottish court culture in the age after the loss of the Court, and with a patriotic discourse of essential or authentic Scottishness, which came into its own after 1707. In it, the Union and the overthrow of the Stuarts were seen as acts of collective disloyalty to a past of valour and simplicity, like that of Republican Rome before it was corrupted by the gold of empire. The beginnings of this critique were already evident in the seventeenth century, when poems like Johnston's lament for the Earl of Stirling's absorption into English court culture, or his 1626 poem on the rupture of the Auld Alliance, foretold the shape of things to come.[151] In December 1706, on the approach of the Union, an Aberdeen schoolmaster wrote this elegy for his country in terms which sum up the conservatism of the north-east, with its evocation of nationalism combined with an injunction to pray for the dead:

> Here lies, entombed in her own ashes, yet with the hope of a blessed resurrection, the famous nation of the Scots . . . she, full of years, though yet in undiminished vigour of limbs, losing control of her mind, yielded helpless to fate. Pray for her![152]

It was thus this least Presbyterian area of Lowland Scotland which provided so much of the impetus for the Jacobite risings of 1715 and 1745.

The Rage of Party

Before James's accession to the English throne, his court poets and propagandists projected a fantasy of a Britain not only ruled by a Scottish king, but one which manifested Scottish values. These 'Scoto-Britanes' were of necessity proved wrong, but there are few signs that this small high cultural segment's fragmentation into careerism and disappointment had much impact on Scottish nationality. Yet although the effects of the Court's departure in 1603 have been exaggerated (as Keith Brown observes, there is not much evidence for a large-scale exodus of nobility),[153] they were nonetheless significant. The high cultural idealization of the monarch found in his court circle had its demotic counterpart in the accessibility and familiarity of the king, and the closeness between king and people long remarked on in Scotland, of which James V's incognito travellings and reputed contribution to folk song ('The Gaberlunzie Man') were only the most recent examples. James's easy relations with his subjects could not be successfully transferred to the English Court. The resulting damage to the lines of communication between the king and his community led in the first instance to the pleading tones of some of the poetry of *The Muses' Welcome*, published on the occasion of James's progress into Scotland in 1617. The language of longing visible in poems such as William Drummond's 'Forth Feasting' was later to explode throughout the subgenres of Jacobite nationalist poetry, with their frequent replication of the voice of a longing Caledonia calling for the return of her king to make the land whole, the 'JAMES of my Heart', in the words of Alexander Robertson of Struan (1670–1749).[154]

This sense of loss, visible in particular among more conservatively nationally minded Scots, particularly Episcopalians, northerners and Gaelic speakers, was complemented by a more lively political sense of resentment, frequently focused on innovations in worship and ever-watchful of popery. It was both prophetic and ironic that the court staff which James left behind him in 1603 was that of the Chapel Royal, for it was to be the perceived intrusion of English sacred music and worship which was to cause increasing discontent and finally explode in his son's face in 1638.

The National Covenant of that year, drawn up in response to the imposition of a high Anglican prayer book on Scotland (James had already secured the future of an episcopal hierarchy), revisited the politics of the Lords of the Congregation in the 1550s, and through a combination of vicious militancy and high-flown rhetoric, reoriented Scottish politics once again away from a Stuart monarch and towards the Reformed interest in England, where Archbishop Laud's attempts to bring order to the Church were alike unpopular. The result was two brief wars, with the king's unenthusiastic forces cowed by battle-hardened Scottish continental veterans. These in turn paved the way for the spread of war to England, where the king set up his standard in 1642.

James himself had a strongly developed concept of Britain, one perhaps less unrealistically geared to the delusions of a Scottish takeover found in his court circle. He was glad to have escaped from the 'twa Kings and twa Kingdoms' theocratic ideology of the likes of Andrew Melville (1545–1622) in Scotland, which argued for the separation of Church and State, and the effective autonomy of the former. This proto-Covenanting case was opposed by the Estates in 1584, when clergy were subjected to the crown, but partially accepted by the recognition of kirk privileges in 1592. James no doubt wished an end to such wrangling, but was unable to 'force the English Parliament to proceed with the Instrument of Union': all that occurred was an act for the repeal of 'mutually hostile legislation', which reached the statute book on 2 May 1607. Nonetheless, James was repeatedly depicted as 'King of Great Britain' ('Emperor of the whole island of Britain' on his 'accession medal'), with the separate realms of Scotland and England elided;[155] and he sought not only political union but also ecclesial conformity. Designs for a new Union flag and a variety of other images of state, including the Great Seal, were pursued. The flag was agreed after much bickering but fell out of use after 1625 (it could in any case 'only be flown in conjunction with one or other of the two national flags'); the design for the Seal 'conjoined not only the English and Scottish arms but also those of Cadwallader and Edward the Confessor, respectively the last undisputed kings of Celtic Britain and Anglo-Saxon England'. In an age when royal imagery defined the public space of national identity far more thoroughly than it does now, James's hail of icons were a sign of decided pressure on a separate Scottish identity.

There was, however, little enthusiasm for Britain in England, and a Scottish king's policy of granting at least a fair share of English offices and perquisites to Scotsmen did not improve sentiment. By 1607, the English parliament had finally rejected 'a full incorporating union',[156] while James mused on the possibility of taking York for his seat of government.[157] Some Scottish interests likewise regarded Unionist tendencies with suspicion: the Convention of Royal Burghs was increasingly conscious of the demands of centralized power, and by 1613 it needed to employ an agent in London to defend its interests: 'the age of the political lobbyist had arrived'. In discussing Union, the Scottish Parliament feared it might turn the country into 'a conquered and slavish province'.[158]

Although Scots had greater freedom of movement in England, few of them shared the king's vision of British unity. Scotland effectively lost its separate representation overseas, and with it the opportunity to follow an independent foreign policy: this had potentially serious consequences, as the country might be dragged into English continental quarrels at worst (as happened with the Spanish war in the 1620s), or find its trade disrupted by them at best.[159] On the other hand, separate Scottish colonial endeavours under the umbrella of British power began with the Nova Scotia project of 1617. Nonetheless, Scottish national identity was cramped in its public expression abroad, and areas of Scottish society were under pressure at home. James's assault on local autonomy in the Borders and Highlands was a clear sign of his centralizing tendencies, confirmed by the backing for Episcopalianism borne witness to in the Five Articles of Perth in 1617, although here James was in sympathy with many of his northern subjects, for Presbyterianism's grip was loose indeed north of the Tay. Nonetheless, the pro-Episcopalian policy of the Stuarts in London may have helped to make possible the final victory of a Presbyterian Church of Scotland in 1690, for 'the Kirk steadily became a metaphor for Scottish identity' in the face of increasing pressure for British ecclesial conformity.[160] The National Covenant was the fruit of this process.

Yet once again the issues are more mixed than the assumptions of simplistic history have made them. James's vision of a unified Protestant Britain had more appeal in the age of the Thirty Years War to the evangelical and zealous Presbyterian and Nonconformist than to the tame bishops of a caesaropapist monarchy, whose use of the Royal Touch for scrofula and other diseases harked back to the sacred claims of mediaeval kings rather than forward to the age of Thomas Muggleton and George Fox. The Kirk may have been increasingly the vehicle for Scottish national identity in the central Lowlands, but that identity itself was defined against Stuart centralism rather than, as of old, England as a nation. In the Bishops' Wars, northern English were often supportive of the Scots: Charles's policy of conformity to a ubiquitously high Anglican church had its enemies south as well as north of the Border. The scene was set for a Scotland divided in religious and dynastic war, which in one way or another lasted half a century (a century if one counts the Jacobite Risings, though after the Union nationalism was once again feeding the Stuart cause). This process undermined the nation's ability to function on a variety of levels. In the end, the vaunted Scottish patriotism of the Covenanters subsided into the imperial Protestant Britain not of the seventeenth, but the eighteenth century.

The signs were there even before the 1640s. Increased loathing of the Catholic Irish combined the denial of Scots-Irish commonality of origin and culture with the largely Scottish colonization of northern Ulster. Fear and hatred of the Irish in Scotland was now at, or beyond, English levels: the nation was severing its historic links, and new ones beckoned. The War in the Three Kingdoms from 1638 to 1651 both bound Scotland and Ireland together in a new way and also divided them through colonization (the plantation of Ulster was already serving as 'a permanent wedge' between Ireland and Scotland) and confessional issues, as well as the ferocity of the Covenanting response to Irish troops and camp-followers in Scotland: 'whereas the process of law', Allan Macinnes observes, 'tended to be applied to Catholic clansmen, all Irish troops were summarily executed on capture or surrender'. The pressure to declare loyalties pushed the clans decisively into 'Scottish as against pan-Gaelic politics', a phenomenon reinforced by the intensity of the Marquess of Montrose's (1612–50) campaign for the king in 1644–45.[161]

Unsurprisingly, therefore, the first strong signs of Scottish enthusiasm for Union emerge in the Covenanting period. The resistance of the self-styled Scottish national church to Episcopalian innovation promised by the National Covenant of 1638 gave way in the Solemn League and Covenant of 1643 to demands for common forms of worship and a symbiotic political union throughout the British Isles, with 'something like a federal Britain as the natural corollary of religious union'.[162] A clear ideology of Unionism was gaining ground in some quarters, driven by a Protestant interest which saw itself as having more in common with the anti-Anglican England of the Commonwealth than with its Caroline predecessor. Covenanting proto-unionists tended to want to see joint British action in foreign policy and trade (areas which were to remain in friction until 1707), together with autonomous but religiously uniform churches and separate parliaments to conduct internal affairs.[163] A language was beginning to develop to reflect these priorities. Campbell *fine* (nobles), for example, 'were to the fore in using the terms "North British" for Scotland and "British" for colonists settling in Ulster'.[164] At the same time, it is important to register that (despite propaganda to the contrary) the Covenants were not universally popular: as Colin Kidd observes, 'the Scoto-British presbyterian ideal of an Anglo-Scottish union on the basis of the Solemn League and Covenant of 1643 was anathema to the great majority of Anglican churchmen and Scots episcopalians alike'.[165] Sections of northern society welcomed Laud's Prayer Book and resisted the Covenants. It was hard to raise Covenanting troops in north-east Scotland, and many deserted: in 1640, 1200 deserted the Earl Marischal, and in 1644, 2600 from 3000 deserted the

Gordon forces raised for the Covenant.[166] Yet the Covenanting movement was national (and supranational, given its Ulster impact) in scope, with the capacity to raise up to 25 000 in arms. It also had an important impact in the north, because those raised in opposition to it by the Royalists were, particularly after Montrose deserted the Covenanting interest, often Highlanders. The clans in particular and the 'conservative north' in general were thus drawn more closely into the orbit of a wider British politics than had hitherto been the case.

Covenanting federalism in the 1640s was, however, like the Scoto-Brittanism of the 1590s, delusive in that it posited an acceptance by English interests of Scottish terms. When the War of Three Kingdoms ended in 1651, it was not with a federal Presbyterian Britain in which Scottish ministers could lord it over a repentant Anglican squirearchy, but with the incorporation, in December 1651, of Scotland into 'the free state and Commonwealth of England', later the 'Commonwealth of England, Scotland and Ireland'. A 'Council for Scotland was set up in 1657', and Scots gained limited rights of representation at Westminster, but taxes rose and an army of occupation was required.[167] Cromwellian writers described Scots as 'Barbarians', 'cattle' (Lilburne's word) and 'an inexhaustible Magazeen of Auxiliaries' for the armed forces. As one Cromwellian soldier complained, 'they charge me with the killing of a woman, and she was but a Scotch woman'. Virulent anti-Scottishness combined with the desire to utilize their fighting qualities in the British army was to surface again many times in the future: in the 1650s, it cannot have helped to make the Cromwellian regime more popular.[168]

At the Restoration of 1660, Union formed part of the 'demonology of the restored regime' (though moves towards 'economic union' were nonetheless made in the the late 1660s).[169] Between 1660 and 1662, the king's return was accompanied by that of Scotland's law, parliament, privy council – and bishops: a 'centrifugal reflex' replaced the Cromwellian 'centralizing surge'. Problems with armed Covenanters remained: but these were largely confined to the south-west, though there were more dangerous sporadic outbreaks. In the 1680s about 180 Covenanters were 'executed' or 'cut down by troops in the field', a number which hardly justifies the martyrology which has long surrounded what were, albeit often for the sake of conscience, rebels who were either armed or supported those who were. Michael Lynch has argued that greater severity was used in the Highlands, supposedly the barbarian allies of Stuart Episcopal tyranny:[170] if this was the case, it foreshadowed the differential policy of the British state towards the Highlands and Lowlands after Cul-loden, when Lowland Jacobite townships escaped relatively unscathed.

In the 1630s and 1640s, many of the Stuarts' problems had centred on the fact that they were the only post-mediaeval British dynasty to have poor relations with the core of the nascent British state: south-east England. Heartland as it was in many ways of mercantilism and English Protestantism, the Stuarts repeatedly displayed their incom-patibility with much of the outlook of London and southern society: there was relatively little support for Charles I there in 1642. After the Res-toration of 1660 in particular, the Stuarts were conscious of the value of potential centres of loyalty outside the English core, and Charles's settlement in 1662 displayed this fact: 'it was deliberate royal policy to keep the settlement of the three kingdoms apart from each other', as Michael Lynch observes.[171] Indeed,

> The decoration and redevelopment of Holyrood Palace in Edinburgh during Charles II's reign may have been part of a royal plan to bolster the country's status as a separate kingdom, both perhaps to minimize the complaints of Anglicization which had led to the explosion of 1638, and also to reinforce Stu-art authority and legitimacy as kings of Scotland.[172]

Stuart court culture in Dublin had shown vibrancy as early as the 1630s, and when James held court at Holyrood as Duke of Albany in 1679–82, many Scottish nobles returned to the northern kingdom, and 'Edinburgh became the centre of a thriving court with an unmistakably Scottish flavour.'[173] A patriot cult of tartan, perhaps evident as early as the sixteenth century, was encouraged at Holyrood in the 1680s. It stressed the antiquity and valour of the Scottish nation, a discourse which was to become a staple of anti-Union rhetoric: as Allan Macinnes notes, Jacobitism 'deliberately promoted a Highland identity' as the visible sign of Scottish nationality.[174] Scots had held a declining proportion of court offices in London since the palmy days of James VI and I; by the Restoration they had no important offices, and thus much less to keep them in the English capital.[175] In Edin-burgh, an Episcopalian regime and tightly controlled parliament strongly endorsed the restored Stuart government, despite repeated Covenanting insurgency in the west. Whether or not with the aim of trying to quiet more general Scottish alienation, James developed the intellectual and artistic infrastructure of Edinburgh as a distinctly Scottish royal capital, a move endorsed by his brother in the commission 'for De Wet to paint at Holy-rood in 1684–6' a 'series of portraits' of Scottish monarchs from Fergus, designed to closely align the Stuarts with the patriotic history of the nation. Apologists such as the King's Advocate, Sir George Mackenzie, insisted on the patriotic nature of belief in 'the immemorial antiquity' of the Scottish Stuart line.[176] The Stuarts were once again stressing their Scottishness, in an attempt to avoid the collapses in their authority of 1559–68 and 1638–43. It was not to be. After James succeeded in 1685, the dynasty once again appeared to reach out towards the feared and hated spectres of prelacy and popery, and Scotland was once again convulsed, although it is also true that James's reign witnessed 'a marked upsurge in apostasy from Protestantism' in the 'conservative north'.[177] After the Convention Parliament disowned James in April 1689, a northern magnate, like Montrose in 1644–45 and Mar in 1715, rose in arms against the new religious and political settlement. Fighting for Episcopacy and royal power, Viscount Dundee fell in the latter moments of his costly, brief and in the end ineffectual victory at Killiecrankie in July 1689. Most of the political nation sat on their hands and watched the fate of his small force.

The Scottish Parliament's relations with its English equivalent and the English Crown were structurally far more of a problem than they appeared. In 1689, the Convention had largely endorsed its English counterpart's decision; but it was wrong to assume, as some in England no doubt did, that it would be so compliant on every occasion. Nonetheless, the securing of the established Presbyterian Kirk meant that 'old-style presbyterian nationalism was dead':[178] henceforward, apart from some sentiment at the fringe of opinion, the Presbyterian interest drifted steadily into alignment with the wider interests of Protestant Britain.

Economic issues began to bulk large in Anglo-Scottish relations, particularly in the wake of the collapse of the Darien colonial venture at a time of domestic economic crisis, with thousands dying of famine. English war with France was responsible for 'blighting Scotland's sinking trade',[179] and the Darien collapse highlighted not only English failure to support Scottish colonization (whereas Scottish troops had already been used abroad by England), but also the effect of English foreign policy on the Scottish economy. In 1698, the patriot, parliamentarian and political theorist Andrew Fletcher of Saltoun (1653–1716) analysed the problem with his customary precision, arguing that envoys to foreign courts, as appointees of the English Crown, could not be guaranteed to further Scottish interests.[180] Discontent rose, and twice in the last two years of William's reign moves were made by England 'to regain control of Scottish politics' by means of Union.[181] In the years around 1700, a ferocious pamphlet war raged between those who argued for the historic sovereignty of the Crown of Scotland (and therefore the Scottish kingdom's right to pursue its own interests separate from those of England), and those who defended historic claims to English suzerainty, which reached back into the murk of Galfridian precedent. Some of these claims were still being accepted at face value as part of the history of Britain in respected textbooks in the twentieth century.[182]

After the accession of Queen Anne in 1702, events moved steadily to a crisis. Following the fiasco at Darien, the Scottish Parliament was increasingly unwilling to endorse the 1701 Act of Settlement by which its English counterpart excluded Catholics from the throne. English expectations that Scotland would as tamely accept the Act of Settlement as they had the parliamentary deposition of James in 1689 proved unfounded. By the Act Anent Peace and War (1703) the Scottish Parliament sought to secure for itself the possibility of an independent foreign policy, while a year later the Act of Security threatened that of Settlement directly, by introducing the possibility of a separate Scottish succession to the throne after the death of Anne, 'unless in this or some subsequent Parliament such conditions of Governance had been enacted as should secure from English or from foreign interest the honour and independence . . . of Scotland'.[183] The Scottish Parliament wanted a renegotiation of the regnal union, which had only intermittently flourished as a true 'composite monarchy' under the Stuarts in London and not at all under their successors.[184] The Act of Security was, as John Robertson points out, designed to exact a price for future co-operation with England; it was supported by those like Andrew Fletcher of Saltoun, who favoured wider confederal arrangements.[185] No longer was Scotland to be, in Fletcher's words, 'a farm managed by servants'.[186] As Colin Kidd observes:

> The most common argument in Scottish political culture between 1689 and 1707 – a prominent feature of the ideology of both whigs and Jacobites, and of separatists, federalists and incorporationists – concerned a demand for the rectification of the union of the crowns, an imperfect conjunction which had corrupted the Scottish constitution.[187]

Despite the fact that the Act of Security indicated that any separate succession to the Scottish throne would be in the Protestant line (thus arguably opening the door to the Duke of Hamilton, a descendant of James II), it was widely regarded by its opponents, particularly in England, as a preparatory move to let in the Stuarts by the back door. There was unwillingness to have the Queen assent to the Act: in retaliation the Scottish Parliament threatened to withhold supply and disband the army. The threat of open sanctions on Scotland followed, including the Alien Act of 1705, designed to rob Scots of the right to settle and trade in England: they 'would be treated as aliens and their exports excluded from the English market'.[188] Thus would Scotland be driven into the *laager*: its overseas trade disrupted by English policy, while it was also deprived of free trade by the agent of that policy. There was fury in Scotland. The Scottish courts, in an atmosphere of mob hysteria, condemned an English East India captain to death. Following the Duke of Hamilton's move to leave the nomination in the hands of the Queen, commissioners were appointed to treat for Union in an atmosphere of rising tension and barely contained violence: the rumour that an incorporating rather than a federal union was what was on the agenda led to the Scots Commissioners being branded 'Unionist traitors'.[189] Hamilton, who had done so much himself to move Scotland towards Union, continued to play the patriotic card.[190] English threats and promises, including both payments and the manoeuvring of troops, informed the subsequent debates. It might be true, as Fletcher argued, that distant seats of government are 'violent, unjust and unnatural', but the Patriot could also recognize *realpolitik* when he saw it:

> in a state of separation from England, my country would be potentially involved in bloody and destructive wars. And if we should be united to that kingdom in any other manner [but that of the confederal equality sought by Fletcher], we must of necessity fall under the miserable and languishing condition of all places that depend upon a remote seat of government.[191]

Not content with either of these gloomy alternatives, Scotland was to experience both in the next 50 years.

2

SCOTLAND'S RUIN?

The Passing of Union

No other event in Scottish history is more controversial than the Union. In the noonday of empire, the events of 1707 were, for most historians, the culmination of Scottish history, whose distinctive qualities had existed only to be subsumed: Bruce and Wallace, those doughty fighters for freedom, were the forerunners of the negotiated partnership of the British Empire, with its stress on the internationalism of the British concept. Sir John Seeley's idea (in his *Expansion of England* (1883)) of a greater British history, which saw 'the internal union of the three kingdoms' as an avatar of 'a still larger Britain comprehending vast possessions beyond the seas' was the high water mark of this perspective, one which arguably diluted Englishness and which gave Scotland, through the global access of its professional classes and pioneers, a status within the British partnership it could never have had while remaining a small overshadowed northern kingdom in an island off the coast of continental Europe.[1]

Once doubt and decline set in, and the British imperial idea hastened to collapse, it was not unnatural that the ensuing provincialization of Scotland had an impact on the interpretation of the Union, the *ur*-event of the British Empire. From a position of commercial, scientific, technological and professional power in 1914, Scotland sank steadily towards the status of a multinational branch economy. The focus of discussion on the Union shifted: it became debated, doubted, even challenged in the courts. Since the 1980s, a popular orthodoxy has emerged which broadly backs elements of Paul Scott's case, first made in *1707: the Union of Scotland and England* (1979), that the Union was a piece of political jobbery, ensured by bribery, which has been of doubtful long-term benefit to Scotland. This has the merit of broadly corresponding to the view held of it by most Scots at the time (as is only evident in the plethora of anti-Union addresses, the strength of anti-Union rhetoric and the reports by English government agents and others of the extent of anti-Union rioting):[2] but it has been attacked by scholars such as Chris Whatley, who have once again stressed the old economic case for Union based on trade.[3] What follows is not a blow-by-blow account, of which too many already exist, but rather a broad view of how the passing of Union was seen in the discourse of nationality in Scotland at the time. Views as to its benefits have tended, in the twentieth as in the eighteenth century, to follow the politics of the viewer, although the Union's early effects were such as to leave even its proponents voicing doubts concerning its wisdom as late as the 1770s: in 1778, for example, Henry Dundas himself, drinking in English company, broke 'out into an invective against the English', saying 'he would move for a repeal of the Union'.[4]

One of the problems with the discourse surrounding the Union is that the Scots and English perspectives on it have always differed. The pamphlet wars of the turn of the eighteenth century are one earnest of this: English writers such as William Atwood (1650–1712) tended always to stress occasions of Scotland's historical subordination to England, while controversialists like James Anderson and the reprinted Sir Thomas Craig in *Scotland's Sovereignty Asserted* tended to sharply contest these views. Equality between England and Scotland was always a Scottish idea. From the English perspective, the Union always more closely resembled a solution to the problem of Scotland's differing outlook and objectives. Since the Union of the Crowns, the northern kingdom had been frequently troublesome: war had broken out there in 1638, 1640, 1644, 1648, 1650, 1654, 1666, 1679 and 1689: Defoe gives as one reason for Union the claim that Scots armies have invaded England 300 times.[5] So deep-seated was this fear, that 'it was 1797 before Westminster felt secure enough to give the Scots their own militia'.[6] Alienated from England, divided in itself, and falling into the poverty which breeds desperation, Scotland after Darien looked like an accident waiting to happen – and this in a context where English foreign policy was playing for high stakes in competition with France, still a disaffected Scotland's most likely ally. As Daniel Defoe's Scottish pamphlet (an example of disinformation by stressing a half-truth as at the core of the opposing position) *The Advantages of the Act of Security* put it, 'without the least hazard of annihilating our *Scots* Name, Sovereignty or Constitution; we may again be all *Frenchmen*, as we once were [i.e. during the regnal union of 1558–60]'.[7]

In the face of such views, English policymakers did right to fear the prospect of James Stuart at the head of a massive armed rising backed by French and Franco-Irish regulars looming as a distinct and unwelcome possibility in the near future. Scotland must be caught in time. Thus as a government agent Defoe, while flatteringly praising the Union as a 'happy Conjunction',[8] more revealingly wrote that 'In this Union here are Lands and People added to the *English* Empire.' Defoe had an answer for those who conceived that the preservation of Scotland's Church, law and institutions by Union was a recognition of the country's entitlement to parity of esteem, an answer calculated to reassure his English readers:

> The Religion and Civil Administration of Justice in *Scotland*, are no more Concern'd in this Matter, than the *Popish* Religion and Methods of Justice reserv'd in *Lancashire* and *Durham*, have been Obstructions to their being annex'd to the *English* Government, and made Provinces thereof.[9]

This was a not untypical view. As Robert Harley, Defoe's political master, wrote in 1709:

> Foreigners say publicly, I mean our own allies, that we [England] are a perfidious nation; and since we have violated our treaty with Scotland, and laugh at the notion of fundamental and inviolable articles [of Union], there is no great wonder if we treat other nations as we do.[10]

Between such an outlook and the Scottish Unionist case there was a great gulf fixed. 'England was not going to stand by' and watch Scotland make what foreign alliance it pleased. Once again, it was the pressing demands of foreign policy which held sway: while Scottish merchants were suffering losses from a French trade disrupted by English war, the Royal Navy was not only pressing in Scottish towns, but was also reluctant to give protection to Scottish ships. Already Scotland had begun to be the recruiting-ground for the nascent British Empire.[11]

Scottish critics of the Union saw the disparity between Unionist rhetoric and reality. The Jacobite nationalist George Lockhart of Carnwath described Defoe as a 'vile monster and wretch', terms which are evidence enough of the damage he was seen as doing to the national cause.[12] Fletcher of Saltoun's view was that an incorporating Union would lead to the 'concentration of all resources on London and its hinterland'. It was not only England that was Scotland's problem, but the concentration of power and resources within south-east England:

if the people of Yorkshire or Devonshire were not obliged to go farther than
York or Exeter to obtain justice, and consequently had no occasion to spend
money out of those countries, how soon should we see another face of things in
both? How soon would they double and treble their present value? That London should draw the riches and government of the three kingdoms to the
south-east corner of the island, is in some degree as unnatural, as for one city
to possess the riches and government of the world.[13]

Fletcher anticipates economic arguments for devolution by almost three
centuries. A similar view is put forward by the author (who may be
Fletcher) of *United and Separate Parliaments*, who argued that 'It is a certain
Consequence of all Power, That whosoever is possess'd of it, he will
imploy it to advance that Interest . . . in which he himself is most concern'd': a telling warning of the inevitability of cronyism and corruption
in an unchecked executive. Opponents of Union feared the concentration
of power in London, and the ability of the illimitable ambitions of Parliamentary sovereignty to abrogate the terms of Union and eventually destroy
the identity of Scotland, which would be abandoned 'whole sale to the
Mercy of that Parliament'. The author of *United and Separate Parliaments*
foresaw both the jobbery of the eighteenth century and the risk to the
Scottish constitution:

> it seems beyond human Comprehension, how these separate distinct Interests,
> and Establishments, can be regulated and supported by one Parliament . . . It
> is much easier to corrupt 45 Scots in *London*, than it is to corrupt 300 at
> *Edinburgh*, and besides, there will be no occasion of corrupting them, when
> the Case shall occur, of a difference betwixt the South-Britons and the North-
> Britons; for the Northern will be out-voted, without being corrupted . . . the
> Scots can be injured in an united Parliament with greater safety . . . Scots Mem-
> bers may dance round to all Eternity, in this Trap of their own making.[14]

There were, of course, supporters of the Union, and not just among
reluctant or suborned members of the Scottish Parliament. Dr John
Arbuthnot preached a sermon at the Mercat Cross in Edinburgh which
stressed the benefits of increased trade, and dismissed anti-Unionist
fears by arguing that Scots would stay at home rather than form an
economic diaspora. Arbuthnot also argued that Scots MPs in London
would be far from powerless (interestingly, he still views them as voting
in a bloc for the national interest), for 'nor in a British Parliament will
parties be so unequally trimmed, that it will be in the power of a lesser
number than the Scots members to cast the balance'. These prophecies
were of course on the incompetent side of Panglossianism, but Arbuthnot

was on stronger ground in arguing that Scottish independence was, though 'undeniable in law, as well as justifiable from history, yet, at present, it is in effect precarious, imaginary, and fantastical'. Scotland's independence was undermined both by the unresolved constitutional settlement of the Union of the Crowns and the economic destructiveness of persisting religious war in a country which lacked the foreign policy autonomy requisite to promote its own economic interests. Arbuthnot argued that 'in lieu of this titular sovereignty and imaginary independency, you acquire by a union true and solid power and dominion', though once again he is over-optimistic in expecting a 'quota of the most eminent posts of the government of Great Britain'.[15]

Even in the arguments of such as Arbuthnot, however, there is evidence of 'an instrumentalist view of Britishness: that the new nation had been created as an anti-Jacobite and anti-Bourbon device' rather than as any cohesive national unit. Union might save Scotland from Jacobitism, and solve the problem of the country's status as a neglected adjunct of English foreign policy, but it did not promote Britishness: Arbuthnot indeed sees Scots as operating in terms of their own national interest within the future British polity. More integrationist views had to wait for their proponents until the advent of the Gothicists in the later half of the eighteenth century, who argued for the Germanic commonality of the English and Scots Lowlanders against the Celticism of Highlanders and Irish, which predisposed the former towards liberty and Protestantism and the latter towards Popish tyranny. Such an ideology dated back to Lutheran times as an attempt to align Protestantism with Germanic destiny: its powerful presence in British history fed a number of myths, not least that of the Jacobite Risings as purely Highland and 'Celtic' affairs, driven by Catholicism and a misplaced affection for arbitrary power. On the other hand, some anti-Unionist thought, such as Fletcher of Saltoun's, may also have been influenced by the notion of a 'shared Gothic inheritance' within Britain.[16]

The Union was certainly deeply unpopular in the nation at large, and this was taken by some of its opponents as good evidence for its illegitimacy. *The Advantages of the Act of Security* argues that the Roman motto *Salus populi, suprema lex* ('the good of the people is the supreme law') undercuts the legitimacy of the Scottish Parliament's acceptance of Union, for 'more than the Authority of Parliament . . . must be made use of to Enforce these Articles upon the Judgements, and Inclinations of the People'.[17] Subsequently this argument was developed in the political theory of leading Jacobites such as Lord Forbes of Pitsligo, who thus provided the basis for an implicitly Whig and contractualist Jacobitism, where 'the greatest happiness of the greatest number' (as Francis Hutcheson put it in a different context) would be achieved by a Stuart restoration and an end to Union.[18] The huge number of anti-Union addresses and petitions, many of them backed by ordinary Scots, provided evidence for the claims which underlay such populist Jacobite theory. There was 'no comparable influx of unionist addresses from areas under court influence', and the view has often been taken that only the double-dealings of the Duke of Hamilton on the one hand and a lack of leadership on the other forestalled a full-scale armed Rising. At the same time, many who signed anti-Union addresses had refused the oaths of loyalty to the Crown, and this fed a desire on the part of the English government to equate anti-Unionism with Jacobite disaffection. The federalist or confederalist anti-Union case was indeed in the main proposed by Jacobites. English troops were sent to northern Ireland and the north of England, prepared to intervene.[19]

Whether or not coupled to a Stuart restoration (and this rapidly became the only realistic route to its repeal under an Act Rescissory of a restored King James), the Union's unpopularity deepened still further in the aftermath of its implementation. The non-Jacobite *Discourse of the Necessity and Seasonableness of an unanimous Address for Dissolving the UNION* (1715) refers to it as 'a Thing most destructive to the Interest of this ancient Kingdom ... violently crammed down our Throats', and makes a point which strikes a chord with many Scots from the eighteenth century to the twentieth: 'sure I am, the Advantage that Nation [England] has, is not equally sensible to them, as our loss is to us'.[20] The disparity between English and Scottish conceptions of the Union was coming home to roost. While the bell-ringers at St Giles were commanded to ring 'the old Scottish ballad "Why should I weep on my wedding day"' to celebrate Union, no marriage of true minds had taken place.[21]

Nonetheless, it needs to be noted that Scotland continued to conduct its own internal affairs in the aftermath of 1707. The 'status of the general assembly' of the Church of Scotland was raised 'to that of a quasi-parliament', since that Church retained all its authority in Scotland. The self-confidence of the Scottish education system, bolstered by a series of Acts culminating in 1696, was to produce 'the remarkable achievements of the following century'.[22] The years after 1707 also saw the development of many boards or commissions (today they would be called quangos) based in Edinburgh 'which attempted to administer Scottish affairs'. Among them were:

The Scottish Court of the Exchequer, which discharged income and paid taxes to the Civil List; the Board of Excise and the Board of Customs; the Board of Police; and the Board of Trustees: all were created in the first decades after Union. Along with the Courts of Session and Judiciary, the Convention of Royal Burghs and the General Assembly of the Church of Scotland, they were a prime source of jobs and rewards for the Scottish bourgeoisie and its sons, as well as being a focus of 'hands-on' administration based in Edinburgh.[23]

As Alex Murdoch has argued, such developments could be seen to act as a 'buffer' between English 'assumptions' and Scottish 'institutions'.[24] Although Scotland had lost its Privy Council in 1708, and would lose its Secretary of State after 1745, the management of Scottish politics by Scottish magnates continued. The family of the Duke of Argyll and later the lawyer Henry Dundas (Henry 'IX') effectively 'managed' Scotland and its politics for half of the century following Union.[25]

But anti-Union discourse continued to be strong, and one of its most potent forms was that of the appeal to Scotland's history as a struggle for liberty, a battle by a small nation for its independence from a far more powerful neighbour, won only by the heroic and unparalleled quality of Scottish valour and now betrayed for gold by an indolent nobility corrupted by luxury, as once the Roman Empire had been bought and sold by the corrupt descendants of L. Mucius Scaevola, Scipio Africanus and Cato the Elder. This discourse of Scottish nationhood had both presence and resonance at every level of society. On 4 November 1706, as Parliament considered 'the first article' of Union, the Duke of Hamilton put it thus:

> shall we in half an hour yield what our forefathers maintained with their lives and fortunes for many ages? Are none of the descendants here of those worthy patriots who defended the liberty of their country against all invaders...?

Two weeks later, protesters from an entirely different social background who burned 'the Articles of Union at Dumfries' stated their case in remarkably similar terms. Their protest highlighted the 'sovereignty of this our native ancient nation' and criticized the Union for being 'destructive of, this nation's independency'; it spoke of Scotland's 'sacred and civil liberties... purchased and maintained by our ancestors with their blood', and appealed to the 'martial... spirits of Scotsmen' not 'to be disposed of at the pleasure of another nation'.[26] Across society, this discourse took on similar forms: Lord Belhaven's anti-Union speech in the Scots Parliament, which appealed to the long tradition of valour, was versified and circulated as street literature, where it 'continued to incense the common people'.[27] Lockhart stressed the 'brave, generous, hardy' qualities of the 'heroic' people of Scotland.[28] Likewise, 26 burghs signed a Remonstrance against Union in favour of the 'Privileges... maintain'd by our Heroick ancestors'; Scotland was on the verge of a Rising.[29] Eight years later it burst out: in 1715, 'a large proportion of those who took up arms did so for the purpose of restoring Scotland's independence'.[30] Some of those who contributed to the discourse of valour, such as Dr Patrick Abercromby, author of *Martial Achievements of the Scottish Nation*, played a part in that rising. As James McKnight put it in 1858, in a summary of Jacobite motivation which should have been better heeded by subsequent historians:

> The Lowland gentlemen of Scotland, who formed so large a part of the Rebel Army, were the lineal descendants of that fierce and turbulent aristocracy whose stubborn and unyielding valour had preserved the freedom of the country during centuries of desperate and infuriated struggles for independence with their more wealthy and powerful neighbours of England.[31]

The discourse of valour and its umbilical link to nationalist opposition to the Union motivated Lowland gentry and tradesmen to fight for the Stuarts on a scale entirely different from that in the risings of Montrose or Dundee, where only 2000–4000, nearly all of them Highlanders, had joined the fight. The extent of Scotland's engagement with the Jacobite cause in the eighteenth century was a focus for dissatisfaction with the Union.[32]

Reclaiming the Nation

In 1698, Fletcher of Saltoun wrote that 'The Party of the late King James was always insignificant, and is now become a jest.' Yet in 1713 Fletcher applauded the efforts of two Jacobites, Lockhart of Carnwath and Lord Balmerino, to have the Union repealed, efforts which came within four votes of success.[33] The party of King James was now far from a jest: it was to be the main engine of anti-Union feeling for the first 40 years of Britain's existence.[34] As Lockhart put it:

> people of all ranks and perswasions were more and more chagrined and displeased, and resented the loss of soveraignty and were daily more and more perswaded that nothing but the restoration of the royal family, and that by the means of Scotsmen, could restore them to their rights... nothing was to be

heard throughout all the country save an universal declaration in favour of the king and exclamations against the Union and those that had promoted it.[35]

Within a week of Union, many of Scotland's leading magnates or their representatives had signed a memorial calling for a restoration, including the Duke of Atholl, the Marquess of Drummond and the Earls of Nithsdale, Traquair, Galloway, Home, Strathmore, Wigton and Linlithgow. In 1708, acting on the report that 'two-thirds of Scotland were Stuart in sympathy',[36] the French planned a rising which would land James in Scotland with French troops. Prevented from landing the soldiers by the Royal Navy, the French admiral was unwilling to put James on shore alone. Most of his potential Scottish supporters dissolved away before they could be caught. The '08 was a debacle, but also a sign of things to come, in that France concentrated on Scotland (as in the 1790s it was to concentrate on Ireland) as the place where Britain might be broken. Ending the Union suited the French for the same reason as it did not suit Westminster: it was one of the key counterweights in the balance of power between England and France. Indeed, in the 1740s, consideration was even being given in France to supporting a Scottish Republic, and a strong network existed of Scottish and particularly Irish soldiers in the French service, ready to be used in support of armed risings.[37] This was perhaps in part the reason why the Bourbon/Stuart colour of white was adopted 'by the agrarian redresser movements of the 1760s' in Ireland, movements strong in Cork and Tipperary, which themselves 'were two of the leading Irish counties for recruitment into the French army', whose Irish troops were repeatedly pledged to restore the Stuarts.[38]

In the 1710 election, at least 16 out of the 45 MPs sent from Scotland to Westminster were Jacobite.[39] By 1712, partly through their efforts, a limited amount of toleration was being extended to Scottish Episcopalians, which in its turn may have helped harden nationalist resolve. The attempt to levy the Malt Tax in defiance of the Union treaty in 1713 led to the challenge to the Union in that year, supported not only by Lockhart, Balmerino and the Earl of Mar (Secretary of State for Scotland), but also by Argyll himself. Only Glasgow was benefiting significantly from the Union's opening of Western imperial markets: elsewhere 'it appeared that Scotland had become a victim of exploitatively English traders whose merchandise was permitted to invade the north at cheap prices to the prejudice of the Scottish market'.[40]

Following the death of the profoundly Unionist Queen Anne in 1714, 'a petition was launched in Scotland in pursuit of repeal of the Union'.[41]

It was rejected by George I's Whig ministry. The Earl of Mar launched a rising, dedicated, in King James's words, to 'restore the Kingdom to its ancient free and independent state...a free and independent Scots Parliament'.[42] James knew nothing of Mar's intentions until the rising had already begun.[43] During it, at times the king appeared almost redundant: for example Mar promised Spalding of Ashentullie, to whom he offered a colonel's commission, that 'whether James landed or not the intention was to march south, dissolve the Union and redress the grievances of Scotland'.[44] Taxes were restored on the Scots footing: 'No union' proclaimed by the Jacobite banners in the burghs. Although the 1715 Rising was British in conception, 90 per cent of its forces were raised in Scotland, and many of its supporters, like Lockhart of Carnwath, had little previous family association with Stuart loyalism: they wished for an end to Union. It was national in scope: as many as one in twelve adult males joined the rising,[45] a figure more than five, and perhaps as high as seven times the size of Montrose's or Dundee's forces. As Bruce Lenman puts it: 'Nationalist emotions...could only find expression in Jacobite actions.'[46]

Emotions in the period ran high. In 'A speech without doors upon the present state of the Nation', the author laments that Scotland is 'at the disposal of the ministers of a nation ever intent upon our ruin and destruction', and that 'the black designs of the english ... constrain'd us to depend upon a remote seat of government ... this master piece of villany they call by the name of an incorporating union'.[47] Likewise, James Garden's address at Aberdeen stressed the 'loss of the Liberty, privileges and independency of this our Ancient Kingdom: with bondage under a forraign prince'. Only the 'Restauration of his present Matie, James the 8th' could save Scotland from 'the specious name and pretence of an Union with England' into which it had been 'sold and enslaved'.[48] Robert Freebairn printed an address at Edinburgh against 'the late unhappy Union' and the 'packed up Assembly which calls itself a British parliament'.[49] Essentially Whig figures like the Master of Sinclair joined the rising, as an 'honourable and beautifull' sign of resistance to the mercenary Union: 'how concerned I was to see those who pretended to be of the ancient Scots Nobilitie reduced to beg at ane English Court!' says Sinclair, in a neat use of the topos of venal Unionism versus ancient patriot valour.[50]

Argyll led the government troops, yet his 'own clansmen were divided to "the extent of one half in favour of a Scottish rising against Union"':[51] note the lack of mention once again of James, and the thought of the 'rising' as being 'against Union'. The fact that Argyll brought Mar to a halt at the indecisive battle of Sheriffmuir (where the Jacobites had fewer than half their troops in action) was a tribute less to his tenacity than to Mar's inadequate sense of timing and incompetence as a field commander. Nonetheless, sensible of the level of Jacobite support in Scotland, Argyll moved cautiously against those involved in the rising, to such an extent that his own loyalty was suspected by the government: as he wrote in September 1715, 'on the other side of this river [Forth], excepting our few friends in the North and those of my vassals in the West Highlands, they [the Jacobites] have a hundred to one at least in their interest'.[52] He knew that James's call to restore Scotland 'to its former happiness and independency' had many supporters. As James's own father, James VII and II, had written in exile, "Tis the true interest of the Crown to keep that Kingdom [Scotland] separat from England.'[53] The Stuart realms were to be 'a series of at least nominally equal kingdoms held together by royal authority', not Parliamentary dictatorship.[54] Compatible as it was both with Stuart loyalism and Scottish nationalism, this view was at the ground base of Jacobite support. By contrast, the Georges were the symbols of British centralism, for 'the Hanoverian kings . . . no more contemplated holding a court at Holyrood than the Emperor Nicholas at Warsaw'.[55]

Limited Spanish help secured another Rising in 1719 (though disaffection with the 'unhappy union' remained so widespread that the Jacobites even thought it worthwhile approaching the extreme Cameronian Presbyterians for support,[56] but it was 1745 before the last and most famous Jacobite spasm occurred. Disaffection with the Union continued: the Malt Tax's introduction led to riots in Glasgow in 1725, while the politicized crime of smuggling (much practised in the east-coast ports, and designed to evade the imposition of post-Union duties) lay at the root of the Porteous Riots in the capital in 1736. Although the widespread support among the Scottish professional classes which had marked the Fifteen had been vitiated by the ejection of many Jacobite sympathizers from universities, schools and kirk livings, support was still strong in northern Scotland, while on the Continent the War of the Austrian Succession led France to plan an invasion in 1743–44, which failed to sail due to a combination of bad weather and detection by the Royal Navy. Frustrated with French dilatoriness, Charles Edward Stuart (1720–88), James's elder son, determined to force Louis XV's hand by financing a landing in Scotland and beginning his own rising.

What happened next is, of course, as much a part of Scottish mythology as of Scottish history, and there is no need to rehearse it here again in detail. Although Jacobite support was weaker than in 1715 (half as against three-quarters of potential clan support, according to Allan Macinnes[57]), nonetheless, between 11 000 and 14 000 men were involved in the rising, as were many women.[58] Anti-Union feeling was again strongly evident: 'nationalism . . . remained a major plank of Jacobitism at the 'Forty-Five', as Macinnes reminds us.[59] James had declared against 'pretended Union' in December 1743,[60] in a Declaration which explicitly drew on the discourse of ancient and heroic Scotland, called 'a Nation always famous for valour, and highly esteemed'. Charles Edward's entry into Edinburgh in September was accompanied by 'strongly nationalist symbolism'.[61] On 9 October 1745 in the capital (though at other times he was more circumspect), Charles Edward declared 'the pretended union of the Kingdoms . . . at an End'. Stuart opposition to the Union was cemented by the role that it had had in forcing the Act of Settlement on Scotland in defiance of the Act of Security, a process which had involved the deeply insulting exclusion of the entire Stuart family from the throne. As Charles put it on 10 October:

> with respect to the pretended Union of the two Nations, the king cannot possibly ratify it, since he has had repeated Remonstrances against it from each Kingdom; and since it is incontestable that the Principal point then in view was the Exclusion of the Royal Family from their undoubted Right to the Crown, for which Purpose the Grossest Corruptions were openly used to bring it about.[62]

The hopes of some of the Scottish Jacobites to restore 'Scotland's independence' by setting up a 'fortress Scotland' in Edinburgh were, however, thwarted,[63] not just by a vote to march south, but also by the unrealistically rosy prospect taken by such views of British naval might and its power of blockade. Far from the advance on London demonstrating some kind of lack of commitment to a Scottish polity, it was militarily inevitable. Surprise and rapidity were the only hopes the Forty-five had of dealing the Hanoverian state a mortal blow; and the substantial French aid required for the final success of either also demanded a move on England. Retreat sealed the rising's eventual failure, for only a proportion of the troops and supplies sent by France to Scotland got through, and as the conflict dragged on, British power more effectively concentrated its force in the available space. Once the Jacobites were driven from the east-coast ports (as they were by the end of February), it was even more difficult for French help to get through. Thus Charles's successes in March 1746 were pyrrhic and transient: money and supplies were exhausted, and Culloden an inevitable battle to protect Inverness, the last significant burgh the Jacobites held. Whatever the tactical failings of the Stuart high command on that day, much foolish history which ignores the strategic plight of the Jacobites has been written. Victory at Culloden would have changed nothing: what Derby began, the retreat after Falkirk continued: a sixteenth-century obsession with subduing Stirling and Edinburgh castles shows the military limitations of much-praised Jacobite generalship, while Charles Edward's own blitzkrieg instincts to punch a hole in the British state and force a path to London as quickly as possible were vindicated by events. The Forty-five was not commanded by a military genius in Lord George Murray, handicapped by a moody adolescent in the shape of Prince Charles: instead, the one was a fine tactician, the other a good strategist, but neither had much talent in the field of the other's gifts.

Although the Jacobite cause never had the allegiance of the Scottish nation as a whole, nor ever commanded majority support south of Forth, the emplaced opposition to it by Presbyterians and Lowlanders has been exaggerated: as Allan Macinnes informs us, 'clan commitment to Jacobitism has been singled out by polemicists partly to play down the nationalist dimension of the cause in Scotland'.[64] In 1715, one government estimate suggested that only 23 per cent of Mar's troops were clansmen,[65] while in the same rising, Jacobite support among Presbyterians, particularly in areas of majority Jacobite sympathy, was noticeable. One-third of the 58 clergy who came out in Aberdeenshire and Banffshire in 1715 were Presbyterian,[66] and in the 1745 Rising, Lord Lewis Gordon, the Jacobite Lord-Lieutenant of these counties, noted with irritation the increase in Presbyterian opposition to the Stuarts as if it was a surprising development. Presbyterians 'disenchanted with Union' did offer Jacobites sympathy, however, even if they were 'rarely participants'.[67] Cameron of Lochiel's regiment had a Presbyterian chaplain,[68] and Revd John Grant, 'Minister of the Gospel in Urquhart', was among those whose ancestral loyalties appear to have transcended their sectarian ones.[69] Nor were Highland Jacobites simply fighting the Campbells, or, even more slanderously, for plunder. As Jane Dawson points out, 'Scottish Gaeldom had always been deeply committed to the Scottish crown and the kingdom.'[70]

Government reports can tend to conflate Highland and Lowland Jacobitism in a rather confused way, for example in the 'Memoriall Anent the True State of the Highlands as to their Chieftenries' (1745):

DUKE OF PERTH – is no Claned familie, although the head of a Considerable
Number of Barrons and Gentlemen of the Name of Drummond in the Low
Countreys he is brought in here Allennarly Upon account of his command of
about 300 Highlanders in Glenertonie and Neighbourhood.[71]

The confusion here is between a tribal conception of the 'Claned family'
and the status of Perth as 'chief of the name' of Drummond, a privilege
held by many Lowland magnates. The status of one shades into the
other, and the importance of kinship networks in Scotland is far from
isomorphic with any conception of 'clanship': rather it transcends it,
reflecting more on the natural social and political organization of a small
kingdom where important players are 'weel kent' (well known; as is
still the case), rather than on the romantic tribalism of Primitivist fantasy
or its atavistic equivalent in government propaganda.

This confusion still continues. The Murrays of Atholl are often
counted as clan leaders by even modern historians; yet it is highly doubtful
whether the family of the Dukes of Atholl can be validly described thus.
As Forbes of Culloden said (and he ought to have known), 'the Murray's
is no Highland family'.[72] To further confuse matters, 'Lowland' officers
served in 'Highland' regiments, the two were brigaded together, and
'Highland' units were among some of the most regimentally conventional in the Jacobite army, even going to the length of having grenadier
companies. Some writers have, in their eagerness to make the Forty-five
a Highland affair, overlooked the evidence to the extent of suggesting
that 'Scotsmen north of the Forth in 1745 be essentially Highlanders',[73]
a view which would make of Adam Smith a claymore-wielding Gael. To
such levels do historians descend when demonstrable empirical fact
challenges their illusions.

The core of Lowland Jacobitism was of course the Episcopal Church
of Scotland, which could still attract the allegiance of up to 30 per cent of
the Scottish population in the early eighteenth century, and nearer half
in the North. The Episcopalian congregation at Elgin, for example, was
nearly 1000 in the 1720s, while hundreds were being confirmed in
Moray as late as 1770: scriptures and consecration alike could be in
Gaelic.[74] Here also, in and around the Gordon lands (as well as in the
West Highlands), was a heartland of the Catholic faith, still strong
enough in these areas to win converts: in 1704, in a complaint to the
Presbytery of Kincardine O'Neil, the Revd James Robertson cited 168
Catholics, of whom 134 were converts. Both Episcopalians and Catholics
'made use of the rich medieval, religious heritage of Gaeldom' to spead

their message, and, at least in part, consequently sustained strong support in the Gaidhealtachd: more than 70 per cent of the principal clans had 'a significant commitment' to Episcopalianism.[75] Nationalism was very evident: Jacobites in exile 'prided themselves on their patriotism, and . . . correspondingly took considerable pleasure in things Scottish, from the country's history to its tastes and mores'.[76] As F. W. Robertson put it colourfully 200 years later, 'the aim of the Prince's men in 1745 is still our aim in 1946 – a free Scotland'.[77]

The extent to which that represented an unacceptable threat to the British State can be seen in the aftermath of the Forty-five, long notorious, and described by Allan Macinnes as 'systematic state terrorism' in three phases: one of wholesale slaughter (Cumberland); one of selective terrorism (Albemarle), and thirdly the starvation of Jacobite districts 'through the wilful destruction of crops, livestock and property with the stated intention to effect either clearance or death'.[78] Contemporary political cartoons noted the Jacobite Rising as a threat to Union and showed the Jacobite forces carrying Scottish national symbols; yet the nationalist dimension of Jacobitism remains an uncomfortable and neglected fact even today. Jacobites saw themselves as continuing the struggles of Wallace and Bruce (a point explicitly made by Lord Lovat to Charles Edward), yet the risings are still mostly described in Scotland in terms of 'civil war'. But if the country was divided between Jacobites and their opponents, this was also the case in the Wars of Independence: and whereas in the fourteenth century many Scots had fought against Bruce, relatively few outside Argyll and Munro lands could be found to fight the Jacobites. In 1715 in particular, the Jacobite cause can be termed a national rising. One must not forget that history's semantics of defeat and victory are different: had Bruce failed, the Wars of Independence would now be termed a British 'civil war', yet Bruce v. Baliol and George v. James are not so distinct as history's vocabulary pretends, nor was there ever a time in major Anglo-Scottish conflicts when there were not Scots who supported the English side. 'The legend that the Jacobite revolts were national risings against English rule' has a sturdy substratum of fact.[79]

Jacobite imagery and rhetoric were potent means of communication among the cause's sympathizers, and their adoption of the topoi and language of folk literature arguably had an enduring effect on the future Scottish literary tradition. In particular, the image of the neglected, feminized Scotland found in sources as diverse as Drummond's *Forth Feasting* of 1617 and in the anti-Union speech of Lord Belhaven (1656–1708), which has its counterpart in the feminized nationality of Ireland, has formed a basis for literary representations of national identity from the pens of Scott, John Buchan, Lewis Grassic Gibbon, J. M. Barrie, Neil Gunn and many other writers. Jacobite campaigns 'deliberately promoted a Highland identity' as a synecdoche for the 'true' Scottish one of antique valour and traditional loyalties, overturned by the buying and selling of 1707, the 'significant elements of a specifically moral identity, grounded in the idea that the Scots were especially noble, loyal and courageous', remarked on by David Allan.[80] Jacobite gentlemen were drawn to Scottish history and tradition, particularly to those aspects which endorsed a reputation for valour,[81] and to the discourse of classical Rome, with its stress on decadence in the work of Juvenal and Tacitus and great topos of the exiled and returning king in Vergil's *Aeneid*. The songs, symbolism and devices of the movement strongly endorsed imagery of renewed fertility, military conflict, and a feminized nation restored to freedom through the eroticized violence of her loyal sons. All these ingredients were later to be present in modern Irish Republicanism: the restoration of Cathleen Ni Houlihan to her rightful place of honour is a discourse which has its roots in the voices of eighteenth-century Scottish and Irish Jacobitism, as some of Pearse's contemporaries made clear. In this sense, the rhetoric of Jacobitism has been enormously influential on future nationalist rhetoric.[82]

What did the Jacobites believe in apart from a repeal of the Union? Were they unthinking, divine-right loyalists of the deepest reactionary dye, as they are sometimes caricatured by historians with too much integrity to call them mindless savages, or is there any truth in James Young's assertion that 'a Jacobite is just a frustrated Jacobin'?[83] The very fact that Scottish republicans can even discuss the point in the 1990s indicates that it is one worth making. As Hugh MacDiarmid put it:

> There can be no minimising the high significance of a cause . . . which retains such unexhausted evolutionary momentum as to reappear with renewed vitality after being suppressed for a couple of centuries of unparalleled change.[84]

Whether or not one accepts MacDiarmid's 'unexhausted evolutionary momentum' as an appropriate description of Jacobitism, it was nonetheless bound up with radical impulses: many areas which were Jacobite became Jacobin in the 1790s. Part of its appeal lay in the long symbiosis between Scotland's native kings and the independence of the country; part in Episcopalian sacramentalism; part in the overwhelming legitimacy of the Stuart line: but much also derived from 'the bias to the poor and support for traditional gentry duties which the Stuart regimes had evinced', and, 'lying at the core of Jacobite ideology in Scotland', Scottish nationalism itself.[85]

Reclaiming the Culture

Any discussion of Scottish nationality and its nationalist (with however large or small an 'n') expressions needs to steer clear of the Scylla and Charybdis of Jacobite nostalgia and economic improvement. On the one hand, nationalist historians have sometimes presumed that 'essential' Scottish identity lay entombed after 1707, to be reawakened from its Unionist doze in revenant vitality in the twentieth century; on the other, Unionist historians for their part (Lord Dacre most notoriously) have argued that 1707 was the settled sea-change which allowed a culture of value to develop in an 'essentially' violent and divided society. Both these 'essentially' simplistic accounts show how vulnerable scholarly history is to the inherited prejudices defined by the status quo, which in their turn lead either to its endorsement or rejection.[86]

They share, however, one thing in common: an agreement on the importance of the eighteenth century as the rite of passage for Scotland and Scottishness. Sometimes it seems that accounts of that century are mutually exclusive: Union, the Risings, the Clearances and the destruction of Highland society on the one hand; Enlightenment, economic change, the Edinburgh New Town and agricultural improvement on the other. Yet close examination suggests far more points of contact between these two Scotlands than is sometimes assumed, just as there are many more cultural links between pre- and post-Union Scotland than is often supposed. Many Jacobites, for example, were improvers, such as Lord Lovat, the Earl of Cromartie and Mackintosh of Borlum. There were intimate connections between Jacobites and mainstream intellectual eighteenth-century figures: for example, Dr John Arbuthnot, physician to Queen Anne and friend of Pope and Swift, had a brother who was a Jacobite spy and a nephew who was a captain in Lord John Drummond's Royal Scots in 1745,[87] while Jacobitism ran in Lord Monboddo's family to the extent that Dr Johnson congratulated his son in terms which looked forward to a Stuart restoration.[88] The Scottish diaspora, with its export of native expertise, remained a continuing cultural phenomenon: its destination, however, began to shift from continental Europe to the Empire, a change which largely commenced in the eighteenth century.[89]

This was the century which arguably defined many of the lineaments of modern Scottish society. As Bruce Lenman points out, 'a new generation of articulate Scots had emerged which looked forward to a degree of integration with and participation in the British state',[90] which henceforth was to be 'a major transmitter of Scottish political distinctiveness'.[91] The thesis put forward in Lindsay Paterson's *The Autonomy of Modern Scotland* (1994) stressed the importance of an autonomous Scottish civic society, run by a domestic bourgeoisie, to a preservation of national identity after 1707. Many of the members of this bourgeoisie were themselves gentry in origin, because the salaries which professionals could command in British and imperial markets exceeded the rewards of a relatively poor local nobility. It was through the law, medicine, the churches and universities that this group established themselves: in the early days, offices frequently passing from father to son. To take one example, the holders of the Snell Exhibition from Glasgow University to Balliol College (given, since 1699, to one or more of the outstanding Glasgow graduates of the year) largely follow this pattern in the eighteenth century. Out of some seventy-three Snells in the period, eighteen became clergymen (this was the original goal of the exhibition), eight doctors, five lawyers and four professors: almost a quarter of this group of professionals being gentry.[92] Even today, membership of one of the established professions is one of the goals to which the Scottish middle classes aspire for their children, and the merchant company schools and independent successors of the Scottish burgh grammar schools turn out doctors and lawyers in large numbers: thus it is that popular arts subjects which require the same entry points as medicine in English universities can be up to 8–10 entry points adrift in Scotland, where entry to law at Glasgow or medicine at Edinburgh is highly prized. It was these same professional classes, together with their associated elites, who largely ran and to some extent still run public life in Scotland and its culture and society. The rise of the professional classes in Scotland in particular, which has served to generate the stereotype of the Scottish doctor or engineer for more than a century, depended on many points which continued to distinguish Scottish from English society, although of course the professions gained ground there too in the early modern period.

Yet there were substantial distinctions, largely based in the professional's ability to out-earn the Scottish landowner. Hence their relative monetary prestige *vis-à-vis* a native nobility which was both larger and poorer than its English equivalent was greater. The power of the 'idea of the gentleman',[93] which led English professionals to envy the landed classes, was less strong: moreover, many of the lower Scottish nobility (e.g. the Boswells of Auchinleck or Erskines of Dun) themselves combined their social and professional status. After 1707, Scots law and the General Assembly were two of the main remaining guardians of national sovereignty: thus they attracted a native elite, and retained and augmented their position. The Scottish universities, too, had already developed the rudiments of a professional training which improved rapidly as the century progressed: Edinburgh's doctors were usually more than a match for English apothecaries and Oxbridge amateurs. The intimacy of the major Scottish cities, where rich and poor lived cheek by jowl in huge tenements, succoured the sociability which helped to produce the Enlightenment: ironically, the Enlightenment's architectural expression in the more spaciously laid-out New Town undermined its own roots in the sociability of enclosed spaces.

The Scottish Enlightenment's chief feature was a commitment to the application of reason to knowledge in a context of material improvement: from this basis sprang the New Town of Edinburgh, the 'heavenly city of the Enlightenment philosophers',[94] the development of economic theory, 'common-sense' philosophy, teleological historiography, and a whole host of eighteenth- and nineteenth-century inventions derived from 'useful learning', the byword of the Royal Society of Edinburgh, founded for 'useful knowledge' in 1783, and of John Anderson, who in Anderson's College (now the University of Strathclyde) founded in 1796 the most quintessentially Enlightenment higher education institution in the country.[95] Presbyterian belief in a useful life usefully lived was present even in the secular reaches of the Enlightenment (perhaps in places as diverse as the development of small public libraries and widespread Scottish opposition to slavery), and the connection between Calvinist theology and Enlightenment thinking is as yet inadequately explored; in the Kirk of Scotland itself, the development of Moderatism led to the beginnings of what is now known as the 'social gospel', where the advancement of the well-being of the needy in a context of peace and justice appeared just as important in the Kirk's mission as the eternal salvation of souls through the metanoia of repentance. 'The integration of religion and society' lay at the heart of Moderatism: 39 of 54 Moderators of the General Assembly between 1752 and 1805 were Moderates,[96] and in this succession is to be found the roots of Scotland's strong development of social commitment and collective action in an atmosphere of greater equality than that always found in England. Women (who had in any case greater social, financial and educational rights) were students in Scottish higher education as early as 1796, while the opposition to slavery of Beattie, Hutcheson, Smith and many other figures was crowned by the Scottish Lord Chief Justice Lord Mansfield's (William Murray, 1705–93) 1771 ruling, which technically freed every slave in Britain: hence possibly the anti-slavery subtext of Jane Austen's *Mansfield Park* (1814) is obliquely reflected in its title.

Our inherited bifurcated vision of the Scottish eighteenth century is to a great extent the product of the Enlightenment thinkers themselves, who sought to remove the threat to Scotland's reputation within the Union from still-rampant English prejudice and the taint of Jacobitism. During the Seven Years War (1756–63), writers like Alexander Carlyle, who in his memoirs privately acknowledged the prevalence of Jacobitism round Edinburgh, publicly argued in favour of a Scottish militia on the basis that had such existed in 1745, 'five thousand undisciplined militia from the most remote parts of the kingdom' would not have been able to stage a 'pitiful insurrection'.[97] The Highlands were being alienized as 'other' in order to bring Lowland Scotland more closely into the Anglo-British orbit, and the discourse of Teutonism advanced by writers such as John Pinkerton, who argued that 'Scotland was being held back by its degenerate Celtic population',[98] provided an ethnic mythology in support of these moves, one which either stigmatized the 'Celtic' Highlander as lazy and indifferent to the fruits of industry, or apotheosized him in the strictly limited terms of the Noble Savage. In the heritage industry which surrounded the development of the Noble Savage idea, the discourse of patriot valour which had animated Jacobite nationalism was caricatured as an inclination to atavistic and purposeless violence. Anti-Highland feeling prevalent in the more Presbyterian parts of the Lowlands succoured this redefinition of the patriot Jacobite symbol as that of a savage whose time had passed. As was the case with the Protestant United Irishmen in the nineteenth century, Lowland Jacobites were more easily integrated than Gaelic speakers, so the whole of anti-Jacobite opprobrium fell on the Gaelic 'other'.

At the core of Enlightenment historiography was a teleology of civility, the aim of which 'was to trace human development through certain common stages of progress from barbarism to refinement'.[99] David Hume (1711–76), William Robertson (1721–93) and Adam Smith (1723–90) all subscribed to this in their different ways. In this teleology, patriot valour ranked very low, for the subtext of all these writers'

historiography was that English society represented a higher norm to
which Scotland should aspire, and that Scotland's place in the Union
would be secure and the opportunities and status of her intelligentsia
improved, to the extent that her 'civility' resembled that of England:
nonetheless, the older discourse of classical corruption and decline
could still be found, though now more as a threat than a statement of
Scotland's current problems: 'ancient virtue' now no longer entailed
Scottish nationalism.[100] In Enlightenment thought, the ability of Scots to
rapidly conform is partly predicated on their Germanicity, the common
Teuton roots of Lowlander and Englishman alike. The Germans, the
greatest lovers of 'valour and . . . liberty' in the ancient world (one now
suitably remote), subsequently (in Hume's words) 'subdued Britain',
bringing with them 'that invaluable possession . . . ancient democracy'.[101] 'Britain' of course was not 'subdued': Nechtansmere was forgotten, and 60 years after Scots prided themselves on their ancient
valour in resisting the Saxon under their heroic kings, one of the 'greatest' thinkers of the century was telling posterity that Scotland, like
England, was the home of Saxon democracy. Hume likewise describes
Scottish attacks on England in the Middle Ages as 'invidious and unjust',
while of England in the same period he says that few regimes have used
'less violence and injustice . . . to gain considerable advantages over their
neighbours'. Nonetheless, England has rightly imposed a 'just terror' on
the 'deluded Irish', who were 'from the beginning of time . . . buried in
the most profound barbarism and ignorance . . . [were] still savage and
untractable'. As far as Hume was concerned, Robert I might never have
described Scots and Irish as 'our common people'. As for his fellow-
countrymen, Hume notes their 'native ferocity' and status as a 'barbarous
enemy',[102] while Robertson's identification of pre-Union Scots as
'bold and licentious' effectively endorses the stereotypes of eighteenth-
century English-derived propaganda.[103] Both historians, sometimes
directly as above, sometimes more subtly, strive to provide a vision
which stresses the ubiquity of an Anglo-Germanic ideal throughout the
British Isles. As Colin Kidd observes, 'Robertson's *History of Scotland*
(1759) presented a negative picture of Scotland's feudal backwardness
which subsequently became the defining cliché of Scottish historical
writing.'[104]

The fruits of this historiography are with us still (though there were
many intermittent challenges to it long before our own day, such as
those of Alexander Law in 1826 and William Burns in 1874.[105] Complaints about the lack of structured Scottish history teaching in schools

themselves go back a long way, but this is hardly surprising when the immensely influential Robertson argued that 'Nations, as well as men, arrive at maturity by degrees, and the events, which happened during their infancy or early youth...deserve not to be remembered.'[106] Scotland's Enlightenment historians argued Scottish history out of serious existence. Not only is there Robertson's blanket gloss, but throughout the related historiography examples of English division and violence are regarded as exceptional, while Scottish ones normatively bear out a stereotype. This is again still with us today: the idea that Scotland is a land with a violent history, riven by turbulent and bloodthirsty internal strife, is one losing ground with those re-entering Scottish history as scholars ('the dismantling...of the legend of late medieval Scotland as a benighted magnate anarchy', as Kidd terms it,[107] but still overwhelmingly dominant in hand-me-down popular history and the symbiotic tourist industry. In the age of Robertson and Hume, Stirling Castle, seat of a great Renaissance Court, was turned into an army barracks by those obedient to the prejudices underlying Robertson's imprecation: it took until the last years of the twentieth century to begin to restore it. Such are the empirical manifestations of Scottish Enlightenment culture's paradoxical contempt of Scottish culture's past.

There were of course, more moderate voices, from James Macpherson (1736/8–96), who sought to treat the discourse of patriot valour with respect, while acknowledging that it had been (sadly?) superseded, to Adam Fergusson (1723–1816), who in his *Essay on the History of Civil Society* (1767) shows awareness that progress involves losses as well as gains, seeing 'an immanent tension between material progress and moral advance'. Fergusson's 'noble savage' is possessed of 'a penetration, a force of imagination and elocution, an ardour of mind, an affection and courage' beyond that of civilized man. Yet nonetheless, in pursuit of 'economic progress, social refinement and a well-balanced constitution', 'not only the individual advances from infancy to manhood, but the species itself from rudeness to civilization'. Fergusson argues that there is a worldwide tendency to move away from small nations, praising 'nations' who are 'uniting themselves more firmly together', and specifically states:

> Where a number of states are contiguous, they should be near an equality.... When the kingdoms of Spain were united, when the great fiefs of France were annexed to the crown, it was no longer expedient for the nations of Great Britain to continue disjointed.[108]

Fergusson notes the organization of 'primitive' societies, with chieftains in the Caribbean standing in as a metaphor for Scots, and contrasts the passions which govern 'rude' societies with succeeding civility. A 'plan of enlargement' is seen as a solution to the 'extreme and sanguinary passions' of 'rude nations'. Thus an ideology of British Empire is born by stealth in the outline of Fergusson's argument: 'enlargement' is itself part of civility, and brings benefits of peace and civilization to 'rude nations'. As part of the Union, Scotland can now be an agent in this process rather than its victim, now that 'the nations of Great Britain' are no longer 'disjointed'.[109]

The United Tartan of Great Britain

Fergusson was the only major Enlightenment figure with experience of military service in the regular forces, as chaplain to the Black Watch, and thus such an argument as that above comes particularly fittingly from his pen. For it was the military, and the Scottish soldier more than many, who was the agent of imperial expansion; and it was arguably only in Scotland's military contribution to the British Empire that the discourse of patriot valour remained as a central and accepted part of Scottish identity. For 40 years after 1745, it was only in the British army that tartan, the symbol of patriot valour, could be legally worn; and the success and/or bravery of Scottish regiments at Quebec, Ticonderoga and Seringapatam underlined the survival of this patriot rhetoric which emphasized that despite its misplaced track record of Scottish nationalism, it was now loyally and properly channelled against the common enemies of Britain:

> The tartan of civil threat became the tartan of imperial triumph, as battle honours accrued to Scottish troops who were often used recklessly to gain them. Tartan was the indicator of loyalty and the means whereby a putatively misplaced Jacobite loyalty transmuted into the true loyalty to Great Britain and her role in the world.[110]

Thus amended, the discourse and symbolism of patriot valour were celebrated in books such as Col. David Stewart of Garth's *Sketches of the Highlanders of Scotland* (1822), an extended apologia for the Scottish military contribution to Empire, while the performance of Scottish troops throughout the half-century which culminated in the Napoleonic

Wars set the scene for the rehabilitation of Scottish patriotism as an essential (but depoliticized) aspect of Scottish cultural heritage in the hands of Sir Walter Scott and others in 1822, ably described in John Prebble's *The King's Jaunt* (1988). The result of Scott's efforts was 'to make of the "sixty years since" the Forty-five a gulf which its nationalism could not cross',[111] by romanticizing the past into picturesque remoteness, and dangerous only in a bygone time, one which had nonetheless been outlived by the era of the Forty-five, portrayed as picturesque, but also futile and destructive. Scott cunningly makes Jacobitism a romantic chimera, attractive to English adolescents (Waverley) and immature nations (Highland Scotland) alike. Its charm was preserved, its rhetoric neutralized. As Andrew Hook points out:

> Scottish romance offered little or nothing in the way of a challenge or threat to the rationalism, moderation, or morality of enlightened modern society; it may present . . . a vision of another, more dangerous, world of colour, excitement and high passion–but the location of that world is safely remote both in space and time.[112]

When Scott noted that 'Arms and men' were the 'best things' to show the king he was reanimating the discourse of patriot valour, first in a British rather than a Scottish context, and secondly in the self-consciously antiquarian manner of heritage, for the 'arms' he had on show were those of a vanished Jacobite era (as in the case of the Company of Archers). This was no Red Square parade of military hardware, but rather a rhetoric of patriot valour dressed in safely obsolete form to obsequiously demonstrate British fidelity while picturesquely raising British curiosity. The tartan market boomed, and so did Scott: 'We are THE CLAN, and our King is THE CHIEF.' A 'euphoric mood of resurgent Jacobitism' in British imperial guise swamped the Scottish capital. Mons Meg, the great cannon which was the symbol of a past Stuart arms race with England, was returned to Edinburgh, since 'a Jacobite King sat in London and . . . the grief for Culloden could be shared by all'.[113] As Angus Calder notes, 'adulation of monarchs filled the space which bourgeois nationalisms in Scotland and England might have occupied'.[114]

Whatever 'grief' was shown for the passing of Jacobitism in this discourse, however, was not being so readily 'shared' for the Highland Clearances, by now long under way. Economic improvement and human suffering were inextricably linked and obscured by the pageant of the 1820s: in 1814–20 alone, 15 000 had been evicted from

Sutherland, and the Duchess of Sutherland had appropriated 794 000 acres of clan land. Not all who subscribed to Celticist pageantry failed to attack the Clearances by any means: Stewart of Garth in particular had reservations, and opposed the Pinkertonian view of Highlanders which underlay some Clearance attitudes as 'indolent and useless as cultivators and shepherds, incapable of becoming manufacturers, too impatient for mechanics, and averse to the duties of a military life'. Such a 'Highland character', Garth says, would justify 'any oppression, even to extirpation' were it true: but it is not. The Celticization of Romantic Scotland was distancing itself in such statements from the wilder claims of the Teutonists.[115]

It was, however, to be many years before even this milder view prevailed: Teutonist assumptions about Highland inadequacy influenced official policy well into the century, and it was not for many more years that the conditions of the Highlands aroused general indignation. 'The transfer of remaining Jacobite and nationalist sentiments to wider British imperial loyalties' meant that Scotland's perspective was directed outwards, away from the issues patriot valour would once have addressed.[116] Writers like James Hogg (1770–1835) appeared to perceive this: Hogg's work includes (in *The Three Perils of Woman* (1823)) a critique of eviction and poverty in the midst of plenty which remains more focused on the problems of Scotland than Scott is, though Sir Walter wrote stingingly of the systemic attack on Scottish banking in the 1826 *Letters of Malachi Malagrowther*, by which stage his politics had begun slightly to drift from uncritical Unionist sentimentalism (a similar note can be found in his later fiction, such as *The Highland Widow* (1826)).[117]

If this process rehabilitated Celtic Scotland, it was only in order that patriot valour could be repackaged as romance: an emotive Celtic fantasy which balanced the practical Teuton Unionism of everyday Scotland. Both were myths, but between them they made up the model of a country with an emotionally and impractically Celtic heart and a practical, businesslike Germanic head, an image of Scotland and Scottishness both espoused by many Scots and also adopted by cultural theorists such as G. Gregory Smith and his followers.[118] It was an image which emphasized division, self-disgust, and the irreconcileability of national longings to real autonomy, which the 'Germanic' head dismissed in favour of Unionism. Hence Scottishness was a matter of the heart alone, of sentiment first and then of kitsch, of bothy ballads, douce ministers, strict dominies and all the caricatures of childhood memories served *réchauffé* as adult realities. J. M. Barrie (1860–1937) was both the artist *par excellence* of this disturbing dysfunction, and also one of its sophisticated mockers.[119]

Scotland's identity was formally divided in the long eighteenth century, which is why it remains so important, and also partly why our view of it is bifurcated, as I argued at the beginning of this chapter. Scotland and England were to some 'kindred offshoots from the great Teutonic stem, separated for a time',[120] and to others a marriage of Celtic emotionalism and Anglo-Saxon realism, manifest in each country as the partner attributes in a great Union. 'The incubus of Germanist fixations' of either kind prevented us from understanding that 'Gaelic Scotland has left a marked input on the institutions and culture of later Scotland',[121] but given the relative neglect of Scotland's cultural history for many years after the Enlightenment, this is not surprising. Moreover, the extended idea of Britishness, an international concept valid throughout a great Empire but centred in England, greatly increased the pressure on Scottish identity to be local, symbolic and limited in the statements it made and the challenges it offered to the superpower in whose success it played a disproportionate part. Added to the desire in Presbyterian Scotland to forget its Episcopalian and Catholic contemporaries and ancestors, and perhaps especially the embarrassingly patriotic bishops of Scottish Catholicism, it is little wonder that the cultural history of Scotland and the political discourses to which it gave rise were quiescent. Whereas the Church of England logically, if controversially, adopted pre-Reformation patriot bishops as its own in order to justify its apostolic claims, the Kirk in Scotland was forced to deCatholicize figures such as St Columba in the pursuit of an indefinably, but historically convenient, 'Celtic' Christianity which somehow was itself not only anti-papal, but also compatible with the Teutonic Protestantism of imperial Britain. Such ideas still circulate (for exampe, in the guide history of Dunkeld Cathedral), and are a tribute to the invention of a country which has for so long found much of its history an embarrassment. As David Allan remarks, 'Culdean presbyterianism' (the belief that the Presbyterian Kirk is the true inheritor of the Church of the Celtic saints) is 'a strange creature indeed'.[122] Such strange creatures are part of the paradox of patriot Unionism, so much to the fore in the age of Empire and so neglected a part of the political armouries of the major British parties today.

3

A SCOTTISH EMPIRE

Devils in Skirts?

Michael Lynch has argued that a 'politics of "semi-independence"' marked the period from 1707 to 1832, with Scotland essentially continuing to arrange its domestic affairs through the patronage and networks of its national and local elites. Subsequently, a Victorian tendency to greater British centralization and standardization was counterbalanced by the growth in the ideology of imperial localism, an 'equipoise, in which loyalties to both a reawakened sense of Scottish nationhood and the Empire had kept the British state at arm's length'.[1] Worldwide Britishness, extending not only to the four home nations but also to settler colonies like Australia, New Zealand, Canada and South Africa, was itself the codified reflection of a vision of an international ideal which developed markedly during the Victorian period:

> The imperial/international/institutional theme of parliamentary sovereignty and Protestant destiny which had dominated the representation of England in a previous age was still powerful, but began increasingly to be used for export, to confirm the 'Britishness' of disparate colonies and their societies, by emphasizing the provision of a visible and also metaphorical framework of common law, diplomacy, government and military authority as the binding skein in a patchwork of colourful localisms.[2]

If Britishness was to be the dominant, international feature of all the settler colonies, and one shared intermittently by the elites of southern Asia (and even by 'The Guides at Cabul' in Sir Henry Newbolt's poem, who though 'an alien legion', teach true values to the 'Sons of the Island

81

Race'[3]), they were also to be permitted the counterweight of their own localisms as a balance. For Canada and Australia, among others, this meant Home Rule; for Ireland and Scotland, held more closely in the embrace of Parliamentary sovereignty's inexhaustible claims, it did not. Nonetheless, Scottish imperial localism was a major and important part of Scottish identity: a limited and selective iconization of Scottish history provided a sense of the country's worthiness to be a partner in a Union of which even Wallace and Bruce were seen as avatars. This was 'Unionist Nationalism', a term argued for and defined in Graeme Morton's *Unionist-Nationalism* (1999).[4]

In 1827, the 'management of Scottish civil society was effectively ended by Canning . . . Scottish affairs were then entrusted to the Home Office, although in practice it was the Lord Advocate who controlled matters.' This was one point which can be taken as the beginning of the process whereby Westminster centralism began to impose itself on Scotland in the place of political management by a local elite, developing, as the century progressed, a new set of centralizing institutions which continued to draw power away from Scotland even in the context of administrative devolution, such as that of the Scottish Office in 1885 – at this stage, it must be remembered, based in London. Eventually, however, as Morton argues, the shift away from the control of Scottish society by an elite allowed the growth of mass politics and end-of-the-century pressure for Home Rule.[5] This was naturally abetted, as Michael Fry points out, by the introduction in 1868 of universal male suffrage.[6]

Scottish particularism had its limits strictly set, like that of many colonies. Scots whose Scottishness was regarded as excessive, intrusive or making special national claims were ridiculed through the same kind of 'squabbling-children-saved-from barbarity-by-British civilization' discourse as that applied to India (or indeed Ireland). Ethnocultural and locally colourful Celticism was tolerated, sometimes encouraged, but not claims for space in the body politic: Scottish difference was 'imprisoned in the body itself, the British body whose integrated genetic inheritance parallels its integrative polity'.[7] This, among other facets of the country's history, has led some commentators to argue that Scotland was fully part of the cycle of colonial oppression/postcolonial emergence, which has been in recent years such an important discourse in describing the literary and cultural expression related to the coalescence and dissolution of the great European empires. Michael Hechter's *Internal Colonialism* (1975) was arguably the first book to put this case fully, arguing for a commonality of experience among the Celtic nations based, among other things, on the differential development rates of an exploitative core and its peripheries. Interestingly, Hechter's case is very similar to that put forward by Fletcher of Saltoun nearly three hundred years before: that aggrandizement of power in London will lead to aggrandizement in resources. Nonetheless, it is a case which is open to criticism: as David McCrone and others have argued, Scotland's status as the 'first industrial nation' is inexplicable in terms of the Hechter thesis.[8] It is less inexplicable, however, in terms of the legacy of the Enlightenment: the strength of the intellectual push for material improvement which rested on the major legacies of Scotland's pre-1707 intellectual and cultural institutions, and their long dialogue with continental practice, ensured their transformation while often denying their value. Scotland's first census had been carried out in 1757; the next year there was a public library in Montrose; in 1768, the *Encyclopaedia Britannica* appeared. The poor were eager for education, and up to 30 000 of Scotland's 1.5 million people were engaged in literary activity or teaching. The Moderate Presbyterianism of many of the leading figures in the Central Belt led to the development of a social Christianity which owed something to seventeenth-century academic theologians such as Henry Scougal (1650–78): but its scope, and that of an education system developing to meet greatly increased imperial opportunities, grew rapidly.[9] As Bruce Lenman tells us, 'the Scottish university system in this era happened to be in a phase of rapid expansion at the very end of a long phase of contraction in the universities of most of western Europe'. Career opportunities for a new Empire-bound Scottish diaspora were also growing. In Bengal, where a majority of legal and financial agents were Scots in the later eighteenth century, 'exemption from taxation, political pressure, and brute force enabled [East India] Company men to become extremely rich remarkably fast'. Glasgow's mercantilist opportunism and advancing commercial systems enabled Scotland to capture more than half of the British imported tobacco trade in the peak year of 1769.[10] Rich Scots nabobs returning home enriched their families and endowed their localities, and may, as recent research is suggesting, have themselves played a part through the funds they made available in the strength of Scotland's industrial revolution.[11]

If the military purpose of the Scottish regiments was initially to have potential subversives 'slaughtered fighting the French', as Bruce Lenman argues,[12] it was not long before these troops, or at least their leaders, entered wholeheartedly into the imperial enterprise. Of the three million men who have served in the Scottish regiments, half have been killed or wounded on active service,[13] a colossal global figure which conceals numerous particular instances of Scottish troops proving themselves worthy partners in Empire through heroism or alternatively being used as cannon fodder. In the War of 1756–63, they lost men at four times the American or English rate: at Ticonderoga, the Black Watch lost half their men, 'a rate they almost repeated at Magesfontein in the Boer War'.[14] At Waterloo in 1815, the Royal Scots Greys distinguished themselves by capturing the French guns; during the Indian Mutiny, the Scots were prominent in highly dangerous storming duties.[15] Their generals 'led the fray at moments of imperial crisis': the Master of Lovat in the Seven Years War, Baird at Seringapatam in 1799, Sir John Moore at Corunna in 1805, Lord Clyde in India in 1858, Earl Haig in the First World War, conflicts in which they expended their countrymen and sometimes themselves.[16] In both the first and second world wars, Scottish soldiers were between 40 and 100 per cent more likely to die than their English equivalents.[17] A quarter of those who served in 1914–18 died.[18]

The rhetoric of popular culture and populist verse ran together the valour of Scotland's heroic past with her current role as a supplier of imperial troops. In William Allan's imperial Unionist *Rose and Thistle* (1878) ('The Rose and the Thistle thegither are gane…An' wae to the loons wha their growin' wad mar'), 'Prince Charlie's Address to his Highlanders at Culloden' is 'Charge! and Scotland forever'; it is followed by 'Second to None: Or the Scots Greys' Charge at Waterloo': 'We charge but to conquer, wherever we are.'[19] Similarly, A. C. MacDonell's 'Rush on Coomassis' (1896) places the 'bravely reckless Celt' as a kind of civilized and 'improved' version of the Ashanti the Scots face: the 'wild shock' of the Scottish Celtic war band is rendered irresistible by the 'Sniders' and 'deep Artillery gun' of Anglo-Saxon military infrastructure. The heroic sacrifice remains, converted from futility to utility.[20] Its metaphor has become the Empire: and so it was to remain, despite some interesting recollections of the Auld Alliance in both world wars, which occasionally threw up intriguing images: for example, E. A. Mackintosh, a Scots subaltern killed in action in December 1917, wrote a poem celebrating Scots help to France as that of 'Fingal's warriors…against the Saxon hordes' in a conflict where 'Breton and Gael stand side by side, / against the ancient foe'. Such expressions of anti-Saxon Pan-Celticism appear to have been rare among the servants of Empire, however.[21]

Our Highland Home

The images of Scottish imperial localism drew strongly on the new limited discourse of patriot valour to be found in the recrudescent Highlandism of the Romantic period. The middle classes wore 'highland dress on Sundays' to attend a Kirk which had little history of favouring Highlanders. Scottish baronial architecture, so popular from the 1870s, was itself an attempt to re-create domestically images of valour and strength now happily emptied of all their threat.[22] To some commentators, this has seemed a benign process. As Michael Fry argues in what looks close to an apologia for imperial localism, these myths 'helped to distil the complexity of the real world as they [the Scots] sought to advance themselves without sacrificing their identity'.[23]

The popularity of the 'Highland home' as a vision was increased by the political circumstances of the early nineteenth century. As Katherine Haldane (now Katherine Haldane Grenier) argues:

> the Napoleonic Wars . . . made Scotland virtually the only (even partly) foreign place to which English tourists could safely travel at the turn of the century, aside from Gaelic Ireland. . . . The very popularity of the cult of Scotland tied the country to a fixed image.[24]

The creation and accentuation of this 'fixed image' came in three stages: the Ossianism of Macpherson, the showmanship of Scott, and the endorsement of Queen Victoria. As Andrew Noble points out, 'Romanticism provided – as the Enlightenment could not, for all its brilliance – a surrogate identity . . . of synthetic symbols fabricated by not unrewarded literary intellectuals.'[25] As early as 1800, visitors were carving their names in Fingal's Cave in Staffa, as the Highland image, courtesy of James Macpherson, moved from that of savage to *Kulturvolk*.[26] The mediation of Ossianic heroism through Jacobite sentimentalism followed in Scott's *Waverley* (1815) and elsewhere, while the noonday of Scottish Highlandism came with the accession of Victoria, the first modern monarch to 'adopt' Scotland as integral to the image of the monarchy. Not only was the newly fitted-out Balmoral swathed in tartan, but the Queen's own civic engagements also publicly represented the swollen cultus of a glamorized and nostalgic Scottish valour. In 1842,

> in Crieff, Victoria and Albert were met by 100 of the local tenants, dressed in tartan, some with Lochaber axes . . . at Dunkeld . . . the sovereign was met by an imposing collection of the Atholl Highlanders complete with claymores and

battleaxes . . . Many . . . were men of gigantic stature, especially the battleaxe
phalanx and those who were equipped with bucklers.[27]

The idea of the primitive, picturesque Scot as a giant was one also
found in many Victorian postcards and popular depictions of vast and
hairy Scots soldiers (usually privates and NCOs: officers, despite being
better fed, are shown as somewhat trimmer). Clad in the red of Britain,
these were the domesticated versions of ancestors who had provided
material for the 'stories of . . . lawlessness and ferocity' for which the
Victorian tourist had an 'insatiable appetite'. Emphasis was repeatedly
put on the 'strong', 'hardy', 'sturdy' and 'robust' qualities of Scots, indicative of 'a sort of preindustrial vigour and strength'.[28] Enlightenment
historiography had drifted down to the level of a populist discourse of
Scotland's past, which stressed not martial valour against a common
enemy, but centuries of aimless strife and civil rancour (ended of
course, only by Union and English civilization). This Victorian image
still carries immense power today, with its presentation of Scottish history as an 'ideologically neutral pageant',[29] devalued and distorted to
destroy any prospect of its effectiveness. When even a moderate Unionist body like the National Assocation for the Vindication of Scottish
Rights (see below) raised issues of unequal treatment for Scotland in the
Union, the English press sneered that Scotland had 'no disabilities (save
the Celtic temperament, which could not be expected to prosper)'.[30]
Any politicization of Scottish difference risked this condemnation, as
I argued at the beginning of this chapter. Germanic as Unionist Scots
felt themselves to be, the images of Celtic tourism could still be used to
dismiss the whole country whenever it was the source of complaint or
remonstrance, however mild. This was nationalism, and even 'unionist-
nationalism' could get above itself and exceed the rights of imperial
localism.

The latter was visible in the popularity of recreational Highlandism,
such as the Highland Games, first developed in the 1780s, and Highland
dancing, whose popularity dates from much the same time.[31] History
was often adduced merely to serve this recreational dimension, as in the
Dundee Highland Society of 1814 and the Dundee Ancient Caledonian
Society of 1822, which aimed to preserve 'the dress and several of the
antiquities of the ancient Caledonians', though it also offered charitable
relief to Highland immigrants into the town.[32] Scenery helped to make
history recreational. As Thomas Tallard wrote in *Glencoe, or the Fate of the
MacDonalds* (1840), 'the chief interest which the author can hope that

any will find in perusing this drama, will consist in the bringing to their minds the features of the stupendous glen to which it refers'.[33] In other words, the massacre of the MacDonalds is an exercise in sublimity: an artistic social reflection of the beauty and terror of Glencoe. Such images were reinforced by the careerist and relentless Highlandism of those colourful claimants to the Stuart throne, John and Charles-the Sobieski Stuarts, for whom Lord Lovat built a Celtic fantasy palace, 'decorated...in a manner which exceeded the kitsch of Balmoral itself'.[34] Their 'Jacobitism' had its counterpart in the sentimental cult of the drawing-room Jacobite song, given a boost when the Queen herself requested 'Oh! wae's me for Prince Charlie' on her first visit in 1842.[35]

More scholarly recreational history developed through the great nineteenth-century clubs which printed much useful primary material on Scotland: the Bannatyne (1823), the Maitland (1829) and the Spalding (1840) among them. The Gaelic Society of Inverness followed in 1871, after the beginnings of a 'Gaelic revival' in the previous decade.[36]

Even Wallace, the 'Great Patriot Hero! Ill Requited Chief!' was brought into the discourse of Highlandism as a warrior chieftain,[37] although stress also continued, rather incoherently, to be laid on the Germanicity of both Bruce and Wallace as 'mighty northern Englishmen' in the poet John Davidson's words. 'Germanist fixations' continued, as William Ferguson argues, to undermine understanding of the 'marked imprint' left by Gaelic society 'on the institutions and culture of later Scotland'.[38] If, as William Burns (1809–76), one of the few nineteenth-century opponents of Teutonism, remarked in *The Scottish War of Independence* (1874), 'the Scots and the English were "kindred offshoots from the great Teutonic stem, separated for a time by an unfortunate war... then, the history of our country ceases to have any meaning"'. How can 'the Scottish Nation' be 'a portion of the general Saxon aggregate' and maintain its nationality? This was, of course, part of the point of the Teutonist cult: Burns set against it 'the two grand ideals of national consciousness and religious freedom'.[39] Five years after his book appeared, W. F. Skene's *Celtic Scotland* did much to rehabilitate Gaelic society, albeit in a still romanticized form. Nonetheless, Skene's views of Celtic landholding practice arguably filtered though to the Napier Commission of 1885 and the development of crofters' rights.[40] Ironically, one of the great reforming measures of the nineteenth century was based on a Romantic perception.

Dissenting Voices

The development of radicalism in Scotland following the French
Revolution of 1789 forms a minor, but still controversial, part of the
narrative of Scottish national identity. Jacobin and reformist activity in
Scotland is taken by some as a version of a wider British model; by
others as more in tune with the nationalist radicalism of the United
Irishmen, though sophisticated commentators have pointed out that
United Irishmen and Friends of the People radical activity was not neces-
sarily to be compartmentalized in this way. The central questions about
Scottish radical dissent from the British state during the period 1790–1820
nonetheless remain threefold: how far were the United Scotsmen and
Scottish Friends of the People 'nationalist' in any sense; how popular
was their cause, and did it leave any lasting legacy?

The extreme case, put forward with particular reference to the rising
of 1820 by writers such as Peter Berresford Ellis, Seamus MacGhiobhainn and Frank Sherry, is that Scottish radicalism contained the lineaments of a nationalist struggle, at least in the central Lowlands. In
a perspective which is more broadly focused on the whole of Scottish
radicalism in this period, other writers such as Colin Kidd have stressed
the radicals' use of a rhetoric of English liberties far removed from the
discourse of patriot valour.[41] In the middle are writers such as Graeme
Morton, who point out the significant element in the United Scotsmen
who wanted to dissolve the Union and restore a 'Scottish Assembly or
Parliament', while nonetheless acknowledging the British language of
radicalism:

> The radical weavers in Renfrewshire in 1819 demanded their rights in line
> with the Magna Carta while the Lancashire cotton spinners sang *Scots wha hae
> wi' Wallace bled* to express their freedom as workers and the power of their
> trades union against tyrants.[42]

Certainly in the 1790s there was evidence of widespread radical discontent of some sort in Scotland. Trees of Liberty appeared 'in places as
unlikely as Auchtermuchty and Fochabers',[43] and there were riots in 1792
in Perth, Aberdeen and Edinburgh.[44] Some onlookers were convinced
that this was nationalist disaffection. Elements in the French government
were 'persistently deluded' that Scotland 'was panting to throw off
the English yoke. It was not true.'[45] Nonetheless, the idea that there was
'a nationalist tinge' in Scottish radicalism in the 1790s has proved hard

to eradicate.[46] The Earl of Buchan, for example, who founded the Scottish Society of Antiquaries in 1780, argued 'for an independent Scottish republic',[47] as did the Jacobin Thomas Muir of Huntershill (1765–99).[48]

Echoing Wolfe Tone, agitators suggested that 'Scotland has long groaned under the chains of England and knows that its connection there is the cause of its greatest misfortunes': sentiments such as this were widespread enough for nationalist ambitions to be credited to the United Scotsmen throughout the 1790s.[49] The United Irishmen themselves appealed 'to the Scottish republican tradition', while Scottish radicals like James Thomson Callendar claimed that Scotland's MPs were 'the servile tools of English misgovernment'. The aristocratic, patronage-driven political outcome of the Union was a major target for criticism.[50] The Scottish Friends of the People distributed material in the Highlands bearing the iconic figure of Jacobite idealism and the history of Scottish valour: 'a Highland man in full dress, with target and broad sword'.[51] In 1792, Muir stated to his countrymen 'that in this great national question [of reform] you are still-Scotland: the land where Buchanan wrote, and Fletcher spoke, and Wallace fought'. Subsequently, Muir attempted to persuade the French Directory to support 'a landing in Scotland', where 'they might expect the ready assistance of fifty thousand Highlanders'. This bizarre fantasy never stood a chance of success, and the Directory took wiser counsels, even though one of France's own over-enthusiastic envoys appeared to concur with Muir. Nonetheless, Muir is to some extent rightly cited as a nationalist revolutionary: just as in the case of French foreign policy of the Jacobite period, he sought to divide England, Scotland and Ireland into three separate republics.[52] Nor was he alone: the view that Scotland was 'oppressed', and, like Ireland, kept alive 'the hope of ultimately regaining . . . entire independence', eve though 'it is nothing but a dependent colony of the English Government', was not a wholly eccentric one. Scots radicals were also urged to support Wolfe Tone, for otherwise 'Wallace' would have 'died . . . in vain'. Enthusiasm for the Revolution in the West of Scotland ran high: it is tempting, though unsubstantiated, to link this both to the remnants of Covenanting radicalism and the Red Clydeside era of the twentieth century, when the Red Flag was famously raised in central Glasgow, and troops and tanks were called in to overwhelm any revolutionary putsch – yet what was going on was in fact little more than conventional industrial unrest.[53] The legend of the Red Flag in George Square is itself an apt symbol for caution in assessing the true extent of the radicalism of a hundred years before.

It was not surprising that 'the ideological community between Presbyterian Ulster and Scotland' should have been indicative of a certain symbiosis between the United Irishmen and Scottish radicalism. Burns was, indeed, widely used as a source of radical language in the Protestant north in Ireland. As the 'Address from the Society of United Irishmen in Dublin, 1792' put it, 'we greatly rejoice that the Spirit of freedom moves over the Face of Scotland . . . our political situations are not dissimilar . . . our rights and wrongs are the same'.[54] Nonetheless, for all these brave words, it is difficult to pin down specifically nationalist sentiments, and it is as well to remember that the internationalism of the revolutionaries might tend to undercut them. Certainly, some of the patriotic allusions to Scotland seem to indicate a desire to see it lead the way in British reform rather than go its own way entirely. England, Scotland and Ireland are identified as different nations, but 'an Union of the whole people' is still mentioned. On the other hand, it is hard to believe that nationalist sentiments are entirely absent from documents such as the 'Address to the Delegates for Parliamentary Reform, 1793':

> Scotland, for ages, the asylum of independence, and equally renowned in arms and arts. . . . That this same Scotland should have so long forgotten her degraded state, as a nation, slept over her political insignificance, or silently acquiesced in the mockery of a popular representation, among the senators of another people, hath long filled us with inexpressible astonishment . . . your independence . . . blotted . . . from among the nations of the earth.[55]

Here, however briefly, the discourse of heroic valour is reanimated within the frame of an argument for reform.

There were other signs that the discourses of patriot valour and heroic resistance were proving popular. In 1815, there were 10 000 on a Covenanting march in Ayrshire, and, possibly more significantly, 15 000 assembled at Bannockburn the previous year to commemorate the 500th anniversary of the battle.[56] At the same time, the presence of Wallace and Bruce on 1832 Reform banners reminds us that these heroes were in the nineteenth century, as never before or since, associated with Unionism and part of a British political discourse: William Wordsworth even considered writing an epic on Wallace, while Robert Southey adopted him as a hero in the English radical struggle against the Norman Yoke.

The 1820 Rising likewise displayed these mixed features. Sixty thousand took part in the general strike called in the West for 3 April in support of Scotland's 'Provisional Government', and 'Glasgow, Paisley and other centres were immobilised, as weavers, factory workers, miners and other workmen took part.'[57] The members of the 'Provisional Government' appeared to intend 'to regenerate their country and restore its inhabitants to their native dignity'. On Tuesday 4 April, banners appeared among the radical military formations round Glasgow bearing the legend 'Scotland Free or Scotland a Desert'. Five thousand troops were sent to Glasgow, where mounted patrols were attacked in Gallowgate and the Gorbals while the radicals were entrenched on the south bank of the Clyde. The 'Strathaven Volunteers' were compared to Wallace and Bruce: 'justice and humanity forbid us tamely to surrender that freedom which our gallant ancestors fought for and established on the glorious field of Bannockburn. . . . Let "Scotland free- or a Desert" be our motto', it was said. Rapidly defeated as they were at Bonnymuir near Falkirk and throughout the west, the radicals nonetheless had articulated a political language which was reminiscent of their country's dangerous and disaffected past.[58]

Caution is required in interpreting the radical rising, however, not only because of the uniquely ambivalent symbolism of Wallace and Bruce in the nineteenth century, but also because some of the more extreme views attributed to the men of 1820 were in all probability black propaganda from pro-government sources. Yet even the provocative must have something to provoke: the balance of probability remains on the side of a quasi-nationalist dimension in *some* Scottish radical activity in 1790–1820 in the Central Lowlands. The street literature examined by Peter Freshwater, for example, is suggestive of a 'nationalist desire for a totally separate Scottish state' in some areas. Support for Daniel O'Connell's Repeal movement in some Scottish broadsides is interesting in this context, as is the portrayal of the 'martyrs' of 1820 as 'heroes of Scotia': but nonetheless, sentiment and a greater devotion to the cause of Reform than that of the nation is still evident. The balance of Scottish radicalism, despite some bold and oft-quoted statements, turns only slightly to the nationalist side.[59]

If much of Scottish reformism shared in a wider British context in the early nineteenth century, more widespread grounds for social radicalism arguably appeared in the massive depopulation of the Highlands, which had begun after Culloden, continued with the forcing out or voluntary departure of the tacksman class (the chief's subalterns and senior lessees, who sublet) in the 1760s and 1770s,[60] and reached a crescendo in the early to mid-nineteenth century. As early as 1739, MacDonald of Sleat and MacLeod of Dunvegan had made an 'experiment in slave-trafficking from Skye', and as the landlord class became more closely integrated into the British polity, the economic pressure they placed on their tenants increased.[61] The intrusion of vast flocks of sheep into the Highlands (250 000 by 1811, nearly 1 000 000 by the 1840s) has long held the symbolic high ground among the images of Highland depopulation,[62] but the vast areas of the Highlands left under deer were in their way even more apt images of the conversion of a large part of Scotland into a heritage park. 'By 1884', MacLean and Carrell tell us, 'deer-forests covered 1,975,209 acres . . . the vast majority of that area in the crofting counties'.[63] This was not only a massive economic change: it was also one intimately linked to the cult of Highlandism:

> Hundreds of thousands of acres of the Highlands and Islands became 'sporting' land . . . the product of a new set of images of the Highlands, created around the court of Queen Victoria . . . the image of the Highlands as a wild place full of kilt-wearing neo-brigands, and crooning lassies, where a man – well, a Very Important sort of Man – could rediscover the primitive blood-lust of the hunt.[64]

Thus did the romanticization of ancient and traditional Scotland commercialize its ideals through economic change, a development which had been foreshadowed as early as 1784 when 'Macdonell of Glengarry . . . who had taken an active part in clearing his fellow countrymen from their lands, decided to form a society in support of the Scottish language, dress, music and characteristics.'[65] Although there had been concern for 'the parlous condition of much of the Highland population' since the 1830s,[66] effective and concerted action had to wait for many years. In the middle of the century, it sometimes came from emigrant Highland communities in the cities: later it was connected to the rise of the Gaelic revival. In 1880, for example, John Stuart Blackie told the Perth Gaelic Society that 'Gaelic and Highland clubs and associations had a role . . . to campaign for radical reform of the land laws and to work for the modernisation of Highland agricultural practices.' It was in this decade that Land League and crofting politics took up Blackie's challenge, and inaugurated the beginnings of the modern era's debates on Scottish land use. That it took so long is almost certainly partly because of the depth of prejudice about Highland society, somewhat dispersed by the Celtic Revival in which Skene's *Celtic Scotland* of 1879–80 played its part. As the 'Commissioners of Inquiry into the Poor Law' concluded in 1844, the poverty of the Highlands was due to 'the imperfectly formed habits of the Highland labourer, in respect of provident

and persevering industry...deficient in the knowledge of letters...
deficient in...practical education of civilized life'. The language was
also regarded as a barrier: yet the key problem in perception was perhaps that also ascribed to colonial peoples in writings such as those of
Thomas Carlyle: 'Under the stimulus of immediate reward, he [the
Highlander] is capable of making very great exertions, but the task
accomplished, and the price paid, he relapses into his wonted lethargy.'
As an ethnic slur, it clearly did not apply: 22 per cent of Highland-born
in Stirling in 1851 were in managerial or professional occupations, for
example.[67]

One of the reasons for continuing prejudice against the natural abil-
ities and disposition of the Highlander was the view that he/she was
a 'lazy' Celt rather than an 'industrious Saxon'.[68] Teutonists such as
John Pinkerton and his successor Robert Knox (1791–1862), who published *The Races of Men* in 1850, continued to separate 'the industrious,
liberal Scoto-Saxons of the Lowlands' from their idle Celtic counterparts, 'an attitude apparent in a section of the Scottish press during the
relief of the Highland famine of 1846–47', although some papers, such
as the *North British Daily Mail*, showed 'sympathy for the plight of the
indigenous Gael' in tandem with 'racial hostility to the simian Irish
Celt'.[69] It would be fair to say, however, that even trusty Teuton Lowlanders had reservations about some of these theorists:

> Up and down and round the stair,
> Mind your back frae Burke and Hare;
> Burke's the killer, and Hare's the thief,
> And Knox the butcher that buys the beef

as one song put it in reference to Knox's early and notorious career as an
Edinburgh anatomist. Anatomy and Teutonism were linked, particularly
in the field of phrenology, where 'Teutonist attitudes...enjoyed wide dissemination', not least in the work of George Combe (1788–1858).[70]

The Disruption of 1843, when the Kirk of Scotland split on the issue of
lay patronage, was not without its nationalist associations, particularly
since the seceders' case was 'that a British Parliament could not legislate
on Scottish religious matters'. Traces of similar 'low-key' nationalism can
be found in the contemporary movement of Chartism, some at least
of whose adherents, such as 'the Birmingham Quaker Joseph Sturge',
supported Home Rule for Scotland.[71] Some of those who had been to
the forefront in pressing the Free Kirk's case in the Disruption were

subsequently involved in the National Association for the Vindication of Scottish Rights (NAVSR), a group which aimed for greater recognition of Scottish distinctiveness within the Union, more equitable public expenditure (which at that time favoured England) and the restoration of offices such as that of the Secretary of State, suspended in 1747, and Privy Council, abolished in 1708. Other complaints included the fact that more was spent on the Irish famine than in Scotland, that Scotland had too few MPs, and that the United Kingdom was 'Great Britain' rather than England.[72]

The leading lights in this organization, launched in November 1853,[73] included the historical novelist James Grant (1822–87) (Scott's second cousin) and the Earl of Eglinton and Winton, its chairman: Eglinton was another purveyor of pageantry, most notably at the picturesque mediaeval tourney he held at Kilwinning in 1839. The Association's aims were sometimes realized, though often in the longer term: an under-Secretaryship was heavily voted down in 1858, but the Secretary-ship and the desired increase in Scotland's MPs from 53 to 71 were eventually secured, and the term 'North Britain' declined in use, for example. Nonetheless, a slightly unreal air of romanticist flag-waving attended many of the Association's activities.[74] Although some of the members of the NAVSR (such as John Steill) favoured the restoration of a Scottish Parliament, this was by no means a majority position, though there is some evidence of nationalist candidates in Glasgow University rectorial elections in the 1850s.[75] Rather, the NAVSR was principally a vehicle for establishing Scottish imperial localism at a level perceived to be appropriate to the country's standing: indeed, it was to some extent a response directed against moves towards greater British cen-tralism, such as the abolition of the Scottish Board of Customs and Excise in 1843 and the similar loss of 'the Scottish Mint, and the Scottish House-hold'. The NAVSR 'joined the anti-centralisation bandwagon, active in the towns and cities of England, to defend local government', although it is arguable that activists such as James Grant were more than merely localist: Grant's attacks on centralist control and its effects in Scotland are reminiscent of Fletcher of Saltoun:

Centralisation hurled Louis Philippe from the throne of France, Centralisation plunged Hungary in woe and Austria in war, Centralisation blotted Poland from the map of Europe, and Venice and Lombardy from the States of Italy. Centralisation is the curse of modern Europe; let us be aware that it does not become the curse of Britain.

> It has disgraced and demoralised Scotland, it has depopulated her Highlands; it has violated her laws and subverted her institutions; it has levelled the kingdom of the Bruces and Stuarts to the rank of an English county.[76]

Centralization was regarded by NAVSR activists as a breach of Union.[77] Although their objections to neglect of Scotland were often rooted in minor symbolic affronts, Grant and his allies had shown 'that it was possible to get up a nationalist agitation in Scotland, even on a trivial point'.[78] Despite the clarion-call of such sentiments, the NAVSR was in no sense a challenge to Britain and the British Empire in the way more radical contemporary strands of Irish Fenianism were, and its agitation obediently died down and disappeared in response to the Crimean War, where British troops were united against a common enemy:

> By 1856 the association had collapsed: its arguments dissipated by a mixture of the war, the growing willingness of the government to listen to Scottish complaints, and the instability which the wide and heterogenous membership brought.[79]

The importance of external warfare to British identity was a strain of patriot unionism which survived even into the early days of the SNP, when it is perhaps more appropriately called localist nationalism. Nationalist patriots such as Andrew Dewar Gibb continued to espouse a Scottish nationalism within the British Empire into the 1950s: and although the end of Empire liberated Scottish nationalism from this essentially British stance, it can arguably still be seen in modern campaigns run or aided by the SNP, such as the 'Save our Scottish Regiments' of the early 1990s.

Certainly the NAVSR was not at heart a radical body. The Lords Provost of Edinburgh and Glasgow and the provosts of Perth and Stirling lent it their support; but despite this and other elite backing, its overall membership probably fell short of 1000, though it attracted crowds of up to five times this figure.[80] In some ways, it was merely the most visible in a burgeoning number of clan and local history societies which were encouraging interest in the Scottish past at a level suitable to preserving a local identity within the imperial partnership. But the NAVSR is arguably more important than this, because some of its members articulated a dissatisfaction with the essentially unequal nature of Britishness which went beyond the limited purview of localist celebration. In his address to the Glasgow NAVSR in 1853, for example, Eglinton called for parity of esteem between Scottish and English institutions, writers and heroes.[81] This was more than local celebration: this was a request to redefine Britishness as belonging to Scott as much as to Shakespeare, to curling as much as to cricket, to Robert the Bruce as much as to Alfred the Great. This call for recognition, if it had ever been answered, would perhaps have created an enduring Britishness on a new plane: but although the ethos of Britain remained international, its home was in (mainly southern) England. The NAVSR called for a Britishness which Scotland could accept, but that England would never recognize (although, perversely, knowledge of distinctively Scottish literature and history was more widespread in English education in 1940 than it is now). Neglect of the Eglinton case meant that Britishness was tied to Empire, and that the collapse of one would endanger the other.

The monumental celebrations of Wallace which spanned the nineteenth century were to some extent attempts to claim the parity Eglinton sought, from the 1820 Falkirk Wallace statue to the Wallace statue at Aberdeen in 1888, via the Abbey Craig monument and the 1859 attempt to 'build a monument to Wallace and Bruce in Edinburgh', dubbed by Noel Paton 'a National Memorial of the War of Independence under Wallace and Bruce and of its results in the Union of England and Scotland'. But instead of calling forth recognition, they made English opinion uneasy. When the Wallace Monument went up on the Abbey Craig at Stirling the Earl of Elgin emphasized its Unionist message,[82] but *The Times*'s reaction to the project had been to call Wallace 'the merest myth' and comment that 'Scotchmen . . . seem to do nothing but masquerade in the garments of their grandfathers'; it was also suggested 'that the Monument signified the growth of a provincial mentality in Scotland'.[83] Thus 'the only way in which Scotland could demonstrate it was not provincial was to remain a province':[84] indeed, *The Times* compared any Scottish consciousness of neglect to that of an English county.[85] Imperial localism was one thing, national difference another. Figures such as the Revd William Anderson (1796–1872), who called Garibaldi the 'William Wallace of Italy', may have meant no reference to any domestic contemporary nationalism,[86] but such statements had the potential to irritate – and perhaps do more, for Wallace was used as a symbol of liberation in a colonial rising in Nyasaland in 1915. Though in one sense he was a liberator from the Norman yoke in a mould recognizable to English Whiggism, in another he was of continuing relevance as an inspirational figure in struggles for national independence. Indeed, in 1916, an irate Glasgow Irish correspondent criticized Scottish antipathy to the Easter

Rising as inappropriate for the nation that had spawned William Wallace.[87]

Home Rule All Round

The Scottish Home Rule Association (SHRA) was founded in May 1886,[88] on the back of the Land League agitation which had seen the setting up of the Napier Commission, the election of five crofting MPs, the restoration of the office of Secretary of State and the debate over the Irish Question. One of the crofting MPs, Dr G. B. Clark, was among its leadership, as were R. B. Cunninghame Graham (later 'the first president of the National Party of Scotland') and John Stuart Blackie, the Celtic revivalist.[89] Gladstone had promised 'Home Rule All Round' on his famous Midlothian tour (though the phrase itself may have originated with Charles Waddie, the SHRA's founder: this did not of course come to pass, but a Scottish Grand Committee of Scottish MPs was established to review Scottish legislation in 1894 – abolished by the Conservatives, it was re-established by the Liberals on an enduring basis in 1906).[90] The SHRA gained limited influence in the Liberal Party, but the 1906 Liberal Government's failure to move on the issue despite the Conservatives' loss of all their Welsh seats (a result which was unique until 1997) indicated that the Liberals were really only interested in toying with Home Rule ideas in opposition, as Labour were to be after them. Nonetheless, some Liberals set up a 'Scottish Nationalist' group in Parliament in 1910, and the Scottish Liberals continued to back Home Rule in their conference resolutions. Scottish input to the growth of the Labour Party by 1900 seemed set to increase pressure for a fuller degree of Home Rule to be granted. This was evident as early as 1888, when Keir Hardie stood as an Independent Labour candidate in Mid-Lanark:[91] in the longer run, it was the future Independent Labour Party (ILP) which was to be true to this cause for longest. Sentimentalist appeals to a 'patriot band' of Scots revived, in a milk-and-water way, the traditionalist discourse of heroic valour. This kind of rhetoric was aided by the contemporary development of Pan-Celticism, the First Pan-Celtic Congress being held in Dublin in August 1901.[92]

On the fringes of the movement were activists like Theodore Napier (1845–1928) and Ruaridh Erskine of Mar (1869–1952), who nonetheless proved strongly influential on elements in the development of the future SNP (and groups like Wendy Wood's Scottish Patriots), with their stress on Celtic revivalism. Napier also pioneered direct action in areas where he perceived Scotland was discriminated against. His greatest success was that he 'almost single-handed obtained over 104 000 signatures to a diamond jubilee petition to Queen Victoria protesting against the misuse of the national names'.[93] Both Napier and Erskine were neo-Jacobites. Erskine was a member of the Central Executive Committee of the Legitimist Jacobite League, a group which actually favoured restoring the Stuarts, and Napier was its Scottish Secretary.[94] Their programme was thus broadly similar, though Erskine was too divisively pro-Gaelic in Napier's view. Erskine, who 'became passionately absorbed in the Gaelic revival', argued not only for 'complete national independence', but also 'the restoration to Scotland of her Celtic system of Government and her Celtic culture', a programme which sounded very like the Gaelicization of Ireland being sought by Sinn Fein's leadership, itself perhaps influenced by Connolly's popularization of Skene's *Celtic Scotland* via its influence on the Napier Commission. 'The mercenary values of England' were challenged as a key opponent in both the Irish and Scottish Celtic Revivals.[95] The Irish connection is clear in Erskine's 'Celtic Communism' ideal, which found echoing support from the extreme figures of John MacLean (1879–1923), who sought to restore 'the tradition and instincts of the Celtic race' throgh 'the communism of the clans' and Hugh MacDiarmid (1892–1978):[96] through it Erskine, like his Irish contemporaries, 'argued that a collectivist ethos in the Celtic past had been undermined by Anglo-Saxon values of greed and selfishness'. Erskine's post-war Scottish National League (founded in 1919) espoused an 'often outlandish style' of 'romantic celticism and extreme language...anglophobic rhetoric and dreamy mysticism', apparently popular among its frequently expatriate romanticist support.[97] In *Changing Scotland* (1931), a book published when he had already despaired of achieving his goals, Erskine summed up his view that 'Scottish independence must ensure a lasting revival of ancient Celtic institutions.'[98] Erskine was perhaps behind the 'Scottish Party' programme announced in January 1907: if so, then both he and Napier called for the effective establishment of a Scottish national party – the latter had done so several times in his *Fiery Cross* journal, beginning in 1901.[99]

Rather than a single national party, however, there were a variety of smaller organizations which clustered round the SHRA, such as the Liberal Young Scots Society (which claimed 1580 members by 1903 and

58 branches by 1914).[100] The Scottish Patriotic Association, another such group, launched its objection to King Edward using the regnal numeral 'seventh' at Bannockburn in 1901: 1100 signed the Protest, and a vote was subsequently taken in the Convention of Royal Burghs, which was lost 65–6.[101] It was the SPA who were at least partly responsible for founding the Bannockburn Day rally now carried on by the SNP. In 1912, this was attended by 15 000 people.[102] The SPA also campaigned for the teaching of Scottish history in Scottish schools. Here too it was following the Irish agenda, where in 1898 Eoin MacNeill had written that Irish youth knew 'the Armada and . . . the Battle of Waterloo', but nothing of 'the Battle of the Yellow Ford' or 'the deeds of King Daithi': in 1903, the Gaelic League had called for 'the Introduction of Irish History into every school and college in Ireland'.[103]

The establishment of the Scottish National League in 1904 marked a further stage along the road of nationalist development, while journals such as the *Scottish Review*, the *Fiery Cross* (with its clear revivalism of the rhetoric of patriot valour) and Erskine's *Guth na Bliadhna* all enjoyed long runs in print,[104] among shorter-lived peers such as *The Scottish Nationalist* of 1903.[105] The *Fiery Cross* put forward an anti-imperialist Pan-Celticism strongly laced with Legitimist Jacobitism. Napier's journal argued for 'The Teaching of Scottish History in Schools', a 'Union of the Celtic Races' and 'opposition to "*Jingo-Imperialism*" and "*Militarism*"', among a host of constitutional demands including the restoration of the Stuarts and the clan system. Despite this apparent extremism, it appears that, like his fellow-workers in the SHRA, Napier would have accepted a federal union – at least some of the time.[106] In 1912, Napier, 'Jacobite and Scottish Patriot', returned to Australia, where his achievements were later celebrated in *The Jacobite*, which proudly proclaimed itself 'the only Jacobite paper in New Zealand', a distinction which appears to have roused no jealousy elswhere in the press.[107]

As H. J. Hanham percipiently put it in 1969:

> by the 1880s the main patterns of modern nationalism had emerged. On the right nationalism was represented by individual Tory peers like Lord Bute, by romantic Tories in the tradition of James Grant, and by a small band of Jacobites. Nearer the centre were businessmen like William Burns and Charles Waddie, for whom nationalism was a discovery to be propagated in a business-like way. And on the left there were Radical writers like Morrison Davidson, and working-class nationalists like some of the early Labour leaders.[108]

These divisions persisted throughout the twentieth century, though they are by no means always as clear-cut as they appear: Morrison Davidson, for example, was also the author of the historically nationalist *Scotia Rediviva: Home Rule for Scotland with the Lives of Sir William Wallace, George Buchanan, Fletcher of Saltoun and Thomas Spence*, an eclectic bunch if ever there was one.[109]

Cultural revival has, however, played a significant role in consolidating and developing ideas of Scottish identity among a vanguard intelligentsia since the foundation of the SHRA, who themselves often leant more towards Hanham's businesslike middle. Leaving aside the overtly political cultural programmes of Napier and Erskine, the 1890s also saw the peak of a native Arts and Crafts movement in Scotland, as in Ireland. Patrick Geddes, a mild Home Ruler with an interest in both urban and internal renewal, was the first to proclaim 'The Scots Renascence' in his *Evergreen* Celtic Revival journal in 1895, a term which has later come to describe the literary revival of the 1920s. Geddes argued against Anglicization, the 'spoiling of what might be good Scots to make indifferent Englishmen', while moderately showing himself aware of 'the larger responsibilities of united nationality and race' within Britain.[110]

Such cultural revivalism had direct links to Home Rule activism: Charles Waddie, founder of the SHRA, put on plays on Bruce and Wallace 'at some considerable personal expense' at the Glasgow Athenaeum in 1899. Despite MacDiarmid's later view (borrowed from Yeats) that 'there will be no literary revival in Scotland until genuine literary criticism replaces the auto-intoxicated folly of patriotism', the signs were that the cultural impulse had priority over any questions of quality.[111]

English opposition to Home Rule was less visceral than was the case with regard to Ireland, but arguably just as profound. A. V. Dicey's *England's Case Against Home Rule* (1886), which warned of the dangers of 'unilateral devolution', was still being used to bolster anti-Home Rule arguments a century later, as was his warning of the threat posed to Parliamentary sovereignty.[112] Federalism diluted sovereignty, and Home Rule distributed it unequally, while the doctrine of the Westminster Parliament was never to give it away: such a triangle of tension continued to encourage immobility on the issue, an immobility which in Ireland's case had tragic consequences.

The spectre of Irish Home Rule called forth many different reactions in Scotland. The SHRA argued in 1890 'that failure to treat Scotland on an equal basis with Ireland "appears to set a premium upon disorder"'.[113] This argument has surfaced intermittently since in nationalist circles:

but the SHRA's position did not really represent a Scottish consensus. The *Glasgow Herald*, for example, viewed Scottish Home Rule demands as a 'by-product of Irish agitation'.[114] There was, moreover, considerable sympathy in Scotland for the situation of the Ulster Protestants, Home Rule's greatest opponents. John Harrison's *The Scot in Ulster* (1888) promoted an idea of ethnic solidarity,[115] but there is little evidence of popular response to this idea in Scotland. In 1923, in the immediate aftermath of Irish independence, with major unrest both in the Free State and in the newly-partitioned north, 'an Orange and Protestant Party' was formed in Scotland: 'Its one MP Hugh Ferguson, representing Motherwell, took the Tory whip in Parliament. Ferguson was defeated after a year, and ... the fledgling party ... reabsorbed by the Unionists.'[116]

Despite limited sympathy for their Presbyterian co-religionists (one further diluted by an evident distaste for Irish extremism in general), the position in Scotland was more complex than such ventures presumed. For one thing, 'the Liberal Imperialist preference for federal Home Rule all round had of course a particular attraction for Scotland, and helped win many Scots to their side':[117] indeed, the SHRA itself 'tended to act as a ginger group within the Liberal Party'.[118] For another, much Orange activity was itself the expression not of native Scottish, but of northern Irish Protestant immigration: Orangemen regarded themselves as 'shunned ... a mere Irish faction, a foreign import brought to disturb the peace of the country'. Although they had sympathizers (particularly in the Kirk of Scotland in the 1920s), there is not a great deal of evidence that Orange unionism had a strong political appeal in Scotland outside areas of Northern Protestant immigration or back-migration.[119]

The Empire remained a potent focus for 'unionist nationalism', at least through to 1914. The Unionist Party (the name of the Conservatives in Scotland up till 1964) of that year

> stressed the sensitive nature of the Scottish national question, urged party candidates to try to direct Scottish national feelings to the ends of Empire, and counselled them to use the argument that Scottish Home Rule would close off avenues of career development for ambitious Scots in England.[120]

Nonetheless, this Home Rule seemed to be drawing closer. In apparent imitation of the Irish example, attempts were made to give an international dimension to the campaign with the foundation of the International Scots Home Rule League (later Self Government League) in 1913, with

its companion paper, *The Scottish Nation*. By early 1914, 'branches...
[were] formed in America'. The increasing likelihood of Irish Home
Rule had an effect on the prospect of change in Scotland which tantal-
izingly, if inconclusively, emerged in the years before 1914. A second
reading for a 1912 Federal Home Rule Bill was followed by the Scottish
Home Rule Bill of 1913, which passed its first reading on 30 May by
204–159, with Scots MPs 45–8 in favour; in May 1914 it was debated
again, but without result.[121] Within three months, war had supervened.

4

THE SCOTTISH NATIONAL PARTY

Beginnings

In the First World War, Scotland lost 110 000 men, over 20 per cent of Britain's war dead.[1] The absence of the promised 'home fit for heroes' fuelled radicalism both north and south of the Border; and the apparent possibility of the replication of Dublin in 1916 in Scotland inflamed unrealistic fears in some British politicians, most famously in the sending of troops and tanks to Glasgow following the unfurling of the Red Flag in George Square in 1919. What began as a protest for a 40-hour week was described by Scottish Secretary Robert Munro as 'a Bolshevist rising', to be quelled by 12 000 troops, 100 lorries and 6 tanks.[2] This absurd overreaction passed into the mythology of the Scottish Left, perhaps partly because the crisis of 1914–19 really did represent some kind of sea-change in Scotland's economic fortunes. Before 1914, Scotland was a major economic power, producing 120 per cent of average UK output per capita; for the rest of the century it steadily underperformed in relative terms. Twenty-three per cent of those born in Scotland from 1911–80 emigrated; in 1911, Sweden's population was 16 per cent higher than Scotland's, today it is some 70 per cent higher. Such statistics indicate the contraction of twentieth-century Scotland from an economic power-house of native industry to an also-ran assembly plant for US and Asian multinationals. The development of nationalism against such a background is not surprising;[3] what is perhaps more surprising is its limited impact, which can to some extent be put down to the skill of the Labour Party in particular in managing Scottish decline through the patronage of British subsidy, and in presenting itself as the patriotic party within Scotland.

In this Labour has been aided from the beginning by the vanguard nature of much Scottish nationalism, which has often assumed greater enthusiasm from the public for extreme measures than has been justified by the available evidence. This was particularly true in the early years after the First World War, with the example of a fully-formed Irish nationalism being highly influential. But Sinn Fein nationalism had limited appeal in Scotland, and linked to Socialism, it had almost none. The Communist John Maclean's (1879–1923) 'conversion to the policy of Sinn Fein in 1919' and his interest in 'Celtic Communism' could alike be read as opportunistic attempts to exploit contemporary political symbolism in pursuit of 'a Scottish Socialist Republic', perhaps much like that sought by the Hiberno-Scottish James Connolly (1878–1916).[4] In fact, the truly successful revolutionaries of the era were men like Arthur Griffith (1872–1922) and Michael Collins (1890–1922), essentially far more conservative figures than the minority radical tradition represented by Connolly, whose status as a heroic icon owed far more to his sacrifice in a national cause than to the class basis of his politics. In similar vein, Maclean's impact in and after the 1920s derived largely from the nationalist side of his views.

As the war drew to a close, the SHRA was refounded in October 1918. In its aftermath, attempts were made to influence Woodrow Wilson on the issue of self- determination, but these naturally foundered, as similar representations to the UN after the Second World War were to do. The Irish leaders of 1916 had also sought to have Ireland's case included in a post-war peace conference (though they had expected Germany to win), and the Scottish approach may have been a pale imitation of this stance. Certainly, the Scottish National League (SNL), founded in 1919–20 (though an earlier version dated from 1904),[5] showed an early 'sympathy with the Irish cause' at the time when the struggle for the Irish Republic was reaching its bitter height; the SHRA contented itself in its congratulation to the government on its 1922 Irish settlement, with a broad hint that there was a need for a 'comprehensive scheme of self-government for the several nations of Great Britain'.[6] There was clear Sinn Fein influence on the SNL right through the 1920s: it was a close-knit organization, whose members had 'known each other … during their association with the Highland Land League and various Gaelic cultural organisations'. Of its leaders, Ruaridh Erskine was a dedicated Celtic Revivalist, while William Gillies (Liam MacGille Losa) had 'openly supported the Easter Rising' in Dublin: they sought 'to . . . create an unadulterated Celtic state'.[7] Maclean, attracted by 'the League's support for the Irish struggle', chaired 'a public meeting in Arbroath in September 1920 to celebrate the sexcentenary of the Arbroath Declaration', which was organized by the SNL, though he subsequently distanced himself from Erskine's 'blood and soil' tendencies;[8] Erskine's view that 'Celticism contemplates no office that is elective, no rule that is not aristocratic' had understandably limited socialist appeal.[9] At a 1926 rally at the Wallace Memorial, the SHRA was criticized by the SNL for its Westminster-oriented emphasis on requesting a Scottish Parliament from the British state. Instead, the SNL proposed, 'Scottish MPs should pledge not to cross the border at all but to remain in Scotland and legislate for Scotland.' Thus was the Sinn Fein/Irish Parliamentary Party division revived in a Scottish context. As James Mitchell notes, 'the SHRA exemplified the weaknesses of the gradualist approach' and the SNL 'the weaknesses of the fundamentalist approach'.[10] Nonetheless, both strands of thought continued to have an influence in Scottish nationalism for the rest of the century, creating in the SNP after 1934 an intermittent but never entirely absent tension between ideals and the means by which real change could be effected.

An SHRA plan of 1920 suggested the devolution to Scotland of all save the Crown, foreign policy, services, currency and weights and measures. Scottish taxes would go to a Scottish Treasury, and (in anticipation of the West Lothian Question) there would be no Scottish members in the Imperial Parliament: instead, there would be a joint council of both parliaments. In an interesting anticipation of the (muted) radicalism on display when MSPs were made to take the Oath of Allegiance in 1999, no Scottish 'member would be required to take the oath of allegiance' under the SHRA plan:[11] as is often the case, the roots of issues and political stances go back further than many would suppose.

Between 1919 and 1923, no fewer than five Bills and one devolution motion were brought before the Commons, but to no effect.[12] Nonetheless, SHRA hopes of Labour Party action were understandably high when Labour, long the party of Home Rule (for the Liberals had had many opportunities to introduce it in government, and failed to do so) formed its first, minority, administration in 1923. But despite the high hopes and the cheering crowds, the ground was already shifting. As the prospect of power drew nearer, 'within the Labour Party the desire for Scottish autonomy declined'.[13] Indeed, the Scottish Labour team sent off south so hopefully in 1923 were rapidly submerged in British politics. It was by contrast the Conservatives who offered some slight structural concession, upgrading the Scottish Secretary to a Secretary of State in 1926,[14] a year in which the General Strike, which 'enhanced the notion of "British" class politics',[15] moved Labour further from a quasi-nationalist position.

In the same year, *The Scots Independent* was launched to represent 'the aim and standpoint of the Scots National League ... political Independence':[16] it was to become the longest-running of all nationalist papers. The *SI* was founded, however, in a year of flux which arguably inaugurated the beginnings of contemporary political nationalism in Scotland. In 1926, the Scottish National Movement (SNM) was founded from a split in the SNL, mainly taking its members from the Edinburgh and Dunfermline branches. Lewis Spence was its leading figure. The National Party of Scotland (NPS) evolved in the 1926–28 period from three groups: the disappointed remnants of the SHRA, the SNL and Spence's SNM: the influence of the Glasgow University Scottish Nationalist Association (GUSNA) on the NPS's development, though legendary, was exaggerated by John MacCormick.[17] The NPS was 'inaugurated at Stirling on Bannockburn Day, 23 June 1928'.[18] In an editorial in *The Scots Independent*, R. B. Cunninghame Graham called on Scots 'in the name of Bruce, of Wallace, and of Burns ... to join the National Party of Scotland'. Relatively few did so, but those who did included figures such as C. M. Grieve (Hugh MacDiarmid) and Compton Mackenzie. The NPS was called by some the SNP, as when MacDiarmid invoked it as 'The Scottish National Party' at the 1928 Glasgow University rectorial election.[19] Almost immediately it began to contest elections, something no overtly nationalist party had done in Scotland since the days of the Jacobites. In January 1929, Spence stood in the NPS's first by-election, in Midlothian and Peeblesshire, Northern, and gained 4.5 per cent of the vote, even though 'his eve-of-poll speech ... consisted of a lengthy Burns oration in verse in Middle Scots'.[20] By 1931, the NPS had almost 8000 members;[21] in 1932, it gained 12 per cent of the vote in Dunbartonshire.[22]

The Scottish Party, formed in 1932, had its roots in 'a breakaway section of the Cathcart Conservative Association'. Its leading figure, the Duke of Montrose, did not endear many of the SHRA/NPS style of Nationalists to his cause when he 'used the nationalist Press to inveigh against hikers disturbing his grouse moors'.[23] In such circumstances, it was remarkable (and a tribute to his sense of real possibility rather than abstract ideal) that the solicitor John MacCormick (1904–61), with his Independent Labour Party (ILP) background,[24] was able to forge a merger between the Scottish Party and the NPS, which differed from it in so many ways.[25] The SP was opposed to the Catholic-leaning romanticism of the Scottish Renaissance and its Pan-Celticist roots.[26] Some of its members were also anti-Irish, in direct contrast to the Celticists, and their focus on a Scottish Parliament within Britain and the Empire was an indication of their different, essentially localist political stance. As James Mitchell observes:

> A strong element of anti-Catholic bigotry and anti-Irish racism was also evident [in the Scottish Party]. The nationalism espoused ... was wholly different from that of most members of the NPS, where Pan-Celtic cultural sympathies and radical social and economic policies were often combined.[27]

At first, therefore, a merger between the two parties did not seem likely. Montrose attacked the NPS in the 1931 election, in the same year as it had its first electoral success in the shape of Compton Mackenzie's victory in the Glasgow University rectorial election.[28] Moderate Scottish Party opinion attacked the 'Sinn Fein, Free State' element in the NPS. MacCormick, however, was conscious of the importance to the nationalist cause of attracting the elements of the social elite who had gravitated to the SP. Following the joint candidacy of Sir Alexander MacEwen in Kilmarnock in 1933, where he gained one-sixth of the vote, unity between the two parties was achieved on 7 April 1934, and the SNP was born. The merger was a success, only a few diehards leaving as a result. But just as the strands of opinion represented by the SHRA and SNL continued to retain their distinctive profile within Scottish nationalism, so the SP's Home Rule approach, in concert with ex-SHRA elements within the NPS, had a powerful impact on the SNP, at least up to 1950. The merger came at a price: the new SNP's aims of a Scottish Parliament with 'final authority on all Scottish affairs', sharing the 'rights and responsibilities' of Empire with joint Anglo-Scottish defence, foreign affairs and customs, sounded much more like Home Rule than nationalist politics on the Irish model. Dual membership of other (Unionist) political parties continued to be a possibility until the late 1940s: another indication that the SNP in its early stages was more SP/SHRA than SNL in its outlook, although admittedly the NPS itself had designed the policy of a Scottish Convention in 1932, building on ideas in the same vein which dated back to the 1890s.[29]

Both the NPS and (possibly) the Scottish Party were more aware of the cultural dimension in Scottish nationalism than their successor party, at least up till the 1980s. Such estrangement as occurred was, as I argue below, due in significant part to the uncompromising vanguardism of prominent cultural Nationalists, whose extreme opinions and pro-Irish and even Jacobite leanings had little to offer the immediate quest for Home Rule, though their impossibilism arguably had a profound impact in the longer term. Certainly, by the Second World War, there were signs that the SNP was distancing itself from these early allies. In 1946, for example, the SNP issued a policy statement with 'the total omission of a section on Scottish culture';[30] in 1964 an article in the *Scots Independent* commented on the 'Futility of Mere Cultural Nationalism',[31] while as late as 1980 Joy Hendry could state that 'the SNP's neglect of the Scottish heritage has been shameful'.[32] By contrast, the shift towards a stronger and more self-confident Scottish identity in the 1980s was one which was anchored in the cultural project, a development which the SNP responded to, but which it had done little to initiate.

This was by no means the position in the 1930s, a decade which saw the foundation of the National Trust for Scotland (1931) and the Saltire Society (1936), signs of at least limited enthusiasm for cultural particularism. For its part, the NPS 'approached the Scottish Vernacular Society with a view to putting pressure on the BBC to broadcast Scots language programmes', while also supporting the idea of a chair in Scottish Literature at the University of Edinburgh.[33] Nonetheless, in the world of electoral politics, the culturalism espoused by the likes of Ruaridh Erskine and Hugh MacDiarmid (who launched a Celtic League in 1929[34]) was seen as eccentric and marginal, while Eric Linklater's disastrous performance in the February 1933 East Fife by-election could be seen as confirming the competitive advantage held by politicians over *littérateurs*, especially as in the same year Sir Alexander McEwen gained nearly 17 per cent in Kilmarnock.[35] John MacCormick had himself asked Linklater to stand, and this political confidence was rewarded by a melange of misplaced romanticism:

> Eric devised a policy for Scotland based upon a model combining the Court of King James IV with Edinburgh in the eighteenth century, incorporating certain Norse and Celtic values, and ignoring 'the cultural blight of Presbyterianism and the industrial revolution'.[36]

Classic Scottish Renaissance thinking in fact, to be found in writers as diverse as MacDiarmid, Muir, Buchan and Barrie. The electorate gave Linklater 1000 votes and sent him back to the Celtic Twilight. Subsequently he turned against nationalism owing to his belief in the incompetence of its leaders.[37] If this were so, their followers, too, had much to learn.

Developments like this, together with the views of romantics such as Compton Mackenzie, who thought that if the Jacobites had won 'the decline of Scotland into a provincial appendage would have been averted',[38] and opined that 'the kilt asserts a man's freedom' and 'who will dare to laugh at Scotland of the White Rose ?',[39] together with the independent-mindedness of figures like MacDiarmid, who always had the capacity to be an embarrassment to any political party, contributed to the greater marginalization of the culturalists. Erskine of Mar, 'clear-sighted as ever', saw such a marginalization as inevitable.[40] Articles by MacDiarmid such as 'Towards a Scottish Renaissance', where the argument is that 'Scots' is 'not . . . an intermediate step on the way towards English, but on the way back to Gaelic' or 'A Scots Communist Looks at Bonny Prince Charlie', which sees Charles as 'a symbol of the Gaelic Commonwealth Restored', seem almost embarrassingly out of touch.[41] But there was also the nature of the strife between the SHRA roots of many in the NPS and the more colourful right-wing membership of the Scottish Party, most of whom had a much shorter Home Rule pedigree, to take into account. The culturalists also provided many of the 'big names' in the early SNP,[42] and this compounded the tensions which naturally arose from their (often gross) misjudgement of the limitations of their own electoral appeal. It was a breach which took a long time to heal. Thus, although a frustrated MacDiarmid wrote in 1967 that 'In all other countries I know of where independence has been gained or regained the necessary impulse came from poets or other artists',[43] it was not until the 1980s that culturalism resumed a major role in the nationalist movement, and even then arguably not in the SNP itself.

The *Scots Independent*, founded by Lewis Spence in 1926, continued to promulgate culturalist views throughout the 1930s, including some which the SNP would subsequently wish to forget, such as James Anderson Russell's 1936 article on 'Scotland and Germany: A National Comparison' or the 1929 editorial 'Mussolini points the way'.[44] Views such as these were caricatured, for example in the *Evening Times* cartoon 'Picture of Hamish McHitler', which illustrated the consequences should the Nationalists sweep to power in a putative 1940 election.[45] There were certainly traces of this kind of thinking among the SNP's culturalists, which encouraged Goebbels to try and gain SNP support. In both 1936 and 1937 he sent over a representative, and in the Second World War 'Radio Caledonia' broadcast German anti-Union propaganda, promising 'independence after the war had been won by Germany'.[46] Goebbels found few takers. In September 1940 the *Scots Independent* reported that Hitler had abandoned plans to separate Scotland from England.[47]

Despite superficial similarities with the Hitler Youth, Clan Scotland, a quasi-paramilitary youth movement, and the successor of the even more Fenian 'Clann Albann', founded in 1930,[48] had more in common with Irish models and a wider general contemporary interest in youth movements, no doubt linked to the ravages of unemployment. Clan Scotland described itself as the *'Political Army* of the National Party', and was advertised aggressively through the pages of the *Scots Independent*.[49] Clearly modelled on Irish forerunners organized by Pearse, Maud Gonne and Con Markievicz (though with a touching faith in the English boarding-school lexicon as a touchstone of character), it promoted shinty as a national game, and the heroism of Wallace, and combated modern evils such as unemployment. Its aim was 'to train clansmen how to LIVE FOR THEIR COUNTRY . . . if you are a slacker, a softie, or a cadger, don't join Clan Scotland'.[50] Rhetoric of this kind was backed up by appeals to patriotism, such as H. C. MacNeacail's article on William Wallace: Hero, Patriot, Statesman, Martyr', which tellingly compared Wallace to Cuchulain, Pearse's exemplar.[51] Neil Gunn went one step further, writing articles in the *Scots Independent* on Pearse himself;[52] in his 1928 article, 'The Hidden Heart', he drew freely from Daniel Corkery's *Hidden Ireland*, as he was to do again in his novel of the Clearances, *Butcher's Broom* (1934).[53] Augusta Lamont similarly suggested that Fionn would be a suitable hero for Scottish 'Boy Scouts',[54] while MacDiarmid welcomed Irish immigration as sustaining the stock 'of the ancient Gaelic commonwealth'.[55] Another nationalist youth movement of the time, Wendy Wood's Scottish Watch, founded in 1931 and for a time supported by the *Daily Record*, had its name readopted in the 1990s by a group professing to be concerned with 'the Englishing of Scotland'.[56]

Wallace was still a popular Scottish icon, but one which failed to resonate in quite the way the SNP hoped for in the 1930s, or indeed during the Second World War, when the anti-conscriptionist Douglas Young tried to persuade the 1943 Elderslie commemoration that Wallace was a democrat.[57] Nationalists remained (and to this day sometimes remain – was the use of *Braveheart* by the SNP much more convincing to the Scottish public?) puzzled as to why public interest and support in and for the heroes of fourteenth-century Scottish independence failed to translate into twentieth-century nationalist votes.[58] Nonetheless, the analysis of many of the articles published by the *Scots Independent* before the war (for example, on Sir Walter Scott and Highlandism) was to reappear as critical orthodoxy in the1980s.[59] In this sense MacDiarmid was right: cultural analysis of Scotland in the 1930s may have had limited electoral appeal (though such appeal was pretty limited, whatever strategy was adopted), but it nonetheless had a vanguard quality which was to come into its own many years later.

Following the 1934 merger, John MacCormick continued to extend his commitment to gradualist policies, welcoming pro-Home Rule supporters of other parties into the SNP.[60] His realism was prominent, although notable culturalist figures such as Neil Gunn also admired him and themselves prospered in nationalist politics.[61] Electoral success continued to be elusive, but there were respectable showings: in 1935, A. Dewar Gibb gained 14 per cent of the vote as SNP candidate for the Scottish Universities, and the party pressed on issues concerned with improving Scotland's infrastructure, such as a Forth Road Bridge (finally completed in 1964).[62] As was often to be the case in later years, the SNP seemed to have a disproportionate appeal to the youth vote, which it failed to retain as these enthusiasts grew older: in April 1938, school elections indicated heavy support for nationalism, a false dawn to be repeated many times in the next 60 years.[63] MacCormick's gradualism won friends, but not votes, despite his 1937 pact with the Liberals which was to allow 'his party a free run in 12 constituencies of its own choice'; MacCormick later himself stood as a Liberal in the 1945 General Election, but his greatest success came in 1947, where as National candidate in Paisley he gained nearly 21 000 votes without winning the seat.[64]

Government responses were slight. In 1937, the Scottish Office was moved to Edinburgh.[65] In 1941 the Scottish Secretary, Tom Johnston, set up a Scottish Council of State and allowed 'for meetings of the Scottish Grand Committee to take place in Scotland'.[66] The Second World War itself weakened the SNP, with the consensualist bulk of the party supporting the British war effort, while a smaller group of critics opposed conscription by the British State. Among these, the academic Douglas Young, a moderate Home Ruler,[67] was prominent, though there were lower-level protests pointing out that the Dominions avoided conscription 'through Self-Government' (*No Conscription for Scotland!*) and concerning the movement of Scots munition workers to England (*To Scots Girls Ordered to England*).[68] Young appealed to the High Court against the 1941 National Service Act on four grounds: that it was contrary to the Common Law of Scotland, contrary to the Treaty of Union, unknown to the Law of Scotland, as it was an English statute, and that it was a fundamental nullity, on the basis that Great Britain 'is deficient in the qualifications of a legal personality by International Law'.[69] Needless to say, he got nowhere: but it is arguable that Young's stand opened the way for future legal challenges to the Union.

Successes

In the 1945 General Election, Labour's Scottish manifesto made Home Rule its 'second priority after a commitment to the defeat of Japan' but omitted to mention it in its UK manifesto.[70] The writing was on the wall. As John Taylor, Secretary of the Scottish Labour Party, said in 1947: 'I, myself, ceased to desire self-government as soon as we secured a Social-ist Government for Britain.'[71] Although Labour did little in power to further a devolutionary agenda (indeed, rather undermining it through nationalization, which placed the control of Scottish companies in English hands, as the Tories pointed out), this did not mean that Scottish affairs were entirely neglected: indeed, they received a surprising amount of attention given the 1 per cent of the vote obtained by the SNP in 1945, a devastating collapse after Robert Macintyre's by-election victory at Motherwell only weeks earlier. The nationalists were also weakened after the departure of the Scottish Union (later Scottish Convention) moderates in 1942, who claimed 5000 members by 1946. In that year, a Scottish Council for Development and Industry was formed, and the Scottish Tourist Board established; in 1948, a White Paper on Scottish Affairs was published, which suggested a degree of administrative devolution for parliamentary business, economic affairs, the machinery of government and nationalized industries. It also included a proposal for a strengthened Scottish Grand Committee, which was still being trailed as a worthwhile structural reform by the Tories in the 1990s. Not to be outdone at the time, in 1949 the Conservative Party promised a Royal Commission on Scottish Affairs and an enhanced Scottish Office. On returning to power in 1951, significant planning authority (e.g. concerning roads and bridges) was devolved to the Scottish Office.[72] Bill Miller has argued that 'the build-up of the Scottish Office' was 'a Danegeld' which stimulated 'the appetite for self-government', which in the long run is no doubt true:[73] but there was very little evidence for this in the 1950s, despite the somewhat spectacular removal of the

Stone of Scone from Westminster in 1950 by a group of young patriots (a feat, incidentally, considered by Michael Collins 30 years before, and deemed unworkable). In 1952, Lord Elibank suggested the return of the Stone on 'permanent loan' to Scotland, a policy in fact implemented by Michael Forsyth in 1996.[74]

Despite the Stone's disappearing act of radical colour, there was anxiety that 'a devolved Scotland would be permanently Conservative' owing to the strength of Scottish Toryism (Unionism, as it technically was then) in the 1950s, which culminated in the party taking over half the Scottish vote in 1959. Such a fear was, however, somewhat illusory: the increased planning powers of the Scottish Office, along with its growing role in patronage, looked as if they might create a new domestic middle-class cadre who could sustain Britishness via the Welfare State, just as the now-declining Kirk or Anglicizing education system (there was student unrest when Edinburgh became the first Scottish university to enter the British UCCA clearing system in 1962) had sustained its imperial predecessor. As Bill Miller observes, 'the institutions which at first guaranteed Scottish home rule' were in decline during the twentieth century. Even their Victorian successors were suffering: 'at the close of the nineteenth century there were about 200 independent Scottish trade unions but they gradually merged' with their southern neighbours.[75] Scottish Office concessions may have been a substitute for local autonomies, but they did not replace them.

To some extent, these administrative concessions can be perceived as a response to the continuation of nationalist unrest at the margins, most competently exemplified in MacCormick's gradualist agenda. As early as 1930, he had argued for 'A New National Covenant'.[76] MacCormick's eventual Covenant idea of 1949–52 can be seen as the largest in a series of local plebiscites (such as those at Scotstoun in 1950 and Peebles in 1959) which sought to demonstrate that support for Scottish Home Rule on a single-issue basis was significant, and far exceeded that offered to political nationalists at General Elections. The Scottish Plebiscite Society, founded in 1946, carried some of these out: one, in Kirriemuir in 1949, showed 92 per cent in favour of Home Rule. MacCormick had 'tried to institute a Scottish national convention in 1939', following SHRA ideas which dated back to the 1890s. In 1949, a discussion of the Scottish Covenant Association, meeting 'in the Inchrie Hotel in Aberfoyle, later renamed the Covenanters' Inn', led to the launch of the Covenant, which attracted two million signatures in the first years of the 1950s. Westminster brushed it aside, with the predictable response that the

Scots could always express their wishes at a General Election. None-theless, Unionist politicians were in no doubt that the Covenant was expressive of some level of real national feeling. Arthur Woodburn, Sec-retary of State in 1949, admitted that 'interest in the subject in Scotland is always present, widespread and sincere'.[77]

The Covenant's failure marked the beginning of the end for this kind of politics. Although plebiscites continued into the 1960s (with one revival in Falkirk in 1993), the launch of an appeal for £100 000 for a national plebiscite in 1961 was abandoned two years later with less than 5 per cent of the money raised.[78] Meanwhile, the SNP was riven with minor splits and at an electoral low. Revival and electoral success could only come through the more conventional routes of the British political system. MacCormick realized that a vanguard could not deliver Home Rule, and sought always to build a consensus, across society certainly, and across parties if possible, seeking a measure of change which would provide Scotland with the beginnings of the 'freedom to become free'. MacCormick certainly came closer than any other nationalist figure of his era to securing broad-based support for real change.

Critics of MacCormick, who left behind his political testament in *The Flag in the Wind* (1955), have seen him as foreshadowing the limited ambitions and horizons of many in the later SNP, a man who 'preferred to opt for a purely provincial Scotland managed by local politicians without any sense of a higher national purpose', as H. J. Hanham put it. Hanham viewed MacCormick's less able successors in that tradition as 'hostile to the state and incapable of understanding how it is run and what it is trying to do', and certainly, grievance politicians of this stamp were not uncom-mon in the SNP in the 1960s and 1970s at local level.[79] Whatever the truth of such accusations among MacCormick's imitators, the man himself had a keener sense of the possible than many of his contemporaries, and not only in the electoral sphere. His legal challenge to Royal titles in 1953 fell before Lord Guthrie, but on appeal the Lord President, Lord Cooper, while rejecting two of MacCormick's three grounds, took the view that

> The principle of the unlimited Sovereignty of Parliament is a distinctively English principle which has no counterpart in Scottish Constitutional law. . . . I have difficulty in seeing why it should have been supposed that the new Par-liament of Great Britain must inherit all the peculiar characteristics of the English Parliament but none of the Scottish Parliament, as if all that happened in 1707 was that Scottish representatives were admitted to the Parliament of England. That was not what was done.

This judgement 'provoked a reaction among legal thinkers on the nature of the Anglo-Scottish Union'.[80]

There was plenty of nationalist activity in the immediate post-war period, if fewer signs of wider support. In 1947, a Scottish National Assembly, a forerunner of the Convention of 40 years later, was set up and 'attended by a broad range of representatives from Scottish society', while a poll in the *Express* showed very strong support for some degree of Home Rule.[81] In October 1947, a Claim of Right (the same language was to be used by the Convention in the 1980s) was put forward to the United Nations. It argued, among other things, for the old idea of Scottish history as being a valorous struggle for liberty, stating for example that:

> in the armed Risings of 1715 and 1745 a great part of the following achieved in Scotland by the Stuart claimants to the throne came from the Jacobite Party's appeal to Scottish patriotism and their definite pledge to abrogate the Treaty of Union of 1707.

Despite what the *Scots Independent* called 'considerable overseas interest', the UN predictably viewed this claim as a matter for British domestic jurisdiction.[82]

There were signs of sporadic discontent on Queen Elizabeth's accession in 1952, few of which counted for much – although they have nonetheless passed into legend. On 9 February 1953, in a revival of Napier's regnal numeral protest, there was an attack on a pillar box in Edinburgh which bore the inscription 'E2R'.[83] The offending regnal numeral was subsequently removed from pillar boxes in Scotland, and the promise of more substantive concessions followed in the shape of the 1954 Royal Commission on Scottish Affairs' recommendation of the transfer of responsibility for electricity, food, animal health, roads and bridges to the Scottish Office.[84] Slow, incremental and largely symbolic change seemed the order of the day.

Triumphs

In 1956, the Suez crisis confirmed the decline of the British Empire: in the same year, Radio Free Scotland, a pirate station set up by Gordon Wilson, subsequently MP for Dundee East, heralded a new and more dynamic phase in Scottish nationalism. In 1962, when the SNP had only

1000 members,[85] Billy Wolfe won 23 per cent of the vote in West Lothian, using the 'Put Scotland First' slogan first aired in 1946, and after 1962 reworked many times for the SNP. In 1963, the modern SNP symbol, a schematized thistle, was designed; the next year (as again in 1968), a Liberal–SNP pact was mooted (the Liberals were to adopt self-government as their top priority, work for an SNP–Liberal majority of seats, and withdraw from Parliament if Home Rule was refused in return for SNP abandonment of independence for federalism). In the same year, Gordon Wilson began a major overhaul of party organization.[86] In the 1966 General Election, the SNP took 5 per cent of the vote nationally, and the next year Winnie Ewing made history by winning Hamilton from Labour in a by-election on 2 November. The *Scots Independent's* editorial for 11 November saw the Hamilton victory as a clear victory for SNL- style fundamentalism against MacCormick/SHRA-style compromise, last seen in the talks on an electoral alliance with the Liberals:

> We decided years ago that 'going it alone' was the only way to secure freedom. Our experience of alliances, arrangements, compromises and pacts during the years before the present 'hard line' of Nationalist politics was evolved had proved finally that no friends unwilling to put Scotland first . . . were to be trusted when the political battle was joined.[87]

Certainly results appeared to be vindicating this policy. In March 1968, an *Express* poll showed SNP support at 37 per cent, with 61 per cent pro-Home Rule and 26.5 per cent favouring independence; a freak poll in the *Daily Record* suggested 80 per cent support for independence.[88] On 9 May 1968, the SNP gained 30 per cent of the vote in the local elections (37 per cent in Glasgow), and won 108 council seats. SNP membership soared. In January 1968, the 'first sub-committee of any House of Commons committee sat in Edinburgh',[89] and passenger road and sea transport was 'transferred to Scottish Office' control, but more was needed. Not only did Edward Heath, the leader of the Opposition, make the need for Scottish Home Rule the centrepiece of his 1968 Declaration of Perth, but on 15 April 1969, the Prime Minister, Harold Wilson, appointed 'a Royal Commission under Lord Crowther to consider the Constitution'. The success of this classic delaying tactic seemed assured when the SNP vote fell to 11 per cent in the 1970 General Election (though the Western Isles was won in compensation for the return of Hamilton to the Labour fold).[90]

But there was now a new development: clear evidence was emerging of the scale of oil reserves in the North Sea, which transformed the economic prospects of an independent Scotland. In March 1973, the SNP launched the 'It's Scotland's Oil' campaign, the single most successful political slogan ever adopted by the Nationalists. In November, eight days after the publication of the pro-devolution Kilbrandon Report, Margo MacDonald won Govan for the Nationalists, and from the two general elections of the following year they emerged in October 1974 with 11 seats and 30 per cent of the vote,[91] a success unprecedented for a non-British party since Irish independence. Despite lukewarm Labour support for a Scottish Assembly, the prospect of devolution loomed for a weak government which had barely prevailed at the polls and was reliant on a lack of third-party opposition to maintain its control of the Commons. There were other pro-devolution arguments, both in the Kilbrandon Report itself and in the case (then much favoured by Malcolm Rifkind) concerning the 'difficulty of implementing recommendations' concerning changes in Scotland's legal system without a Scottish legislature,[92] but these were supporting cast beside the political pressure on a weak government under threat in its Scottish heartlands. The SNP were second in 36 seats, mostly Labour-held; the Establishment was alarmed, viewing devolution as inevitable. On 19 August 1974, just before the SNP took a further step forward in the October election, *The Times* stated that 'the Scots are all assembly men now' and suggested that matters had already gone too far for a minimal settlement: 'it is better to devolve the widest powers'.[93] But Labour was surprised and badly frightened. Perhaps as a consequence, since 1974, the Labour Party in general has been too frightened of the SNP threat, and thus overestimated it. Now Labour was seething at the perceived 'revanchist chauvinism' of the 'middle-class' enemy, and were grudging in any concessions. Gordon Brown, the future Labour Chancellor, acidly observed that 'there were only two working-class SNP candidates' in the October 1974 General Election.[94] For this most radical of parties, the tag of 'Tartan Tories' was being prepared in response to its success.

Why did the SNP break through? Oil was not the reason, for the first major boost to the party's support came in the 1960s, and the oil campaign's long-term effects were negligible: despite the SNP's accurate predictions of the scale of the revenues and the positive effects they could create,[95] the vast bulk of them were spent outwith Scotland with little sign of protest from the Scottish public. The other parties paid no electoral price for minimizing the North Sea's economic potential and ridiculing the SNP's figures and arguments, which were more than borne out by subsequent events. The causes, then, of the Nationalist rise must be sought elsewhere. As with the Liberals at Orpington in 1962, their success could be read as a third-party protest vote; or it was a means of defending Scotland's deteriorating status as a branch economy; or a response to the 'internal colonialism' of differential rates of development identified by Michael Hechter, which itself echoed Fletcher of Saltoun's critique of the naturally aggrandizing nature of metropolitan power. Most popular has been the view that, ultimately, the rise in the SNP was a response to the decline of the British Empire, and the public process of decolonization which inevitably accompanied it.[96] The Cabinet in 1967–68 saw the SNP threat as either a transient protest or 'evidence that the balance of central and local government had to be recast'.[97]

There were (following Esman) four 'options... available to the political centre' in the face of the SNP surge. First, acculturation and assimilation: a process which was already substantially in place by a number of indirect or peaceful routes, and where further coercion would doubtless be counterproductive. Secondly, there was the path of neglect and ridicule; third, the risky and unlikely route of direct repression; and fourthly the seeking of some accommodation, which could be concessional (higher public spending, a bias to Scotland in new projects, protection for Scotland from certain aspects of UK policies, and so on) or involve structural change, such as Home Rule. The political route chosen by the two main British parties and their allies after 1968 was one which was broadly to remain unchanged for almost all the rest of the century. A vigorous pursuit of the second option (neglect and ridicule) was taken towards the SNP and Scottish nationalism generally; less focused or less extreme Scottish grievances (unemployment, declining heavy industry, the democratic deficit, Scotland not getting a fair deal) were met by concessional accommodation, which helped keep Scottish expectations of public service provision high. The Liberals were, in the early days, more adventurous (in 1971, they suggested that Scotland should get 50 per cent of North Sea Oil revenues, for example), but by the late 1970s and the period of the Lib-Lab Pact, they were ploughing much the same furrow as the other Unionist parties.[98]

Constitutional change was continuously kept under review (at least until 1979), but a series of delaying or spoiling tactics rendered its threat ineffectual, unlike financial and administrative patronage, which came easily: after 1970, the Conservatives took on nationalism through higher public spending, much as their Labour predecessors had done. Some authorities, such as Richard Finlay, have argued that the Scottish electorate saw an SNP vote as a means of unlocking Westminster's bounty through financial concessions: taken to its extreme, such a position can be held to posit modern Scottish nationalism as a kind of game, whereby concessions are extracted from Westminster by an electorate voting for a party it does not believe in, but whom it knows (from all the ridicule piled on it under option 2) is a Unionist bogey. For Finlay, the first nationalist surge was 'a desire to protest at the failure of the London government to meet the aspirations of the Scottish post-war consensus', and the resurgence of nationalism in the 1980s was likewise conducted in defence of a British corporatism now seen as 'a distinct Scottish political culture'.[99]

The only major shifts in the Westminster twin-track policy of higher public spending and constitutional foot-dragging combined with belittling abuse have taken place as a result of the 1988–90 Poll Tax debacle (significantly, the only political issue of modern times which has allowed the SNP to take up a position of illegality without suffering electoral damage), and following the 1997 Referendum, when (again significantly) there have been signs of the granting of structural change resulting in pressure being brought to bear concerning Scotland's right to the value of earlier concessions in public spending. In the first instance, elements of both assimilation and repression were present (Scotland was expected to conform to England, but to do so in advance of England), which led to an unusual degree of tension; in the second, the failure of concessionary change to achieve more than further demands brought home the necessity of structural alterations in the constitution. It remains the case, however, that the price for this is expected by many to be the withdrawal of further financial concessions to Scotland. The dangers of 'unilateral devolution', warned of by A. V. Dicey in *England's Case Against Home Rule* (1886), and subsequently part of political debate for over a century do, apparently, have their price.[100]

A degree of doublethink has prevailed here, notably in the context of the accusation that the Scots are 'subsidy junkies', when their 'subsidies' are themselves part of British state policy to reduce political tension. This dependency argument took on its most recent form in the late 1980s: in November 1987, for example, Nigel Lawson identified 'a culture of dependence rather than of enterprise' in Scotland, and since that date this argument has seldom been absent from the Unionist press. Yet, as Gavin McCrone pointed out as long ago as 1969, Scottish public expenditure may be a necessary counterweight to the generation of an unsustainable boom in the South following any redistribution of public finances, while more recently the SNP have repeatedly pointed out that the identifiable public expenditure figures for Scotland as a percentage of the UK total ignore the benefits provided by spending on so-called 'national assets', such as the Millennium Dome, Jubilee tube line, White-hall departments, the BBC (98 per cent of whose programmes are made outwith Scotland), and so on. As George Rosie and other commentators have pointed out, such 'national assets' have an overwhelming tendency to be based in one city – London. The siting of the Charity Commission, the Tote, the Prison Service, the National Lottery, the BBC, the Jubilee Line and the Millennium Dome are all significant examples, to which may be added the £160 million Foreign and Commonwealth Office con-tribution to the World Service, the £511 million for and £83 million annual budget of the British Library, £265 million on galleries and museums, and much, much more: many of these attractions boost tourist numbers and thus further feed the local economy.[101] (A good example of how local London issues are reported at a level more appropriate for national and international coverage by virtue of the concentration there of the organs of the state can be seen in the media time devoted to the London mayoral contest, which received far more 'national' BBC airtime than anything to do with the Scottish Parliament, even though the Mayor of London has no legislative authority.) In addition, as Richard Finlay has suggested, the dependency argument has damaged the Tory vote in Scotland as 'traditional middle-class voters do not like being told that they are "spongers"'.[102]

There are however, limitations to the view of the SNP as a jackpot lever on a British fruit machine. For one thing, demand for structural change in the constitution, though often weaker than immediate anxieties over inflation or unemployment, has remained relatively high on any measure for many years. For another, there has been a clear shift of rhet-oric since 1987 from even gradualist Home Rulers towards an assertion of Scottish sovereignty rather than the old SHRA idea of it being a grace and favour treatment of Scotland by Westminster. In other words, the evidence is that even gradualists have become more fundamentalist: as James Mitchell points out, pro-devolutionists began to use less Unionist rhetoric after 1979. Labour politicians began to talk about the 'democratic deficit' and the 'Doomsday scenario', of a Tory London administration in a tiny minority in Scotland; Donald Dewar even used the phrase 'independence in the UK' to describe the proposed devolutionary settle-ment.[103] In 1992, Charles Gray, the leader of Strathclyde Region, in the heat of an election night programme, suggested civil disobedience 'in the event of a fourth Conservative election victory'; while in 1995, in a public debate with Alex Salmond, George Robertson, then Shadow Secretary of State, declined to answer whether his second choice for Scottish government (after devolution) was independence or the status quo. The latter would appear to have been the true answer; but its being regarded as a liability to give it was itself indicative of a genuine shift in the parameters of political debate. The vigil for Home Rule outside the old Royal High School in Edinburgh was in place continuously from 1992 to the Referendum victory, while at the December 1992 Home Rule rally in Edinburgh, 'Alex Salmond was rapturously welcomed by the crowd when he demanded that Scotland should be set free.'[104]

There has been a persistent nationalist fringe, usually not directly associated with the SNP, dating back to rumours of a Scottish Republican Army allegedly 'formed in 1916 when several veterans of the Scottish Brigade of the IRA who had seen combat . . . returned home', and continuing through various manifestations such as Fianna na-h-Alba, the Tartan Army, Scottish Liberation Army, Scottish National Liberation Army, Arm Nan Gaidheal, Border Clan, Flame, Jacobites, Army of the Scottish People, Scottish Citizens' Army and various other names. The maximalist case for their activities was put forward by Andrew Murray Scott and Ian Macleay in *Britain's Secret War: Tartan Terrorism and the Anglo-American State* (1990), and was fictionalized in Andrew Osmond and Douglas Hurd's *Scotch on the Rocks* (1971); but, despite the occasional conviction of incompetent loners and small groups, very little evidence of an 'army' of any sort has persuasively emerged. As even Scott and Macleay note, 'the Scottish Republican Army remained one of the great Celtic myths', one which the presence of *one person* in 'full IRA-style paramilitary uniform' at the 1980 Bannockburn Rally does as little to confirm as the odd 'success' of these fearsome organizations in burning or stealing Union flags.[105] Undoubtedly some individuals have been involved in terrorist activities; but the haphazard and limited nature of these activities, combined with the fortunate degree of incompetence with which they have been carried out, do not suggest the presence of much organizational substance or ability.

Peaceful direct nationalist action, on the other hand, has a well-attested history as a minority pursuit. This too has been largely carried on by colourful characters with a penchant for self-publicity, most notably Wendy Wood, originally Gwendoline Meacham, (1892–1981), a former SHRA and SNM member born in Maidstone, whose organization, the Scottish Patriots, grew apart from the SNP after the Second World War. Wood's career of direct action, in which her frequent public addresses and vocal statements marked her out as some kind of Scottish Maud Gonne, began with her leading a group of Nationalists into Stirling Castle in 1932 to pull down the Union flag. She went on to form an Anti-Conscription League, disrupted Blackshirt rallies, spoke at IRA gatherings, incited a London crowd before a Scotland–England football match, and generally made a nuisance of herself. At 31 Howard Place, her Georgian villa in Edinburgh, she placed a Union flag under the stair carpet so she could tread on it every day, and committed her Patriot organization to support breaches of the law providing the 'offence was not of a serious criminal nature and directly against Patriots' policies'.[106] Wood's colourful impossibilism did contribute to some concrete achievement, however. Following her address to the General Assembly of the Church of Scotland in 1961, the Kirk accepted the policy of Home Rule, while in 1966 her pressure was instrumental in persuading the Post Office to issue Burns stamps.[107] In December 1972 she commenced a hunger strike to the death for Scottish Home Rule in an attempt to force the Conservative Government to abide by Ted Heath's 1968 Declaration of Perth. Jim Sillars (then a Labour MP) made a television plea to her to end the strike, and she acceded after the Secretary of State, Gordon Campbell, 'repeated undertakings' to publish a Green Paper 'after theRoyal Commission had reported'.[108] The inflammatory posturing of the Patriots and their leader thus had some impact in defining a distinctive Scottish interest in politics, though in Wood's own day her extremism rendered her marginal.

Revolutionary Vanguard or Broad Church

The lengthy Parliamentary debates in the 1970s over Scottish and Welsh devolution make interesting reading, and in some ways are more illuminating of the attitudes of parliamentarians than detailed accounts of the ins and outs of the Scotland and Wales and (after the guillotine of 19 February 1977) Scotland Bill. Neil Kinnock, for example, described the use of Welsh in education as 'warfare against children who are not capable of defending themselves'; Jill Knight opined that if Scotland wanted devolution, why shouldn't Coventry have it; MPs reminisced about their ancestors and the ethnic Saxonicity of Lowland Scotland.[109] The Labour MP George Cunningham's infamous amendment of 25 January 1978 established that 40 per cent of the electoral roll, irrespective of turnout, must vote 'Yes' in the referendum for any Assembly to be established: as a consequence, dual-registered students and nurses, to say nothing of the dead and those who had moved, were included in any calculation for a 'Yes' vote, although the government made some late allowance for this. In a neglected development, on the same night as Cunningham's amendment was passed, the former Liberal leader, Jo Grimond, successfully sought to remove Orkney and Shetland from any devolved settlement, should they vote No.[110] The spectacle of Scotland being partitioned loomed. The SNP were unhappy, but as the then Margaret Bain said, 'we are still prepared to accept the Assembly because it is the first internal constitutional change in Britain since 1707'.[111] The 'Yes for Scotland' campaign was launched with Lord Kilbrandon as chair in January 1978: the Nationalists were prominent in it and were by far its hardest workers. The anti-SNP Alliance for an Assembly, set up in November, was by contrast toothless and lifeless, like subsequent Unionist Home Rule fronts such as Scotland United and Common Cause, which, like Jim Sillars's short-lived Scottish Labour Party (SLP) of 1976–79, were puffed by their friends in the press far beyond their substance on the ground. In 1978–79, divisions in the Labour Party seriously undermined the Yes campaign, while its No equivalent was well-funded, tightly run and played on people's fears. Meanwhile, the SNP's support was falling steadily from its 1977 poll peak of 36 per cent, and Labour's Donald Dewar's victory over Keith Bovey in the April 1978 Garscadden by-election intensified this process.[112]

The 1 March 1979 Referendum fell on the basis of the 40 per cent rule, described by James Mitchell as 'a brilliant act of anti-democratic political manipulation'. It certainly permitted almost limitless political obfuscation, with the actual 52–48 margin for devolution frequently, if not universally, altered by not only newspapers but even reference books, into a result expressed in terms of percentage of the electorate who voted for each option, or did not vote, with the result that it often appears that only one-third of Scots supported a measure which was carried by any normal democratic assessment. The 40 per cent rule thus not only decided the inefficacy of the Yes vote; it transmuted it in political history. The legal result became superimposed on the actual result, and the *de facto* truth that 'Scotland Said Yes' was lost not only in Westminster, but also in political textbooks and in the self-perception of Scots themselves, who when polled thought that Scotland hadn't wanted what it voted for.[113]

The Conservatives, who in opposition had promised a convention and inter-party talks, and who during the campaign (in the person of Alec Douglas-Home) had talked of a better devolution Bill to those who voted No (the Tory Yes vote halved in the aftermath of Douglas-Home's intervention, according to one poll), predictably did nothing or little once in government. The Scottish Grand Committee met 'occasionally in Edinburgh' and a 'Select Committee on Scottish Affairs' was set up, which quietly disappeared in 1987 when the Tories ran out of MPs to staff it. After that, there was little else forthcoming except concessions in public spending, themselves often handled so badly that the Tories gained no credit for them. It was plain when *Scotland in the Union* was published by the Conservatives in 1993, in response to their 'Taking Stock' promise in the previous year's general election, that their thinking had developed no further than it had ten years earlier: as Mitchell says, this 'was the least informed and most insubstantial of government papers reacting to agitation for self-government since the war'.[114] Especially in the years after George Younger's departure from the Scottish Secretaryship in 1986, the Tories increasingly appeared a small coterie who took advice about Scotland only from those who agreed with them already: the appointment of a very right-wing special adviser to Michael Forsyth in 1995 was only further evidence of this. Stunts such as Forsyth's attending the *Braveheart* première in a kilt and the return of the Stone of Destiny to Scotland fell flat in terms of Tory support, suggesting that Walter Scott's linkage of emotional patriotism to unconditional Unionism was no longer operational.[115] Something had changed, and there was increasing evidence of an appetite for the substance of history, not merely its shadow.

The SNP suffered considerably from the impact of defeat in 1979, partly due to the unrealistic expectations of many activists and a lack of understanding of the limited and provisional nature of much of their own support. Like Labour, they swung to the essentialist Left in response with the formation of the 79 Group, which contained many of the intellectual leading lights of the party, such as Alex Salmond and Stephen Maxwell. Strategically it was, particularly after the accession of Jim Sillars to the SNP folowing the collapse of the Scottish Labour Party, a much more important force than its right-wing Celticist rival, Siol Nan Gaidheal (Seed of the Gael), which had links to neo-Jacobite organizations such as the Knights Templar, and provided a brief and colourful revival of the nationalism of an earlier generation. SNG absorbed older Celticist marginal organizations such as the 1320 Club.[116] Linked groups such as the White Rose League caused unwarranted concern: ironically, the Jacobite and Scottish Renaissance white roses which caused such a frisson in Nationalist circles at the end of the 1970s were, by the opening of the Scottish Parliament in 1999, the badge of every Nationalist representative.

Although both SNG and the 79 Group were proscribed by the party at its Ayr conference in 1982, by then significant damage had been done. The passing of anti-NATO and in particular civil disobedience resolutions through 79 Group influence at the Aberdeen conference in 1981 was a spectacular own goal in the year when the formation of the SDP–Liberal Alliance provided a much more dangerous third-party rival than had hitherto existed. Sillars's inspirational rhetoric committed the SNP to a strategy of civil disobedience combined with targeting the Labour heartlands of the Central Belt. Banal stickers appeared in blue and white, bearing the image of a group of roughs in silhouette, entitled 'Join the Scottish Resistance'. The limited civil disobedience approved on a resolution in 1979 was extended in the 1981 moves to some kind of general policy. Sillars and a few allies succeeded in getting themselves arrested for an attempted break-in at the Royal High School, home of the putative Assembly, in a farcical operation which would have reflected very badly on the SNP had they been important enough for anyone to care. Meanwhile, the Alliance made permanent advances in significant areas of rural Scotland (such as West Aberdeenshire) where the SNP had once been strong, unchecked by the presence of any moderate opposition. In 1982, the ultimate vindication of Sillars's policy was seen when Roy Jenkins won the Glasgow Hillhead by-election for the Alliance, with the SNP coming fourth. By 1983, with the Nationalist vote down by another third from its low base, Alliance paper candidates in the poorest Glasgow seats were beating the Nationalists hands down. The image of Red Clydeside conjured up by Sillars and his supporters was shown to be a delusive myth, a return to the rhetoric of the 1920s, and a serious backward step. Enthusiasm for public services and protection for jobs at risk was not Socialism: and besides, these were targets that Labour was always better placed to meet than the SNP. Only when the outrage of the Poll Tax was combined with limited Labour opposition to it in 1988, did Sillars and the SNP win Govan – and even then, a poor Labour candidate was needed. That by-election victory remains the only first-past-the-post Parliamentary success enjoyed by the SNP in the Central Belt since 1979. In its aftermath, Jim Sillars predicted 'Scotland free by '93', later used as a millstone slogan in the 1992 General Election, in which Sillars lost his seat.[117]

The year 1988 was an important one for the SNP, and marks the beginning of the latest stage in the party's development, for it was then that the policies of the non-payment of the Poll Tax and of Independence in Europe were implemented, arguably the most successful Nationalist policies since 1979. The 'association of states of the British Isles' and comparisons of Scotland with Britain's EFTA neighbours in Scandinavia gave way to a more holistic approach, which was more in tune with early SNP policy than the anti-EEC era of the 1970s and 1980s. As early as 1935, in an article in the *Scottish Standard* on 'The Real Curse of Scotland', William Power had argued 'that Scotland's tragedy was the cultural break with Europe in the 17th century';[118] his pro-European views were echoed by others, such as Marian McNeill.[119] Scotland was compared with other small European countries in articles such as 'A Lesson from Estonia' or 'Latvia: A Little Nation'.[120] In the years after the war, Power's public pro-Europeanism continued: in November 1947 in *Scottish Opinion*, he foresaw 'a United States of Europe with Scotland taking a leading role in the championing of smaller nations'.[121] In 1948, the party voted to support European unity, while a few years later George Dott argued for a 'European authority'.[122] In 1957, the *Scots Independent* proclaimed that 'European Union can be our Hope for the Future', while in 1961, Gordon Wilson observed 'the tactical advantages which may accrue to the Scottish movement from the entry of the UK into the Common Market'.[123] Thus the concept of 'Independence in Europe', finally adopted as an SNP slogan in 1988, the year after a General Election fought on a viorously anti-EEC ticket, was not entirely the volte-face it appeared to many at the time. SNP Europeanism did have a long history: but, if anything, the implicit isolationism of the *It's Scotland's Oil* campaign of 1973 and the years that followed had intensified the hold of an essentially post-colonial emphasis on sovereignty, as the process of handing back (or in some cases inventing) statehood for the far-flung provinces of the Empire both reduced Scottish overseas influence and drew attention to the political powerlessness of a country which had once been among the richest on earth. This emphasis on sovereignty as a narrow concept led to the SNP's mistake of opposing EEC membership in the 1975 Referendum, when the party found itself without allies save on the extreme fringes of Left and Right. In this context it was Jim Sillars's emphasis on the importance of the EEC for Scotland, taken up during his SLP days and subsequently brought by him into the SNP, which was arguably his most important and fruitful legacy to the party. Scottish nationalism could now be viewed as internationalist, increasingly so as the xenophobia of Tory Euro-scepticism became more strident south of the Border.

Certainly, the switch to Independence in Europe as the flagship SNP policy at least coincided with a rise in Nationalist support. It also dealt with many of the old separatist and isolationist arguments, with their jibes about a Scottish army and passports at the Border. The rising influence of the EU, and the clear signs of success for small countries within it, may also have played their part. In a poll carried out for *The Economist*'s 'Undoing Britain?' survey in November 1999, 46 per cent of Scots thought Holyrood would be the most important political focus for them in 20 years' time, 31 per cent the EU and only 8 per cent Westminster. Rising expectations of EU influence were also evident in England and Wales.[124]

The Scottish Constitutional Convention, founded in 1989 on the basis of the 'Claim of Right for Scotland' group,[125] grew out of a long line of similar organizational attempts in the twentieth century, and indeed even had something in common with the policy of Wendy Wood's Patriots to recall the Scottish Estates.[126] It did much to prepare Scottish civic society for constitutional change, and provided a valuable testbed for future Lib-Lab collaboration and coalition, with Labour concessions on proportional representation exchanged for Liberal Democrat abandonment of federalism and a range of other policies. Nonetheless, much of the Convention's activity was window-dressing, in that it had no answer to Conservative refusal to meet its demands, and was unlikely to take any action since its underlying aim was to wait for a Labour General Election victory while officially grounding its case in the sovereignty of the Scottish people. Public figures from the churches and trade unions who appeared prominent in the Convention formed a useful camouflage for the development of Labour Party ideas to which the Liberals would be bound. These would form the basis of the so-called 'new politics', where consensus brought about by the stifling of debate (for the Convention did not effectively consider a reconstructed Union, federalism or independence as options on which the Scottish people would even be *allowed* to decide) would be regarded as a good in itself, reinforcing Labour hegemony in Scotland while claiming the moral high ground of universal agreement, and reinforcing Labour's claims to be the patriot party. The SNP's withdrawal from the Convention anticipated the limited and consensual nature of its remit, and the party was roundly criticized for it by a Scottish media used to printing Labour press releases as exclusives; nonetheless, adroit manoeuvring by Alex Salmond in the mid-1990s allowed the Nationalists to play an effective part in the eventual referendum campaign to endorse a Labour scheme shorn of the rhetoric of Scottish sovereignty which had marked the Convention's own proposals, first unveiled on St Andrew's Day 1995.[127] Quasi-nationalist feeling among Labour Scottish activists was placed squarely by the devolution White Paper in the context of Westminster sovereignty, and a referendum was insisted on by the incoming Labour Government. The mismanagement of the last one had left such a bitter taste that this was opposed, but in the event there was no need for concern, since Scotland voted by 74–26 in favour of a Parliament, and by 64–36 in favour of its having tax-varying powers. Every local authority area backed the first question (by 84 per cent in the case of Glasgow); only Galloway and Orkney voted No narrowly on the second count. On 11 September 1997, on the 700th anniversary of the Battle of Stirling Bridge, Scotland had voted Yes.

Since 1997, the difficulty for the government has been to preserve an appeal to Scottish patriotism while emphasizing and developing a new rhetoric of Britain, 'Cool Britannia' or the 'young country'. This has proved a difficult balancing act. Arguments over the location of the Parliament, pressure for more attention to be paid to Scottish culture and demands for the devolution of broadcasting are among the issues which have caused problems for Labour. Appealing to Britishness is difficult, when so many of the institutions of 'new Britain', like broadcasting, seem old-fashioned in their attitudes: the BBC was criticized by its watchdog for its anti-devolution bias during the Referendum coverage, and only 57 per cent of Scots consider it to be a British (rather than English) institution (as opposed to 95 per cent in the case of the NHS).[128] Another major problem for a British patriotic response to the SNP was and remains the difficulty of 'playing the British card . . . when signs of British decline were evident', and this itself is a clear sign that the 'decline of Empire' thesis for the rise of Scottish nationalism has, prima facie, much to commend it. Such post-imperial Britishness as was successfully constructed rested in large part on the ubiquitous services of the welfare state, and the perceived assault on these in the 1980s further undermined Scottish loyalty to contemporary Britain.[129] Despite the increasing multiculturalism of Scottish society, the proportion of those domiciled in Scotland primarily regarding themselves as 'British' fell from 30 per cent during the SNP surge of the late 1960s to 18 per cent by the end of the century, while 'Scottishness' remained over 70 per cent.[130]

On the other hand, there are contrasting signals, with 75–80 per cent of Scots seeing co-operation with England on a range of issues as important, and support for independence in general failing to rise much above 30 per cent.[131] It could be argued, as it was by the Earl of Eglinton in the 1850s, that the crucial aspect to any project for rebuilding Britain will be to emphasize a general parity of esteem for Scottish examples, culture, tradition, education, and so on. It seems to be the case that there is a great fund of remaining goodwill towards Britain in Scotland, but a rising unwillingness to suppress Scottish identity and outlook or to be taken for granted. Response in this direction is very slow: it was only in 1999, for example, that the BBC deigned to produce a document advising its newscasters to use different terms to describe a range of political, legal and educational developments in Scotland, many of which had been in place since 1707! Meanwhile, the whipping up of English nationalism among some politicians and opinion-formers in response to even limited recognition of Scotland's importance is an unsavoury reminder of Randolph Churchill's Orange Card from another age. We are at a crossroads. The United Kingdom may remain united; but for it to be strongly united, more space must be conceded to Scottish claims. Yet the evidence from England, now as in the past, is that any concession is an irritation, and that parity of esteem is Scotch presumption. 'We do nothing in this House', an irritated Eric Heffer said in the Commons in 1978, 'but debate Scottish and Welsh business': and this was because it was being debated at all.

In the last chapter, I will look at various aspects of Scottish life and culture today with the aim of allowing the reader to make their own decision on these issues, to which no one has the answer. Change, as is common in human affairs, has been slower than many predicted, and what future developments may be can only be guessed; but just as some aspects of Scottish society and culture today retain enthusiasm for British models and ideas, so others present a picture of a separate national agenda, clearly developing in its own way. The relative health and strength of both these kinds of Scotland are critical for appraising the shape of the future of the country and of the United Kingdom itself.

5

A NATION OF TWO HALVES

Political Football

It is a truism of our time that the exponential growth of the visual media as a means of communication has shortened attention spans: an observation which, if true, goes some distance to accounting for the increasing marginalization of history as a curricular subject in schools. At the same time, the speed with which events are reported in the contemporary media is probably a more accurate measure of their nature than subsequent systematization used to allow: overdetermined narratives of historical change are thus put out of fashion. The title of this chapter, though, is not merely intended to be a reflection of that fashion: but to illuminate the speed with which the debate on identity in contemporary Scotland is growing and changing, while recognizing the limitations of journalism's central cliché, which is to exaggerate the freshness of any development, measuring the complex likelihood of historical shifts by the narrow focus of succeeding stories. The cliché of language is a surer indicator of the staleness of thought than the supposed changes it aims to describe: hence journalism of all sorts is saturated in cliché, while purporting to inform us of what is different and new. All football games are different, but it is in itself a cliché of our times that they are usually all described in similar terms.

Since the days of Theodore Napier at least, football has been used as a symbol of Scottish political identity, not merely by cultural pundits (e.g. Jim Sillars's description of the Scots as '90-minute nationalists' following his defeat in Govan in 1992), but also by the fans themselves: 'Gi'e us an Assembly, and we'll gi'e ye back your Wembley' was famously chanted after the breaking down of the Wembley goalposts in 1977, following Scotland's 2–1 win over England.[1] The same year saw the high water mark of SNP support at 36 per cent, while Scotland's dismal 1978 Home Championships performance, followed by the devastating puncture of Celtic hubris in the Argentina World Cup, coincided with the beginnings of a collapse in SNP support. Similarly, the 1974 World Cup, in which Scotland had been undefeated, was a year of triumph for the Nationalists. Such comparisons are slick and unscholarly (history is diverse, and Keith Bovey's principled but unwise comments on defence-related employment in the 1978 Garscadden by-election may have punctured the SNP before a ball was kicked), but are nonetheless appealing, even compelling. The 1970s was the period in which Scottish nationality's link to football seemed closest and most uncontroversial.[2]

If this decade saw the growth of the modern 'Tartan Army', heavily garbed in the patriot dress of the eighteenth century, it was also one in which Scottish supporters (notably at Barcelona in 1972 and Wembley in 1977) were associated with violence every bit as much as their English counterparts. In the 1980s this changed. Particularly after the Heysel disaster of 1985, when English clubs and English clubs alone were banned from European competition, Scottish supporters' behaviour improved noticeably. The desire to contrast themselves with English fans and to virtuously telephone the BBC to complain when 'British' hooligans were mentioned as rioting appears to have been a powerful motive force for change. In the 1990s, there has been a clear move towards revisiting the tartan garb, not as a gesture of naive patriotism (as in Argentina in 1978), but one of postmodern irony. Tartan outfits worn at Scotland games have become even more outrageous, and the pride with which they are worn is suffused with an ironic distancing which no longer passionately expects victory, but good-humouredly awaits defeat.

Club football is just as important as Scotland's presence on the international stage. There are at least three important reasons for this. First, the presence of a national league of respectable standing was one of the most visible expressions of Scottish nationhood in the last century. There is evidence that the pattern of leisure and sport changed in the years around the first Scottish league competition of 1891 (the Cup began in 1874). In the 1880s, for example, the Aberdeen area had dozens of cricket clubs (one of which lost 36–0 to Arbroath in the Scottish Cup while trying to adapt to football); subsequently, they faded away. Cricket became not a British, but an English game, a cinderella sport in Scotland, while football prospered.

Secondly, football has had a function in binding together Scottish communities, and in this role is a game for which Scots have been more enthusiastic, per capita, than their neighbours in the south. Rangers and Celtic are among the dozen or so best-supported clubs in the world, remarkable in such a small country: when both play at home, the average gate is equivalent to one-quarter of the adult population of Glasgow city. At the other end of the scale, Scotland supports a number of league clubs from towns with a population of under 20 000, such as Brechin City, Montrose, Peterhead, Cowdenbeath, Stenhousemuir, Stranraer, East Fife, Forfar Athletic and Ross County, where the club plays an important part in cementing the social life of a significant section of local society.

Thirdly, there is the issue of sectarianism, to a considerable extent kept alive by the Rangers/Celtic divide, with its fainter echo in Hearts and Hibs in Edinburgh and its hardly discernible whisper in the traditions of Dundee and Dundee United (once Dundee Harp).[3] It is not merely confined to these clubs however, for a Protestant national identity is arguably still a strong part of the Scottish game, leading (among other results) to a paranoiac attitude towards referees and occasionally the football establishment by Celtic in particular. In the 1950s, the footballing authorities threatened Celtic with expulsion from the league for flying the Irish flag; more recently, it continues to be clear that sectarian anti-Catholic songs have a wide currency outside the gates of Ibrox, Rangers' stadium. As Joseph Bradley points out, supporters of Hearts, Dundee, Ayr United, Kilmarnock, St Mirren, St Johnstone, Airdrie, Motherwell, Falkirk, Queen of the South, Morton and Inverness Caledonian Thistle have all been responsible for singing

> Hello, hello, we are the Billy Boys,
> Hello, hello, you can tell us by our noise,
> We're up to our knees in Fenian blood, Surrender or you'll die
> For we are the Billy Billy Boys.

This homely tribute to the noble deeds of the followers of William of Orange thus has a currency which stretches across the whole of Scottish football, making it 'a nationalistic, political and cultural repository' of a totally different kind from that now found in the English game.[4]

Research into the political attitudes of Scottish football supporters provides a complex, but no less distinctive picture. On the key sectarian question as to whether Northern Ireland should remain in the UK or join the Irish Republic, there is a marked distinction between fans' attitudes, according to a 1990 survey, admittedly one based on relatively small samples. Rangers fans split 73–11 in favour of the UK, with Hearts (the side with the next most Protestant identity) splitting 42–21 on the same question. By complete contrast, Celtic fans split 5–79 in favour of Irish reunification; Hibs fans 0–61 and Dundee United fans 9–64. Eighty-five per cent of Hibs, 84 per cent of Celtic and 68 per cent of Dundee United fans supported the withdrawal of British troops from Northern Ireland, while only 21 per cent of Rangers fans did so. While most fans supported Scotland internationally, 52 per cent of Celtic and 12 per cent of Hibs fans supported Ireland; 13 per cent of Rangers fans were sufficiently Unionist to support England. Unsurprisingly, 73 per cent (57 per cent for Hearts) of Rangers fans were Church of Scotland, with 0 per cent Catholics (10 per cent for Hearts), while 93 per cent of Celtic fans were Catholic. Hibs and Dundee United fans, by contrast, were 39 per cent and only 5 per cent Catholic respectively, despite the views expressed on Ireland. In terms of following a faith rather than a label, however, there was a massive distinction, with an extraordinary 64 per cent of Celtic fans attending Mass at least once a month, compared to the mere 13 per cent of Rangers fans to be found in church; Aberdeen's fans, at 29 per cent, were the next most likely after Celtic's to be churchgoers.[5]

Opinions in Scottish politics again varied significantly between the supporters of the various teams. The SNP was most strongly supported (41 per cent) by Dundee United fans, who tended to live in what were already strong Nationalist areas; Motherwell fans registered 37 per cent, while a third of both Aberdeen and St Johnstone supporters (though only 4 per cent of Celtic fans) backed the SNP. Support for Labour was overwhelming at Celtic (85 per cent), with Kilmarnock (58 per cent) also registering strongly. The Conservatives failed to get above 15 per cent and were frequently in single figures, except at Aberdeen (17 per cent), St Johnstone (29 per cent) and arch-Unionist Rangers (32 per cent). The Rangers figure in particular is striking, given the weakness of the Conservative vote in Glasgow.[6]

Asked to choose heroes who expressed their identity, further telling differences emerged. Of Rangers fans, 51 per cent lived up to stereotype by choosing John Knox, as did a remarkable 34 per cent of fans at Hearts and Motherwell, while 23 per cent of Celtic fans offered Padraig Pearse. By contrast, Robert the Bruce, who averaged 45 per cent (except among members of the Orange Lodge, who ranked him much lower), gained only 17 per cent endorsement at Celtic Park. High proportions of Aberdeen and St Johnstone fans (around 30 per cent) chose the folk group *The Corries* as expressing their identity. Again, these figures show a divided political consciousness, but also a remarkable sensitivity to history and national, as opposed to popular, music. Of Rangers fans, 57 per cent voted for Burns: one wonders how many Aston Villa supporters would have mentioned Shakespeare?[7]

Thus there are a number of indications of the strength of individual football clubs as a home for national allegiances, albeit ones riven by sectarianism, as a feature of Scottish culture which renders largely redundant the kind of Gaelic Athletic Association (GAA) movement which proved so important to the Irish cultural renaissance. The GAA did organize in Scotland,[8] and there are still teams which are descendants of those founded at the turn of the twentieth century, just as shinty has a following in the Highlands. But with the partial (and rather sectional) exception of rugby, no other game has the impact which football has on defining the nature of national and religious allegiances publicly in Scotland.

Lest it be thought that this case is overstated, the explosion of controversy about Scottish identity and sectarianism following the Rangers' vice-chairman's taped singing of sectarian songs after the 1999 Scottish Cup Final was not confined to a ten days' wonder, but rather led to widespread questioning of the status and level of sectarianism in modern Scotland. Polling evidence suggested that there was still widespread belief among Catholics of discrimination against them.

At the same time, commentators such as Tom Gallagher, who stress sectarianism as a key component of Scottish society, have little hard evidence to support them and are regionally biased: anti-Catholicism in east-coast Scotland north of Edinburgh is a rarity, for example. Even in its western heartlands, attempts by the Orange Order to launch a Unionist party in Scotland of a Northern Irish stamp have been intermittent and unimpressive.[9] The presence of Catholic schools still causes a knee-jerk reaction in some quarters in the west of Scotland, but is largely a non-issue where they exist in the rest of the country. The Monklands by-election of 1993 did produce a poll showing more than 60 per cent of Protestants voting SNP and an even larger proportion of Catholics Labour, but Catholic hostility to the SNP is a rapidly declining phenomenon. Although only 5 per cent of Catholics voted Nationalist in the October 1974 General Election, by the 1990s there had been a major shift. In 1992, one poll in *The Universe* suggested that 35 per cent of Catholics intended to vote SNP,[10] while the Bishops' Letter before the 1999 Scottish election came close to suggesting that the SNP was the party to vote for.

There is widespread evidence of integration and shared values: Catholic marriages to non-Catholics in 1998 stood at 43 per cent at the level of the lowest diocese, Motherwell. The case remains very different in divided parts of Northern Ireland. Sectarianism in Scotland is not be ignored, but the available evidence is that it is more evidenced in perception than behaviour.[11]

Political Difference and National Difference

Scottish society differs from that of England in many other, and ulti-mately more important, respects. Not only are the Scottish church, banking and educational systems historically distinct: they also attract strong popular support. Even in 1981, when confidence was low in the aftermath of the Referendum, it proved politically impossible to coun-tenance the sale of the Royal Bank of Scotland to Hong Kong Shanghai (later HSBC). Education, the law and (to a declining extent, perhaps) the Kirk are all seen by the domestic professional classes as bulwarks of national identity. The numerical strength of Catholicism (775 000 baptized Catholics) has led increasingly in recent years (particularly after the 1982 papal visit) to an official role in Scottish society, one strategically supported by the appointment of two successive Cardinals, Gray and Winning, the first since the sixteenth century. The Episcopal Church, meanwhile, is a shadow of its counterpart south of the Border, the Bishop of Oxford alone having authority over four times as many clergy as all the Episcopal bishops in Scotland combined.[12]

The legend of Scotland's excellent education system has long been over-taken by the realities of a cosy corporatist consensus which, if it largely avoids the levels of the worst-performing schools elsewhere, falls some way short of the best. In Mathematics and Science, Scotland ranks eleventh out of 17 developing countries at the age of 10, and fourteenth at the age of 14, surpassing England on only one measure out of four.[13] With an over-provi-sion of higher education per capita in Scotland (compared to the UK norm), Scots tend to continue to attend their own universities rather than go south of the Border: in 1999, despite the demise of grants in a system which takes a year longer to reach an Honours degree, under 9 per cent of Scottish-domiciled students who took up university places went to England and Wales,[14] a factor which certainly made the decision to abolish tuition fees for Scots-domiciled students studying in Scotland only more politically

possible than it would otherwise have been. Historically, Glasgow, Strathclyde and Aberdeen were all very heavily based not only on a Scottish, but a
local intake: these three universities only joined the central admissions system in the 1980s. In 1988, 87 per cent of students at Strathclyde and 85 per
cent of those at Glasgow were Scots-domiciled, with only St Andrews and
Stirling having a minority of Scottish students.[15]

Newer institutions such as the media also attract loyalty on a national
basis: indeed, Scotland has a distinctive national media to an extent
often overlooked south of the Border. The *Daily Record* had a circulation
of 651 000 in 1999, while the *Sunday Mail* had 770 000. The *Sunday Post*,
which once reached *The Guinness Book of Records* for its saturation coverage
of 1.14 million sales, was by 1999 down at 470 000. Nonetheless, the
Scottish tabloid Sundays sold 1.25 million, as against the 630 000 sold by
English titles, even those which marketed a peculiarly Scottish edition.
Matters were as pronounced among the quality papers. In 1999 *The
Times* had 28 000 Scottish sales, the *Guardian* 14 000, *The Independent*
7500 and the *Daily Telegraph* 24 000, while Scotland's two quality
national newspapers, *The Herald* and *The Scotsman*, sold 101 000 (despite
the 48p cover price) and 78 000 respectively. The Sunday versions of
both these newspapers currently muster over 150 000 sales between
them, and have peaked at nearly 200 000 (including a good number
south of the Border), a figure at least level with the total for all English
broadsheets, even though these have received heavy price-cutting and
run dedicated Scottish editions. It must also be noted that many Scots
buy one of the big regional quality titles on a daily basis, such as
the *(Dundee) Courier* (94 000) or the *Press and Journal* from Aberdeen
(102 000), which also prints a separate Highland edition.[16] Only in
Lothian do the English papers sell strongly.[17] In these circumstances,
the continued pressure for BBC TV to reflect Scottish priorities is
understandable. The unwillingness to concede a 'Scottish Six' in 1999
led to the rather inadequate compromise of *Newsnight Scotland*, cynically
dubbed *Newsnicht* north of the Border on acount of its tokenism. The
issue here is, of course, broader than a merely Scottish one: for although
Scotland makes only 2–3 per cent of programmes in return for nearly
10 per cent of the licence fee, the position is nearly as bad in the English
regions. The BBC's use of its £2200 million annual subsidy to ensure
that 'the biggest, sweetest slice by far goes to London' is, or should be, an
issue of British, not merely Scottish concern.[18]

Economically speaking, 'global and European performance and prospects' matter more in Scotland's 'outward-looking economy' than is the

case in the rest of the UK.[19] Scotland sells around 52 per cent of exports in the rest of the UK, and 48 per cent elsewhere.[20] There are widely differing geographical characteristics within the Scottish economy, such as oil in the North-East and Shetland and 'Silicon Glen' in the Central Belt. Agriculture, forestry and fishing are 67 per cent more important to GDP than is the case in the UK as a whole, while inward investment from US firms alone increased from six to 178 between 1945 and 1981: overseas-owned manufacturing accounted in 1996 for 53 per cent of manufacturing jobs in West Lothian and 63 per cent in Inverclyde, an immense reversal from Scotland's leading-edge capitalism in 1914, and one which has consequences for R&D spending, which is often a 'headquarters' operation: Scottish businesses's R&D spend is less than 45 per cent of the average in the rest of the UK. Low transport costs have helped to ensure Scotland's success in the electronics industry, but prominence here and in financial services have not offset the decline in traditional manufacturing and the underdevelopment of 'business services'. GDP per head in Scotland was 13 per cent lower than the rest of the UK in 1996 (6 per cent higher if 80 per cent of oil revenues are included[21]), and Scotland has a tendency to miss out on economic upswings, house-price booms, and so on, which has led in recent years to SNP criticism of interest-rate policy as a regional tool for south-eastern economic conditions being implemented on a UK-wide basis.

The population of Scotland has remained steady at five million or so since 1970. By far the highest proportion are concentrated in the former Strathclyde region, which had 49 per cent of the population in 1971 and 44 per cent in 1997. The fulcrum of the Scottish economy switched from the east to the west coasts after the Union and during the British Empire; following the end of Empire, the pendulum has been swinging slowly back towards the East (36.7 per cent in 1971, 44 per cent in 1997), a process which looks to be accelerating under the influence of the development surrounding the re-establishment of the Scottish Parliament. The economic imbalance is even starker: between 1977 and 1995, Grampian rose from 114 per cent to 136 per cent of average Scottish GDP, with Edinburgh at 150 per cent of GDP. By contrast, there is a serious problem with entrepreneurship and new business growth in parts of the old industrial belt in particular: in 1996, Aberdeenshire had 400 VAT-registered businesses per 10 000 population and Angus had 300, while three local authorities in greater Glasgow, with its greater parochialism, lower mobility and perceived dependency culture (as Peat and Boyle observe, 'this caricature' is 'true'), had under 150. Out of thirty-two local authorities, not one of the top ten for business population per capita was in west central Scotland. In this context, commentators who stress the need for Scotland to move from a dependency to a business-oriented culture have a good deal of hard evidence on their side, though the structural limitations of a branch economy also play their part.[22]

Among the Scottish cities, this shift is also reflected. Glasgow city has shrunk by over a third sice 1939, and Dundee has declined by 20 percent since the 1960s, while the Edinburgh and Aberdeen urban areas have increased in size. In recent years, net outmigration has declined from its high points in the 1920s, 1950s and 1960s: nonetheless, it is only since 1990 that there have been small gains in population rather than five-figure net losses. Many Scottish families have at least one relative in North America, Australia or New Zealand.[23] Scotland has thus been considerably less successful than Ireland in reducing population loss. Many of the new immigrants to Scotland have, particularly in the Highlands, been dubbed 'white settlers', partly on account of a perceived wish among some of them to maintain the 'character' of the place they have come to by keeping it picturesque and backward, in a paradigm where 'remoteness' (in space, time and manners) and 'attractiveness' are synonymous. Insofar as this is the case, it is due to the fact that many have had their first experience of Scotland through tourism, and it is in tourism that they often work: 'incomers . . . are seen to be encouraging, and making a living from, other transitory and seasonal outsiders'. As one local remarked in Jedrej and Nuttall's survey on the issue:

> Maybe we're not primitive enough! Put us back in black houses, and we'll make pretty pictures for the tourists, out in the fields with the beasts and cutting the hay. And then we'd be worth protecting.[24]

There is a natural resentment among diverse local communities in being subjected to a tourist gaze even by those who live among them, and many object to their reduction to a stereotype of 'authentic' or 'inauthentic' local by those who profess to be part of the community on which they sit in judgement. On the other hand, incomers may sometimes have reason on their side when they protest at an unwillingness to innovate in the local economy.

There are thus major distinctions both in the institutions and structures of Scottish society, as well as many very marked regional disparities. Edinburgh is more than 50 per cent richer than Glasgow in GDP per capita, while Aberdeen's wealth exceeds that of parts of its

Highland hinterland by almost as much. Such marked disparities might be expected, combined as they are with widely varying levels of social mobility, to cause regional tensions. If the Highland–Lowland divide has lost much of its force as a construction which splits Scottish identity, others were tried in the 1970s, when the No campaign in the Referendum laid considerable stress on the fear that northern Scotland in particular might feel at rule from the Central Belt. If exaggerated and distorted, there appeared to be some grounds for these claims. Much was made of the fact that Grampian, the Borders and Dumfries and Galloway all voted No in 1979, but in each case this was by a slender margin, as were all but one of the Yes votes.

In the 1980s and 1990s, it became increasingly difficult to identify these regional disparities to the same extent. The Edinburgh–Glasgow rivalry might plod on, fed by the snobbery of the capital and the insular complacency of its commercial rival, but even though Edinburgh's prosperity soared while Linwood, Gartcosh and Ravenscraig closed in the west, the capital moved politically with the rest of Scotland. In 1979, Glasgow had two Tory MPs; by 1982 it had none. In 1987, Edinburgh Central (including the New Town) and Edinburgh South fell to Labour; gradually the rest followed, with the exception of a Liberal seat in Edinburgh West. In 1997, Edinburgh Pentlands even threw out the Foreign Secretary, Malcolm Rifkind, the most senior Cabinet minister to lose his seat in living memory. Meanwhile, the presence of a strong Liberal/SDP vote allowed a Tory to cling on occasionally in Aberdeen South, but by 1997 Labour had 20 of the 21 seats in Scotland's four cities, with one Liberal as ballast. In the rural areas, Labour gained too, but here the SNP or the Liberals were often the main challengers. All over Scotland, professional areas, boom towns, farmers, fishermen and industrial workers, although they did not unite in a crusade to get the Tories out, steadily drifted away. Only once since 1970 has the Conservative Party polled more than 30 per cent in Scotland, and that was in 1979, when the Tories benefited disproportionately from the SNP's status as the party of disappointed expectation: there was still a small swing to Labour. By 1997, the Tories' loss of all their seats indicated that what support they retained did not have a regional heartland, though their vote held up best where the SNP was the main rival. In the 1999 Scottish election the Tory vote was highest in Ayr (38 per cent – subsequently won back in a by-election in 2000), and below 10 per cent in Shetland, the Western Isles, Caithness, Sutherland, Easter Ross, Ross Skye, Inverness West, Fife Central, Dunfermline, Greenock and Inverclyde, Paisley, eight out of ten Glasgow seats, Cumbernauld and Kilsyth, Falkirk, Coatbridge and Chryston, Airdrie and Shotts, Linlithgow, Livingston and Midlothian. In four seats in the Highlands, six on the east coast and sixteen on the west, the Tories fell below one vote in ten. In only two seats from six in the booming capital did they manage 25 per cent; in wealthy Aberdeen, they averaged under 15 per cent across three seats. Whatever Scotland's regional disparities might be, there was a clear political bias against the Conservative Party running nationwide.

Unsurprisingly, then, what is reflected in any comparison between the 1979 and 1997 referenda is the extent to which changing levels of support for the proposal indicated a much higher level of national acceptance, and far fewer signs of mutual suspicion and regional division than appeared to some to be present at the earlier vote. Turnout, in comparison with the figures in 1979, was fairly consistent, never rising by more than 5 per cent (Western Isles), nor falling by more than 5 per cent (Highland, Lothian). But the areas which voted No in 1979 showed major changes. The Yes vote in Shetland rose from 27 to 62; in Orkney from 28 to 57; in the Borders from 40 to 63 and in Dumfries and Galloway from 41 to 61. The highest Yes-voting area in 1979, Fife, rose from 57 to 76 per cent Yes, but it was matched by Central and beaten both by the Western Isles and Strathclyde, where Glasgow (84 per cent) and West Dunbartonshire (85 per cent) recorded the highest Yes votes in the country. Tayside, where the Yes vote rose from 50 per cent to 63 per cent, showed the weakest increase in support: intriguingly, although it is the heartland of the SNP,[25] it attracted (outside Dundee) two of the five highest Tory votes in 1999.

In the Scottish Parliament elections of 1999, the SNP took 29 per cent of the vote and 35 seats. Although this was regarded as something of a disappointment given the pre-election hype, it was a result which represented a solid willingness to vote Nationalist in many parts of the country: north of the Tay, the SNP was the largest party. What was also little remarked on by the media was the fact that two of the minority parties, the Scottish Socialists and the Greens, who gained 8 per cent of the vote between them, were also pro-independence. The 1999 survey of Scottish opinion showed that whereas in 1979, only 38 per cent of Scots would describe themselves as 'Scottish' rather than 'British' when faced with these as alternatives, 20 years later 77 per cent were prepared to do so.[26] Gradually rising levels of perceived Scottishness thus conceal a much more rapid escalation of the primary focus of national identity, one which was also reflected in *The Economist* survey's identification of the

Scottish Parliament as the main future focus point for those domiciled in Scotland.[27]

History, Heritage and the Future

After the 1979 referendum, an exasperated Neal Ascherson 'wrote in the *Scotsman*, that while Scotland waits for the next chance, we can agitate, drink, or grow up'.[28] Most commentators, while acknowledging that the second is always with us, would say there had been clearly some of the first, and hopefully some of the third. If that is true, one of the distinctive routes by which they have come is that of Scottish culture.

In this Cairns Craig was a visionary commentator, arguing from the early 1980s that the flowering of Scottish culture which can be dated from around the appearance of Alasdair Gray's *Lanark* (1982) was itself a kind of 'cultural independence', a term used in the Polygon *Determinations* series which Craig edited.[29] Certainly, Scottish cultural life has increasingly been setting its own agenda since the 1980s, to the extent that government ministers are demonstrably shy of its nationalist potential. Whatever the rights and wrongs of these fears, it is certainly the case that Scottish culture has been one of the aspects of a Scottish agenda which has created a marked divergence in the outlook and nature of debate in Scotland and England. This marching to a different drum has been one of the main ways in which, it has been argued, Unionism in Scotland has lost even the means to access its traditional grounds of appeal. Comparisons with the Celtic Revival's role as the cultural avatar of politics in Ireland have been made, but despite maximalist readings of the 1980s and 1990s such as Tom Nairn's *After Britain* (2000), it is the present author's view that the strength of Britishness as a cultural and social glue remains seriously underestimated by contemporary nationalist commentators. Their views are understandable; arguably more disturbing is the fact that in the last few years, right-wing Unionist commentators have sought to undermine Britishness by printing and disseminating exaggerated and inflammatory stories of Scottish anti-Englishness, which have little basis in fact.[30]

On *Newsnight Scotland* on 6 January 2000, Professor Tom Devine, author of the highly influential *The Scottish Nation 1700–2000* (1999), put forward the case that traditional Unionism had lost nearly all the grounds of its historic appeal, a point echoed from a different part of the political spectrum by the Tory commentator Michael Fry in *The Herald* on the same day. Fry argued that the last grounds on which the Union was defended were those of subsidy politics, realized through the defence of Scottish public expenditure levels: in this, he and Finlay (see Chapter 4) are broadly in agreement. However, Fry also claimed that devolution became inevitable because this policy on its own was not enough, and that Michael Forsyth's last-ditch attempt to rescue the symbolism of Scottish sovereignty through the return of the Stone of Scone to Edinburgh on 30 November 1996 was an implicit if inadequate acknowledgement of this fact. In other words, the cultural divergence of Scottish expectation had moved on apace while subsidy politics was being returned to again and again as the only structural strategy which could hold change at bay. It had had great success, but its lack of window-dressing in the terms set by a Scottish cultural revival was noted too little too late by the government of the day.

Both Fry and Devine agree that the grounds of the Union's appeal have been substantially eroded, but while Fry sees this as likely to be an ongoing process, Devine argues that the innate conservatism of human nature makes a further drift towards independence for Scotland unlikely without a major contributing cause, such as an ideological conflict of a left/right (rather than nationalist/unionist) kind between governments in Edinburgh and Westminster. Both arguments ignore the European dimension: yet it has arguably long been clear that, just as the historic foundation of the British state as a Union state rather than a multiple monarchy lies in the Revolution of 1688 and its legacy of the overweening claims of Parliamentary sovereignty, so any challenge to that state must ultimately take the form of a challenge to that sovereignty. After 1922, Ireland's challenge was written out of the record books as Ireland's Britishness was disowned and airbrushed out of a history which had seen it as organically linked only 25 years before. As Norman Davies, points out, the idea that 'the southern Irish' 'never' consented to Britishness is a modern slant which threatens to leave figures the the Duke of Wellington (or, indeed, the Earls of Burlington and Orrery in a previous century) entirely out of account.[31] Since 1973, the much more broadly-based challenge of EU government and institutions has been encroaching on Britishness. Any increase in Scottish sovereignty which may take place will arguably depend on the success or otherwise of the European project – that is, in the absence of any positive attachment to Unionism. As Stuart Trotter observed in *The Herald* on 10 March 2000:

If, over the next decade or two, the EU takes on most or all of the primary powers of government, Westminster will become, in effect, a second tier of government and it may seem pointless to refuse Holyrood similar status. Thus 'independence in Europe' may come about although it will not be the 'independence' that was in the minds of the founding Fathers of Nationalism.[32]

This is a level-headed supposition: but there are always 'ifs', and the 'if' here depends on our accepting Fry's and Devine's view that positive Unionism is an irrecoverable political project. But are Fry and Devine right? Is a positive Unionism (as opposed to fears, suspicions and old attachments) in steep decline in today's Scotland? and are they right in seeing the decline of the Conservative Party (until 1964, called the Unionist Party) as isomorphic with that decline?

During the General Election campaign of 1992, John Major called the Scots 'an intensely proud, patriotic race',[33] but neither he nor any other recent leader of the Conservative Party has understood why this does not add up to Conservative votes, for the Conservatives have long positioned themselves precisely as the patriotic party. But is this now an alien patriotism? The Conservatives dislike their identification as 'the English party' in Scotland, but when their leader 'beats the drum for England' and blames such inoffensive Unionists as 'Robin Cook and Donald Dewar' for 'the rise of nationalism in Scotland', it is clear that the party's instincts continue to have difficulty accepting the very idea of Scottish patriotism in its modern guise.[34]

Perhaps the crucial change is once again one which is contingent on the decline of Empire, not just (as some Tories would argue), the shift away from the title 'Unionist' in the 1960s. In those days, a 'Britain and Empire' patriotism was international and inclusive: Scottishness was one of many 'local' nationalities within the *Pax Britannica*. Slowly but surely, the general Tory reaction to the loss of Empire has been a drift, not towards other forms of internationalism, but to an increasingly narrow English nationalism. Michael Forsyth's last-gasp efforts to swathe himself in tartan as Secretary of State failed to overcome many years of perception (explicitly endorsed by the timing of the Poll Tax's introduction to Scotland) that the Conservative Party considered sectional English interests as their priority. Revealingly, one of the last upsurges of explicit Britishness occurred during the Falklands War of 1982,[35] one famously titled by the American press 'the Empire strikes Back'. Foreign policy seems to be one of the last strongholds of positive Unionism: but even here, the SNP were able to speak out against the war in Kosovo (when Britishness once again showed signs of being important) in 1999 in a way which had not been available in 1982. Although this intervention quite possibly damaged their electoral prospects, it did not destroy them as it might once have done.

English nationalism itself is clearly of growing importance, though it is unclear this is because it has been assiduously promoted by a group of political and cultural leaders who have little interest in rebuilding Britain on a more inclusive and dialogic basis. This itself has a weakening effect on positive Unionism: the repeated and misleading attacks on Scotland as the beneficiary of the London taxpayer during the mayoral campaign in the capital in 1999–2000 were fundamentally anti-Unionist in that they sought to set the regions and nations of Britain at each other's throats over resources. Claims that 'Scotland robs London' not only create resentment in themselves, but threaten to lead to a closer examination of the aggrandizement of the London economy, through heavy expenditure claimed to be of national benefit which nonetheless disproportionately feeds that local economy (see Chapter 4).[36] That such claims are made both by candidates on the Right (Steve Norris) and Left (Ken Livingstone) indicate the national, rather than party political quality of English anti-Unionism at the turn of the twenty-first century. In such a situation, what remains of positive Unionism is indeed under threat.

The situation continues to change rapidly, and any conclusions must be provisional. However, there does appear to be clear evidence that positive Unionism is declining and being undermined, often from non-Scottish sources. The changes of the post-1970 period represent an opportunity for Britain to develop a series of more equitable internal dialogues between its peoples: as Norman Davies says in the Introduction to his influential study of *The Isles* (1999), there is an 'inability of prominent authorities to present the history of our Isles in accurate and unambiguous terms'. Davies might have added 'unwillingness': although 'the old Anglocentric straitjacket is bursting at the seams', many key decision-makers in British society still think Britain will not be Britain unless it fits.[37] But insisting that it fits only provokes anger and division. The devolution of power in the United Kingdom must undermine the post-1688 assumptions of metropolitanism and the infinite sovereignty of Parliament if it is to adapt either to the European Union or to a Britain where too many have noticed that the straitjacket no longer fits. To take only one example, the revival of great interest in Scotland's culture and history within Scotland would benefit from dialogue with other British cultures and histories. But to create that dialogue requires a rethinking of the central single agenda of British-ness implied by the 1997 devolutionary settlement, but still unrealized.

The rediscovery of Scotland's history adds another dimension to this process. The cultural reputation of Scotland's history entered a new phase in the 1980s with the campaign to demythologize it.[38] This process of demythologization, which had its academic counterpart in works such as Eric Hobsbawm and Terence Ranger's *The Invention of Tradition* (1983), sought to discard the leftover fragments of kitsch Romantic identity (tartan chief among them), by claiming them to be the spurious products of their age, and not part of Scottish identity at all. This demythologization became quite an industry, without anyone appearing to notice that it represented yet a further attack by Scottish history on its own value:

> The attack on tartanry is only a further attack on self . . . the self-belief evident in the sculpture of the Children of Lir in Dublin is very different from the mater-ial manifestations of kitsch in Scotland; but this is not the problem of myths but the problem of what is done with them. The fragmentary, detached and exag-gerated qualities of the Scottish past are the result of a previous defeat by a his-torical rhetoric which now revisits them in order to berate them for what it has made them.[39]

It was the Enlightenment construction of Scottish history which left it a mixture of pointless legends shining amid the dross of an irrelevant and forgotten culture; and it is better to re-enter and revalue that culture than waste contemporary energies blaming a caricature drawn by your society of itself, thus caricaturing it in its turn, and setting up a procession of self-abasement and blame, while encouraging people to sneer at their own history.

Demythologization thus damages Scottish history just as much as mythologizing did; but broader-based assessments of the significance of the past, though intensely popular reading, are still set to the margins of the educational curriculum. There is clear evidence that the major British political parties regard Scottish history as politically dangerous. Although in a last-ditch attempt to preserve his position as Scottish Secretary, Michael Forsyth argued for a Scottish History Higher, his Scottish Parliamentary successors appear to want nothing to do with it. A report commissioned by the government-appointed Scottish Con-sultative Committee on the Curriculum from the Scottish Culture Review Group concluded in June 1998 that 'Scottish culture has not yet been given an adequate place.' Their report, *Scottish Culture and the Curriculum*, showed that government and its agencies were out of touch with the strength of appetite for Scottish culture on the ground. A poll of 1125 institutions, including 250 schools, carried out by the group revealed that some 90 per cent of respondents thought there should be a curriculum in schools with a Scottish emphasis, and that 97 per cent wanted an emphasis on Scottish history, 93 per cent on Scottish literature, 91 per cent on Scottish music and 80 per cent on Scottish art, while even in Modern Languages and the Sciences, around 45 per cent wanted Scottish content or examples promoted.[40] The SCCC report was a demand for self-respect. Although the incoming administration in Holyrood in 1999 promoted a consultation on the formation of a National Cultural Strategy, it was clear that the specifics of Scottish culture are still regarded by many as a genie best kept in its bottle. A Scottish Arts Council report in 1999 showed widespread prejudice against traditional music, but there is limited sign of a will to address this either, save through special school initiatives in the Gaeltachd. The SCCC report itself (by no means composed by political Nationalists) was watered down into an official version which merely offered 'a ponderous declaration that politics, business education, and values are the true heart of what teachers should be doing about Scottish culture',[41] a decision branded as 'incredible and reprehensible' by the hardly nationalist *Times Education Supplement*.[42] The effect of this suppression is to exclude confrontation with the Scottish past and its surviving and developing cultural expressions. The unwillingness to integrate it is a rejection of the parity of esteem called for by the Earl of Eglintoun 150 years ago. As Ian Bell wrote in *The Scotsman*:

> Change is upon us now . . . with a chance, finally, to let in a little light and a little air . . . the Establishment constituency is too narrow, the connections too intimate, the lack of incentive for radicalism too small.[43]

This is a problem both for wider British society and what Tom Nairn has memorably called the 'pickle-jar nationalism' of Scotland's own determinedly unadventurous corporatist society, the elements of which have 'matured too much and for far too long in their own company'.[44]

Scotland, in other words, though a strong focus of interest among a segment of the population at large, often continues to be unimaginatively apprehended by the managerial and corporatist culture of its social and political leadership, raised in 'the closed circles of provincial self-management and establishment'.[45] At the same time, cartoons in not only *The Spectator*, but also *The Times* and the *Guardian*, continue to show the exponents of Scottish nationality in the claymore-wielding, poverty-stricken garb of the Jacobites thus caricatured 250 years ago. Both elements feed each other: the self-congratulation of elements in a local elite are identified as provincial braggadocio by the metropolitan eye, which as a result sees no reason to alter its own perspectives. Scotland is behind not only London but much provincial English practice in a number of areas, from business formation to tourist development. While county towns such as Worcester and Shrewsbury develop historical tourism at the cutting edge of European practice (Worcester Commandery, Shrewsbury Quest), Scotland's largest free attraction (Kelvingrove Museum) has not been upgraded since the 1970s, while even costly Edinburgh Castle has only just introduced the audio tours which have been a feature in minor English Heritage sites for years. There are many other examples. For a useful dialogue to be possible within Britain regarding Scotland requires not only a suspension of metropolitan prejudice, but also the courage in Scotland to confront the country's limitations, unflinchingly comparing its achievements to those outside its borders, from Cheshire to California. The desire for the Scottish Parliament to achieve great things and for it to be an expression of a Scottish consensus are mutually contradictory: time will tell in what manner this strain will become apparent. As the composer James MacMillan has recently observed (*The Herald*, 31 March 2000), 'Scotland needs more consensus and conformity like it needs a hole in the head';[46] yet eerily, the 'New Politics' called for from so many quarters for the Scottish Parliament were intended to deliver just this.

Scottish nationality, then, has, in the development of a nation, institutions, Enlightenment, culture, science, discovery, military achievement and social innovation, a long and complex history. To understand that history is not to endorse it; but to see it steadily and see it whole is an important, nay a crucial, premiss in the development of the Scotland and Britain which it will be possible to create in the future. This book has sought to tell this story fully, if briefly, in order to promote an understanding of that complexity and to diminish the prevalence of caricature born either of an exaggerated sense of self-worth or an ignorant desire to dismiss. If it can inform enough to allow a settled discussion of the nature of Scotland's presence in today's United Kingdom, and its dialogue with that larger entity, it will have done its work.

NOTES

Introduction

1. Cited in Graeme Morton, *Unionist–Nationalism* (East Linton: Tuckwell Press, 1999), 147.
2. Angela Morris and Graeme Morton, *Locality, Community and Nation* (London: Hodder & Stoughton, 1998), 9.
3. Benedict Anderson, *Imagined Communities* (London: Verso, 1983), 15; John Hutchinson and Anthony D. Smith (eds), *Nationalism* (Oxford and New York: Oxford University Press, 1994), 47; G. W. S. Barrow, *Robert Bruce*, 2nd ed. (Edinburgh: Edinburgh University Press, 1976 (1965)), 322; Murray G. H. Pittock, *Celtic Identity and the British Image* (Manchester: Manchester University Press, 1999), 21.
4. Robert Tombs, review of Adrian Hastings, *The Construction of Nationhood*, in *Historical Journal* (June 1999), 583–4 (583).
5. Geoffrey Barrow, *Robert the Bruce and the Scottish Identity* (Tillicoultry: Saltire Society, 1984), 18.
6. Morris and Morton (1998), 80.
7. Morton (1999), 57.
8. Hugh Trevor-Roper, 'The Invention of Tradition: the Highland Tradition of Scotland', in Eric Hobsbawm and Terence Ranger (eds), *The Invention of Tradition* (Cambridge: Cambridge University Press, 1983), 15–41.
9. Michael Lynch, *Scotland: A New History* (London: Century, 1991), 299.
10. Cf. Declan Kiberd, *Inventing Ireland* (Cambridge, MA: Harvard University Press, 1996).
11. Blin Hary, *Wallace*, tr. William Hamilton of Gilbertfield and ed. Elspeth King (n.p., 1998), 6.
12. Kennedy Index IX: 61, 362, Aberdeen City Archives; David Ditchburn, 'Who are the Scots?', in Paul Dukes (ed.), *Frontiers of European Culture* (Lampeter: Edwin Mellen, 1996), 89–100.
13. Homi Bhabha, in Hutchinson and Smith (1994), 306.
14. Barrow (1976 (1965)); Dauvit Broun, 'The Pictish Origins of the Scottish kinglist', unpublished paper, Glasgow–Strathclyde School of Scottish Studies Traditions of Scottish Culture Seminar, 15 February 2000.

15. Pittock (1999), 21–2.
16. Oscar Wilde, *The Picture of Doran Gray* ed. Isobel Murray (Oxford: World's Classics, 1981), xxiii.
17. Richard Jenkyns, *The Victorians and Ancient Greece* (Oxford: Blackwell, 1980); Virgil, *Aeneid* i:33.
18. Ernest Renan, cited in Hutchinson and Smith (1994), 17–18.
19. William Ferguson, *The Identity of the Scottish Nation* (Edinburgh: Edinburgh University Press, 1998), 306.
20. Edwin Muir, *Scottish Journey*, with an introduction by T. C. Smout (Edinburgh: Mainstream, 1979 (1935)), 227.
21. Morris and Morton (1998), 9.
22. *Ibid.*, 73–7.
23. The quotation is from W. B. Yeats's unpublished poem on Major Robert Gregory, 'Reprisals'.
24. For this kind of view of the Scottish soldier, see Stephen Wood, *The Scottish Soldier* (Manchester: National Museums of Scotland, Archive Publications, 1987).
25. Alice Brown in Brown *et al.* (eds), *Politics and Society in Scotland* (Basingstoke: Macmillan Press – now Palgrave, 1996), 211; cf. *Sunday Herald*, 20 February 2000.
26. Cf. J. G. A. Pocock, 'The New British History in Atlantic Perspective: An Antipodean Commentary', *American Historical Review* (April 1999), 490–500 (491).
27. Sir Henry Newbolt, *The Island Race* (London: Elkin Mathews, 1914 (1898)), 54, 56, 67.
28. Tom Nairn, *The Break-Up of Britain* (London: NLB, 1977), 152.
29. *Ibid.*, 13.
30. *Ibid.*, 256.
31. Richard Hoggart, *The Way We Live Now* (London: Pimlico, 1996 (1995)), xi–xii.
32. Morris and Morton (1998), 110.
33. John Osmond, *The Divided Kingdom* (London: Constable, 1988), 127.
34. Murray G. H. Pittock, *Inventing and Resisting Britain* (Basingstoke: Macmillan Press – now Palgrave, 1997), 139–40.
35. Mark Hauppi, 'Scottish Nationalism: A Conceptual Approach', unpublished Ph.D. thesis, University of Colorado (1980), 112.
36. Morris and Morton (1998), 98.
37. Brown *et al.*, 201.
38. *Sunday Herald*, 20 February 2000.
39. Yves Meny, 'The Political Dynamics of Regionalism', in Roger Morgan (ed.), *Regionalism in European Politics* (London: Policy Studies Institute, 1986), 1–28.
40. Paul Scott, *Defoe in Edinburgh and Other Papers* (East Linton: Tuckwell Press, 1995), 164.
41. David McCrone, *Understanding Scotland* (London: Routledge, 1992), 60; Hauppi (1980), 128–9.
42. Michael Hechter, *Internal Colonialism* (London: Routledge & Kegan Paul, 1975).

Chapter 1

1. Cf. Colin Kidd, 'Sentiment, race and revival: Scottish identities in the after-math of Enlightenment', in Laurence Brockliss and David Eastwood (eds), *A Union of Multiple Identities: The British Isles c1750–c1850* (Manchester: Manchester University Press, 1997), 110–26.
2. A. A. M. Duncan, *Scotland: The Making of the Kingdom*, The Edinburgh History of Scotland Volume 1 (Edinburgh: Oliver & Boyd, 1978 (1975)), 188.
3. Michael Lynch, *Scotland: A New History* (London: Century, 1991), 59.
4. Colin Kidd, 'Gaelic Antiquity and National Identity', *English Historical Review* (1994), 1197–214 (1205).
5. See Derrick McClure, *Why Scots Matters* (Edinburgh: Saltire Society, 1988).
6. Dauvit Broun, 'The Pictish Origins of the Scottish Kinglist', unpublished paper, Glasgow–Strathclyde School of Scottish Studies Traditions of Scotish Culture Seminar, 15 February 2000.
7. Cf. Charles W. J. Withers, *Urban Highlanders* (East Linton: Tuckwell Press, 1998).
8. D. E. R. Watt, 'Education in the Highlands in the Middle Ages', in Loraine MacLean (ed.), *The Middle Ages in the Highlands* (Inverness: Inverness Field Club, 1981), 79–90 (79).
9. John MacInnes, 'Gaelic Poetry and Historical Tradition', in Maclean (1981), 142–63 (144, 155).
10. Allan Macinnes, *Clanship, Commerce and the House of Stuart* (East Linton: Tuckwell Press, 1996), 38.
11. *Ibid.*, 1.
12. William Fergusson, *The Identity of the Scottish Nation* (Edinburgh: Edinburgh University Press, 1998), 306.
13. Macinnes (1996); Leah Leneman, *Living in Atholl* (Edinburgh: Edinburgh University Press, 1986), 44, 168.
14. Cf. Lynch (1991), 66.
15. G. W. S. Barrow, 'The Sources for the History of the Highlands in the Middle Ages', in Maclean (1981), 11–22 (19).
16. George Rosie, 'Museumry and the Heritage Industry', in Ian Donnachie and Chris Whatley (eds), *The Manufacture of Scottish History* (Edinburgh: Polygon, 1992), 157–70.
17. Duncan (1978 (1975)), 1–2.
18. Peter G. B. McNeill and Hector L. MacQueen (eds), *Atlas of Scottish History to 1707* (Edinburgh: University of Edinburgh, 1996), 238.
19. *Ibid.*
20. John Morrill, 'The British Problem, c1534–1707', in Brendan Bradshaw and John Morrill (eds), *The British Problem, c1534–1707* (Basingstoke: Macmillan Press – now Palgrave, 1996), 1–38 (7).
21. Lynch (1991), 68.
22. Duncan (1978 (1975)), 20–22.
23. Tacitus, *Agricola*, tr. H. Mattingley and S. A. Handford (Harmondsworth: Penguin Classics, 1970 (1948)), 80–1.
24. *Ibid.*
25. *Ibid.*, 61.

26. *Ibid.*, 76.
27. Duncan (1978 (1975)), 28.
28. *Ibid.*, 19, 26.
29. Peter Marren, *Grampian Battlefields* (Aberdeen: Aberdeen University Press, 1990), 2.
30. Duncan (1978 (1975)), 36, 37, 40.
31. *Ibid.*, 41, 45, 53, 59, 62, 65.
32. Alfred Smyth, *Warlords and Holy Men: Scotland AD 80–1000* (London: Edward Arnold, 1984), 31, 257.
33. Duncan (1978 (1975)), 53.
34. Smyth (1984), 31.
35. Duncan (1978 (1975)), 61.
36. Smyth (1984), 39–40.
37. Duncan (1978 (1975)), 54.
38. *Ibid.*, 58; Smyth (1984), 258.
39. Broun (2000).
40. Smyth (1984), 258.
41. *Ibid.*, 27; Duncan (1978 (1975)), 64, 65, 90–1; Norman Davies, *The Isles* (London: Macmillan, 1999), 264; Steve Driscoll, 'Scone and its Comparanda', unpublished paper, Glasgow–Strathclyde School of Scottish Studies Traditions of Scottish Culture Seminar, 25 April 2000.
42. Smyth (1984), 215, 218, 258.
43. McNeill and MacQueen (1996), 65.
44. Duncan (1978 (1975)), 81–3.
45. McNeill and MacQueen (1996), 60–1, 65.
46. Marren (1990), 50.
47. Duncan (1978 (1975)), 91, 94.
48. *Ibid.*, 92.
49. Cf. *ibid.*, 93.
50. *Ibid.*; Davies (1999), 254.
51. Smyth (1984), 260.
52. Duncan (1978 (1975)), 94–6.
53. Murray G. H. Pittock, *The Invention of Scotland: The Stuart Myth and the Scottish Identity 1638 to the Present* (London: Routledge, 1991), 27–8.
54. James Anderson, *Scotland Independent* (Edinburgh: n.p., 1705), 18, 263.
55. Duncan (1978 (1975)), 97–8.
56. *Ibid.*, 99; McNeill and MacQueen (1996), 76.
57. Duncan (1978 (1975)), 123–5, 128, 132, 134; Davies (1999), 280.
58. McNeill and MacQueen (1996), 77.
59. Duncan (1978 (1975)), 264, 521–3, 538, 547, 550, 551, 581.
60. McNeill and MacQueen (1996), 30.
61. Gordon Donaldson (ed.), *Scottish Historical Documents* (Edinburgh and London: Scottish Academic Press, 1974 (1970)), 33.
62. Duncan (1978 (1975)), 559.
63. Donaldson (1974 (1970)), *Register of Dunfermline*, 36–7.
64. *Book of Pluscarden*, cited Lynch (1991), 111.
65. G. W. S. Barrow, *Robert Bruce*, 2nd ed. (Edinburgh: Edinburgh University Press, 1976 (1965)), 97, 113, 119, 167–8.

66. Lynch (1991), 112–13.
67. Resolution 155, which created National Tartan Day in the USA in 1998, was linked when it was set up to the Declaration of Arbroath and its connections to the Declaration of Independence.
68. Donaldson (1974 (1970)), 57.
69. Duncan (1978 (1975)), 101, 103–4, 111, 116; *Scottish Parliament factsheet 2* (Edinburgh: The Scottish Office, 1999).
70. Broun (2000) advances this idea of regnal unity as the basis for Scottish nationality.
71. McNeill and MacQueen (1996), 52.
72. Donaldson (1974 (1970)), 177.
73. Duncan (1978 (1975)), 530–1.
74. Macinnes in Maclean (1981), 143; Barrow (1976 (1965)), 69.
75. Lynch (1991), 94.
76. Duncan (1978 (1975)), 126, 141.
77. Fergusson (1998), 26–7.
78. Duncan (1978 (1975)), 182.
79. McNeill and MacQueen (1996), 336.
80. Lynch (1991), 93, 100.
81. *Ibid.*, 94.
82. *Ibid.*, 96, 100, 101, 107.
83. *Ibid.*, 93; Smyth (1984), 230.
84. Lynch (1991), 55–6, 58, 60.
85. Barrow (1976 (1965)), xv, 430.
86. Lynch (1991), 61.
87. Cf. Alexander Broadie, plenary address on Thomas Reid, Reid Conference, University of Aberdeen, 1996.
88. Cf. Murray G. H. Pittock, review of Antoin Murphy, *John Law, Eighteenth-Century Ireland*, forthcoming.
89. Cf. Ken Simpson, *The Protean Scot* (Aberdeen: Aberdeen University Press, 1988).
90. Geoffrey of Monmouth, *Historia Regum Britanniae/The History of the Kings of Britain*, tr. Lewis Thorpe (Harmondsworth: Penguin, 1968 (1966)), 10.
91. W. F. Skene, *Celtic Scotland* (Edinburgh: David Douglas, 1880), 94.
92. Roger Mason, 'Scotching the Brut: Politics, History and National Myth in Sixteenth-Century Britain', in Mason (ed.), *Scotland and England 1286–1815* (Edinburgh: John Donald, 1983), 60–84 (62–3, 66).
93. Fergusson (1998), 14.
94. Skene (1880), 94.
95. Dauvit Broun, 'The Birth of Scottish History', *Scottish Historical Review* (1997), 4–22 (9).
96. Philip O'Leary, *The Prose Literature of the Gaelic Revival, 1881–1921* (Philadelphia: Pennsylvania State University Press, 1994), 179n; Tim Pat Coogan, *Michael Collins* (London: Random House (Arrow), 1991 (1990)), 77.
97. Skene (1880), 128–30.
98. Cf. Archie McKerracher, *Perthshire in History and Legend* (Edinburgh: John Donald, 1988), 32–42.
99. Otta F. Swire, *The Highlands and their Legends* (Edinburgh and London, 1963).

100. MacInnes in Maclean (1981), 142–63.
101. I am indebted to Professor Alexander Broadie for this information.
102. Fergusson (1998), 304–6.
103. Barrow (1976 (1965)), 446n.
104. McNeill and MacQueen (1996), 99.
105. Lynch (1991), 128–30.
106. Donaldson (1974 (1970)), 66.
107. Keith Robbins, *Great Britain* (London and New York: Longman,1998), 4, 5, 8.
108. Cf. Murray G. H. Pittock, *Inventing and Resisting Britain* (New York: St Martin's Press, 1997).
109. Gordon Donaldson, *The Scots Overseas* (London, 1966), 25; David Ditchburn, 'Who are the Scots?', in Paul Dukes (ed.), *Frontiers of European Culture* (Lampeter: Edwin Mellen, 1996), 89–100 (96).
110. Ditchburn (1996), 91, 96.
111. J. S. Smith, 'The Physical Site of Historical Aberdeen' and J. Charles Murray, 'The Archaeological Evidence', in J. S. Smith (ed.), *New Light on Medieval Aberdeen* (Aberdeen: Aberdeen University Press, 1985), 1–19 (4–5, 13, 16, 18).
112. William Watt, *A History of Aberdeen and Banff*, The County Histories of Scotland (Edinburgh and London: W. Blackwood, 1900), 37; W. Douglas Simpson, 'The Region before 1700', in A. C. O'Dell and J. Mackintosh (eds), *The North-East of Scotland* (Aberdeen, BAAS, 1963), 67–86 (81); Elizabeth Ewan, 'The Age of Bon-Accord: Aberdeen in the Fourteenth Century', in Smith (1995), 32–45 (32, 34).
113. Ditchburn (1996), 95.
114. Donaldson (1966), 26.
115. Jonas Berg and Bo Lagercrantz, *Scots in Sweden* (Stockholm: The Nordiska Museet, 1962), 23, 68, 70.
116. Ditchburn (1996), 96, 99.
117. Berg and Lagercrantz (1962), 7, 45.
118. Nicholas Hans, 'Henry Farquharson, Pioneer of Russian Education, 1698–1739', *Aberdeen University Review* XXXVIII (1959–60), 26–9 (27); Murray G. H. Pittock, *Jacobitism* (Basingstoke: Macmillan Press – now Palgrave, 1998), 126; Dimitry Fedosov, *The Caledonian Connection* (Aberdeen: University of Aberdeen, 1996).
119. Ditchburn (1996), 89–90, 91.
120. Cf. Fergusson (1998) for a more comprehensive picture.
121. Barrow (1976 (1965)), 96–9.
122. Ditchburn (1996), 93, 95, 96.
123. Lynch (1991), 101.
124. Cf. Theo van Heijnsbergen, "'Slee' Poetry and Scottish Writing", unpublished paper, Glasgow–Strathclyde School of Scottish Studies Traditions of Scottish Culture Seminar, 29 February 2000; Simon Blackburn, *The Oxford Dictionary of Philosophy* (Oxford: Oxford University Press, 1996 (1994)), 111.
125. Lynch (1991), 104.
126. *Barbour's Bruce*, ed. Matthew P. MacDiarmid and Jane A. C. Stevenson, 3 vols (Edinburgh: Scottish Text Society, 1985), Book I, ll 1 ff, 5, 36, 225–8; Book II, 343–4.

127. I am indebted to the researches of Dr John Durkan for this piece of information.

128. Leslie Macfarlane, *St Machar's Cathedral in the Later Middle Ages* (Aberdeen: St Machar's Cathedral, 1979), 10.

129. Lynch (1991), 106.

130. Council Register 6:27, Aberdeen City Archives.

131. Burgess Regulations 1632–94, p. 27; Kennedy Index, Aberdeen City Archives.

132. Jean Munro, 'The Lordship of the Isles', in Maclean (1981), 23–37 (31).

133. Lynch (1991), 68.

134. *Ibid.*, 161–2.

135. *Ibid.*, 205–7.

136. *Ibid.*, 186–7.

137. Allan White, 'The Reformation in Aberdeen', in Smith (1995), 58–66 (59).

138. Lynch (1991), 187–91, 196, 197.

139. Murray G. H. Pittock, 'Scottish Court Writing and 1603', in Eveline Cruickshanks (ed.), *The Stuart Courts* (Gloucester: Alan Sutton, 2000), 13–25 (20); M. A. Bald, 'The Anglicisation of Scottish Printing', *Scottish Historical Review* 23 (1926), 107–15; M. A. Bald, 'Contemporary References to the Scottish Speech of the Sixteenth Century', *Scottish Historical Review* 25 (1928), 163–79.

140. *Extracts from the Council Register of the Burgh of Aberdeen 1398–1570* (Aberdeen: Spalding Club, 1844), 325–6; Fenton Wyness, *Spots from the Leopard* (Aberdeen: Impulse Books, 1971), 23.

141. Leslie Macfarlane, in John S. Smith (ed.), *Old Aberdeen* (Aberdeen: n.p., 1991), 20; *Registrum Episcopatum Aberdoniensis* (Aberdeen: Spalding Club, 1845), lxvi, lxxxvi, xci.

142. Kennedy Index II:311, Aberdeen City Archives; Agnes Mure Mackenzie, *Scottish Pageant*, 4 vols (Edinburgh and London: Oliver & Boyd, 1946–50), III:103.

143. Cf. Murray G. H. Pittock, *The Myth of the Jacobite Clans* (Edinburgh: Edinburgh University Press, 1999 (1995)), 47.

144. Bruce McLennan, 'The Reformation in the Burgh of Aberdeen', *Northern Scotland* (1975), 119–44 (133).

145. Lynch (1991), 304.

146. Cf. Gordon Donaldson, *Scottish Church History* (Edinburgh: Scottish Academic Press, 1985), 191–203.

147. Watt (1900), 218; D. Macmillan, *The Aberdeen Doctors* (London: Hodder & Stoughton, 1909), 173–4.

148. Cf. Alexander Broadie, plenary address to the Thomas Reid Conference, University of Aberdeen, 1996.

149. John Laird, 'George Dalgarno', *Aberdeen University Review* XXIII (1935–6), 15–31 (19).

150. Donaldson (1985), 191.

151. *Musa Latina Aberdoniensis*, ed. Sir William Duguid Geddes and William Keith Leasle, 3 vols (Aberdeen: New Spalding Club, 1892–1910), I: 180, 219.

152. Mackenzie (1946–50), III: 329.

153. Keith Brown, 'Scottish identity in the seventeenth century', in Brendan Bradshaw and Peter Roberts (eds), *British Consciousness and Identity* (Cambridge: Cambridge University Press, 1998), 236–58 (253).

154. Cf. Pittock, in Cruickshanks (2000), 22, 25.
155. Jenny Wormald, 'The union of 1603', in Roger Mason (ed.), *Scots and Britons* (Cambridge: Cambridge University Press, 1994), 17–40 (23, 24); Davies (1999), 464, 466, 565.
156. Lynch (1991), 239; Davies (1999), 556.
157. J. G. A. Pocock, 'Two kingdoms and three histories?' in Mason (1994), 293–312 (307).
158. Lynch (1991), 237, 239.
159. Brown in Bradshaw and Roberts (1998), 237.
160. Lynch (1991), 243.
161. Macinnes (1996), 58, 89, 92, 94, 100.
162. Lynch (1991), 275.
163. David Stevenson, 'The Early Covenanters and the Federal Union of Britain', in Roger A. Mason (ed.), *Scotland and England 1286–1815* (Edinburgh: John Donald, 1987), 163–81 (164, 177).
164. Macinnes (1996), 60.
165. Colin Kidd, 'Protestantism, constitutionalism and British identity under the later Stuarts', in Bradshaw and Roberts (1998), 321–42 (322).
166. Cf. Pittock (1999 (1995), 71; Edward M. Furgol, *A Regimental History of the Covenanting Armies, 1639–1651* (Edinburgh: John Donald, 1990).
167. Lynch (1991), 283.
168. Derek Hirst, 'The English Republic and the Meaning of Britain', in Bradshaw and Morrill (1996), 192–219 (201, 205, 208).
169. Kidd in Bradshaw and Roberts (1998), 323.
170. Lynch (1991), 287, 295, 308; Davies (1999), 598.
171. *Ibid.*, 288.
172. Murray G. H. Pittock, *Inventing and Resisting Britain: Cultural Identities in Britain and Ireland, 1685–1789* (Basingstoke: Macmillan Press – now Palgrave, 1997), 7.
173. Keith Brown, 'The vanishing emperor: British kingship and its decline, 1603–1707', in Mason (1994), 58–87 (86–7).
174. Lynch (1991); Macinnes (1996), 169.
175. Brown in Mason (1994), 58–87.
176. Pittock (1997), 7, 19.
177. Macinnes (1996), 174.
178. Lynch (1991), 304.
179. *Ibid.*, 309.
180. Andrew Fletcher of Saltoun, *Political Works*, ed. John Robertson (Cambridge: Cambridge University Press, 1997), 40.
181. Lynch (1991), 309.
182. Cf. Cassell's *History of Britain* (London, 1923); Pittock (1991), 27–8.
183. Patricia Dickson, *Red John of the Battles* (London: Sidgwick & Jackson, 1973), 34.
184. John Morrill in Bradshaw and Morrill (1996), 11.
185. Fletcher of Saltoun, *Political Works*, ed. Robertson (1997), xvi, xvii.
186. *Ibid.*, 185.
187. Kidd in Bradshaw and Roberts (1998), 331.
188. *Ibid.*, 332.
189. Dickson (1973), 102.

190. Lynch (1991), 312.
191. Fletcher of Saltoun, *Political Works*, ed. Robertson (1997), 213–14.

Chapter 2

1. Norman Davies, *The Isles* (London: Macmillan, 1999), 865–6; J. G. A. Pocock, 'The New British History in Atlantic Perspective: An Anti-podean Commentary', *American Historical Review* (1999), 490–500 (491).
2. G. B. McNeill and Hector L. McQueen (eds), *Atlas of Scottish History to 1707* (Edinburgh: University of Edinburgh, 1996), 152.
3. Economic historians often tend to see the importance of this dimension to the Union: cf. R. H. Campbell, *Scotland Since 1707: The Rise of an Industrial Society*, 2nd ed. (Edinburgh: John Donald, 1985 (1965)).
4. John Dwyer and Alexander Murdoch, 'Paradigms and Politics: Manners, Morals and the Rise of Henry Dundas, 1770–1784', in John Dwyer, Roger Mason and Alexander Murdoch (eds), *New Perspectives on the Politics and Culture of Early Modern Scotland* (Edinburgh: John Donald, n.d [1983]), 210–48 (217).
5. Daniel Defoe, *An Essay at Removing National Prejudices Against a Union with Scotland* (London: n.p., 1706), Part I: 19.
6. Keith Brown in Brendan Bradshaw and Peter Roberts (eds), *British Consciousness and Identity* (Cambridge: Cambridge University Press, 1998), 236–58 (247).
7. Daniel Defoe, *The Advantages of the Act of Security* (n.p., 1706), 32.
8. Cf. the discussion in Leith Davis, *Acts of Union* (Princeton: Princeton University Press, 1998).
9. Defoe, *An Essay* (1706), Part II: 5, 7.
10. Agnes Mure Mackenzie, *Scottish Pageant*, 4 vols (Edinburgh: Oliver & Boyd, 1946–50), IV:189.
11. P. W. J. Riley, *The Union of England and Scotland* (Manchester: Manchester University Press, 1978), 28, 198.
12. '*Scotland's Ruine*': *Lockhart of Carnwath's Memoirs of the Union*, ed. Daniel Szechi (Aberdeen: Association for Scottish Literary Studies, 1995), 147.
13. Andrew Fletcher of Saltoun, *Political Works*, ed. John Robertson (Cambridge: Cambridge University Press, 1997), xxvi, 213.
14. Anon., *United and Separate Parliaments*, ed. Paul Scott (Edinburgh: Saltire Society, 1982), 16, 18, 22–3.
15. *The Life and Works of Dr Arbuthnot*, ed. George A. Aitken (Oxford: Clarendon Press, 1892), 396–408.
16. Colin Kidd in Bradshaw and Roberts (1998), 336, 341.
17. *Advantages* (1706), 5, 6.
18. Cf. Murray G. H. Pittock, 'The Political Thought of Lord Forbes of Pitsligo', *Northern Scotland* (1996), 73–86; cf. Francis Hutcheson, *Philosophical Writings*, ed. R. S. Downie (London: J. M. Dent/Everyman, 1994), xxxii.
19. Riley (1978), 282–3, 285, 304.

20. *A Discourse of the Necessity and Seasonableness of an unanimous Address for Dissolving the UNION* (n.p., 1715), 2, 5.
21. Norman Allan, *Scotland: the Broken Image* (Ottawa: privately printed, 1983), 10.
22. Keith Brown in Bradshaw and Roberts (1998), 251.
23. Graeme Morton, *Unionist–Nationalism* (East Linton: Tuckwell Press, 1999), 12.
24. Alex Murdoch, *The People Above* (Edinburgh: John Donald, 1980), 27.
25. Morton (1999), 11.
26. '*Scotland's Ruine*' (1995), 160, 177–8, 179.
27. Riley (1978), 284.
28. '*Scotland's Ruine*' (1995), 240.
29. John Gibson, *Playing the Scottish Card: The Franco–Jacobite Invasion of 1708* (Edinburgh: Edinburgh University Press, 1988), 74, 78.
30. Allan (1983), 10.
31. John, Master of Sinclair, *Memoirs of the Insurrection in Scotland in 1715*, ed. Messrs MacKnight and Lang, with notes by Sir Walter Scott, Bart (Edinburgh: Abbotsford Club, 1858), xxi.
32. Cf. Murray G. H. Pittock, *The Myth of the Jacobite Clans* (Edinburgh: Edinburgh University Press, 1999 (1995)).
33. Fletcher of Saltoun (1997), 44.
34. Cf. Pittock (1999 (1995)).
35. '*Scotland's Ruine*' (1995), 210–11.
36. Gibson (1988), 46.
37. Cf. Murray G. H. Pittock, *Jacobitism* (Basingstoke: Macmillan Press – now Palgrave, 1998).
38. Kevin Whelan, *The Tree of Liberty* (Cork: Cork University Press, 1996), 34, 35.
39. Cf. *Letters of George Lockhart of Carnwath*, ed. Daniel Szechi (Edinburgh: Scottish History Society, 1989); Daniel Szechi, *Jacobitism and Tory Politics, 1710–14* (Edinburgh: John Donald, 1984).
40. Patricia Dickson, *Red John of the Battles* (London: Sidgwick & Jackson, 1973), 157–9.
41. Pittock (1998), 35.
42. Alistair and Henrietta Tayler, *1715: The Story of the Rising* (London and Edinburgh: Thomas Nelson, 1936), 311, 313.
43. Sir Charles Petrie, *The Jacobite Movement: The First Phase 1688–1716* (London: Eyre & Spottiswoode, 1932).
44. John Baynes, *The Jacobite Rising of 1715* (London: Cassell, 1970), 29.
45. Daniel Szechi, *The Jacobites* (Manchester: Manchester University Press, 1994), 77.
46. Bruce Lenman, *The Jacobite Cause* (Glasgow: Richard Drew and National Trust for Scotland, 1986), 51, 53.
47. National Library of Scotland (henceforth NLS) MS 17498 f. 145.
48. NLS MS 1012.
49. Taylers (1936), 46, 314.
50. Sinclair (1858), 2, 7.
51. Dickson (1973), 182.
52. Taylers (1936), 60.
53. Petrie (1932), 197, 226.

54. Bruce Lenman, *Integration, Enlightenment and Industrialization: Scotland 1746–1832*. The New History of Scotland 6 (London: Edward Arnold, 1981), 57.
55. *List of Persons Concerned in the Rebellion*, with a Preface by the Earl of Rosebery and Annotations by the Revd Walter Macleod, Publications of the Scottish History Society Volume 8 (Edinburgh: Edinburgh University Press, 1890), ix.
56. Revd W. H. Langhorne, *Reminiscences* (Edinburgh: David Douglas, 1893), 9.
57. Allan Macinnes, *Clanship, Commerce and the House of Stuart, 1603–1788* (East Linton: Tuckwell Press, 1996), 182n.
58. *List of Persons* (1890); Cf. Pittock (1999 (1995)) for a full discussion of numbers and sources.
59. Macinnes (1996), 194.
60. NLS MS 17498 f. 204.
61. Pittock (1998), 99.
62. Colonel James Allardyce (ed.), *Historical Papers Relating to the Jacobite Period 1699–1750*, 2 vols (Aberdeen: New Spalding Club, 1895/6), I: 177, 183, 189.
63. Stuart Reid, *1745: A Military History of the Rising* (Spellmount, 1996), 49.
64. Macinnes (1996), 162.
65. Taylers (1936), 72.
66. Alistair and Henrietta Tayler, *Jacobites of Aberdeenshire and Banffshire in the Rising of 1715* (Edinburgh and London: Oliver & Boyd, 1934), 218 ff.
67. Macinnes (1996), 173.
68. Alastair Livingstone of Bachuil *et al.* (eds), *Muster Roll of Prince Charles Edward Stuart's Army 1745–46* (Aberdeen: Aberdeen University Press, 1984).
69. Seton, Sir Bruce of Ancrum, Bart, and Jean Gordon Arnot, *The Prisoners of the '45*, 3 vols, Scottish History Society (Edinburgh: Edinburgh University Press, 1928/9), II: 258–9.
70. Jane Dawson, 'The Gaidhealtachd and the emergence of the Scottish Highlands', in Bradshaw and Roberts (1998), 259–300 (296).
71. Allardyce (1895/6), I: 166, 169–70.
72. Jean McCann, 'The Military Organization', unpublished Ph.D. thesis (University of Edinburgh, 1963), 55.
73. Rosebery (1890), xv; Pittock (1999 (1995)).
74. Revd J. B. Cronin, *History of the Episcopal Church in the Diocese of Moray* (London: Skeffington & Son, 1889), 94, 121, 122.
75. Macinnes (1996), 174, 176.
76. Daniel Szechi, '"Cam' Ye O'er Frae France?": Exile and the mind of Scottish Jacobitism, 1716–1727', *Journal of British Studies* 37:4 (1998), 357–90.
77. F. W. Robertson, *The Scottish Way 1746–1946* (n.p., 1946), 1.
78. Macinnes (1996), 211–12.
79. Bruce Lenman, *The Jacobite Clans of the Great Glen, 1650–1784* (London: Methuen, 1984), 163; James Anderson, *Sir Walter Scott and History* (Edinburgh: Edina Press, 1981), 24.
80. Macinnes (1996), 169; David Allan, 'Protestantism, presbyterianism and national identity in eighteenth-century Scottish history', in Tony Claydon and Ian McBride (eds), *Protestantism and National Identity: Britain and Ireland c1650–c1850* (Cambridge: Cambridge University Press, 1998), 182–205 (183).

81. Cf. Murray G. H. Pittock, *Poetry and Jacobite Politics in Eighteenth-Century Britain and Ireland* (Cambridge: Cambridge University Press, 1994).

82. Cf. Pittock (1999 (1995)).

83. Gerard Cavan, 'Bonnie Prince Charlie and a' That', in *Jacobite or Covenanter? Which Tradition* (n.p., Scottish Republican Forum, 1994), 37–44 (37).

84. Hugh MacDiarmid, 'A Scots Communist Looks at Bonny Prince Charlie', *Scots Independent* (August 1945), 1.

85. Pittock (1998), 134, 135.

86. Cf. Pittock (1999 (1995)), introduction.

87. *Prisoners of the '45*, II: 14–15.

88. James Boswell, *The Journal of a Tour to the Hebrides*, in Samuel Johnson and Boswell, *A Journey to the Western Islands of Scotland; The Journal of a Tour to the Hebrides*, ed. R. W. Chapman (London and Oxford: Oxford University Press, 1974 [1924]), 196, 210.

89. Cf. the work being done in Professor Tom Devine's Diaspora project at the University of Aberdeen (unpublished plenary address, Eighteenth-Century Scottish Studies Society Conference, University College, Dublin, July 1999).

90. Lenman (1981), 30.

91. James Mitchell, cited in Catriona MacDonald (ed.), *Unionist Scotland 1800–1997* (Edinburgh: John Donald, 1998), 3.

92. Lindsay Paterson, *The Autonomy of Modern Scotland* (Edinburgh: Edinburgh University Press, 1994); TS list of Snells in the collection of the author.

93. Cf. Robin Gilmour, *The Idea of the Gentleman in the Victorian Novel* (London: Allen & Unwin, 1981); Paul Langford, *Public Life and the Propertied Englishman* (Oxford: Oxford University Press, 1991).

94. James Youngson, *The Making of Classical Edinburgh* (Edinburgh: Edinburgh University Press, 1988 (1966)).

95. Cf. John Butt, *Two Hundred Years of Useful Learning* (East Linton: Tuckwell Press, 1996).

96. Anand Chitnis, *The Social Origins of the Scottish Enlightenment* (Edinburgh: Edinburgh University Press, 1986), 66, 70.

97. John Robertson, *The Scottish Enlightenment and the Militia Issue* (Edinburgh: John Donald, 1985), 99.

98. William Ferguson, *The Identity of the Scottish Nation* (Edinburgh: Edinburgh University Press, 1998), 253.

99. 'Hume', *The Blackwell Dictionary of Historians*, ed. John Cannon *et al.* (Oxford: Blackwell, 1988).

100. John Dwyer and Alexander Murdoch in Dwyer, Mason and Murdoch (1983), 210–48.

101. David Hume, *The History of England*, 6 vols (London: A. Millar, 1754), I: 15, 160.

102. *Ibid.*, Vol. I.

103. William Robertson, *The History of Scotland During the Reigns of Queen Mary and King James VI*, 18th ed., 3 vols (London: n.p., 1809), I: Book i.

104. Colin Kidd, 'The Strange Death of Scottish History' revisited: Constructions of the Past in Scotland, c1790–1914', *Scottish Historical Review* (1997), 86–102 (87).

105. Ferguson (1998): Kidd (1997), 93 ff.

106. Robertson (1809), I: Book i.

107. Colin Kidd, 'The canon of patriotic landmarks in Scottish history', *Scotlands* 1 (1994), 1–17 (12).
108. Adam Fergusson, *An Essay on the History of Civil Society* (Cambridge: Cambridge University Press, 1995 (1767)), 7, 26, 61, 75.
109. *Ibid.*, 61, 75, 84, 104–5, 208.
110. Pittock (1999 (1995)), 113–14.
111. Murray G. H. Pittock, *The Invention of Scotland* (London and New York: Routledge, 1991), 90.
112. Andrew D. Hook, 'Scotland and America revisited', in Owen Dudley Edwards and George Shepperson (eds), *Scotland, Europe and the American Revolution* (Edinburgh: Edinburgh University Press, 1976), 83–8 (88).
113. John Prebble, *The King's Jaunt* (London: Collins, 1988), 100, 104, 131, 211, 359.
114. Angus Calder, 'Tartanry and Frolics', *Cencrastus* (New Year 1989), 9–13 (9).
115. Eric Richards, *A History of the Highland Clearances*, 2 vols (London: Croom Helm, 1985), II: 3, 45, 46, 68; Col. David Stewart, *Sketches of the Highlanders of Scotland*, 2 vols (Edinburgh: John Donald, 1977 (1822)), II: 441, 451.
116. Christopher Harvie, 'Scott and the Image of Scotland', in Alan Bold (ed.), *Sir Walter Scott* (London and Totowa, NJ: Barnes & Noble, 1983), 17–42 (31).
117. Cf. Caroline McCracken-Flesher, '*Pro Matria Mori*: Gendered Nationalism and Cultural Death in Scott's "The Highland Widow"', *Scottish Literary Journal* 21:2 (1994), 69–78.
118. Cf. G. Gregory Smith, *Scottish Literature: Character and Influence* (London: Macmillan, 1919).
119. Cf. R. D. S. Jack, *The Road to the Never Land* (Aberdeen: Aberdeen University Press, 1991).
120. Kidd (1997), 93.
121. Ferguson (1998), 303.
122. Allan in Claydon and McBride (1998), 187.

Chapter 3

1. Michael Lynch, *Scotland: A New History* (London: Century, 1991), 433.
2. Murray G. H. Pittock, *Celtic Identity and the British Image* (Manchester: Manchester University Press, 1999), 9.
3. Henry Newbolt, *The Island Race* (London: Elkin Mathews, 1914 (1898)), 54–5.
4. Graeme Morton, *Unionist–Nationalism: Governing Urban Scotland 1830–1860* (East Linton: Tuckwell Press, 1999).
5. Morton (1999), 21, 45, 197.
6. Michael Fry, *Patronage and Principle* (Aberdeen: Aberdeen University Press, 1987), 82.
7. Pittock (1999), 12.
8. Morton (1999), 55.
9. Anand Chitnis, *The Social Origins of the Scottish Enlightenment* (Edinburgh: Edinburgh University Press, 1986), 1–30, 211.

10. Bruce Lenman, *Integration, Enlightenment and Industrialization: Scotland 1746–1832*, The New History of Scotland (London: Edward Arnold, 1981), 43, 81, 95.
11. Cf. work being carried out at the Diaspora project by Professor Tom Devine, University of Aberdeen.
12. Lenman (1981), 65–6.
13. Patrick Mileham, *The Scottish Regiments 1633–1996* (Staplehurst: Spellmount, 1996 (1988)), 7.
14. Pittock (1999), 108.
15. Mileham (1996 (1988)), 66, 156.
16. Pittock (1999), 108.
17. *Ibid.*; National Library of Scotland ACC 9290 (Archie Lamont papers).
18. Stephen Wood, *The Auld Alliance: Scotland and France, the Military Connection* (Edinburgh: Mainstream, 1989), 155.
19. William Allan, *Rose and Thistle* (n.p., 1878), 3, 91, 92, 99. The line means 'woe to the rascals who would stunt the Union'.
20. A. C. Macdonell, *Lays of the Heather* (London: Elliot Stock, 1896), 41–3.
21. Wood (1989), 146.
22. Christopher Harvie, *Scotland and Nationalism* (London: Allen & Unwin, 1977), 40.
23. Fry (1987), 4.
24. Katherine Jean Haldane, 'Imagining Scotland: Tourist Images of Scotland 1770–1914', unpublished Ph.D. thesis, University of Virginia, 1990, 6, 9.
25. Andrew Noble, 'Highland History and Narrative Form in Scott and Stevenson', in Noble (ed.), *Robert Louis Stevenson* (London and Totowa, NJ: Barnes & Noble, 1983), 134–87 (150).
26. For studies of Macpherson's context, see *Edinburgh Review* 93 (1995).
27. Haldane (1990), 30–1, 34, 108.
28. *Ibid.*, 273, 283.
29. Colin Kidd, 'The canon of patriotic landmarks in Scottish history', *Scotlands* 1 (1994), 1–17 (7).
30. Haldane (1990), 298.
31. *Ibid.*, 292–3.
32. Charles W. J. Withers, *Urban Highlanders* (East Linton: Tuckwell Press, 1998), 191.
33. Thomas Tallard, *Glenco, or the Fate of the MacDonalds* (London: n.p., 1840), ix.
34. Pittock (1999), 43; cf. William Donaldson, *The Jacobite Song* (Aberdeen: Aberdeen University Press, 1988).
35. Magnus Maclean, *The Literature of the Highlands*, new edn (Glasgow: Blackie, 1904), 22.
36. Sydney and Olive Checkland, *Industry and Ethos: Scotland 1832–1914*, The New History of Scotland (London: Edward Arnold, 1984), 138, 166.
37. Morton (1999), 116.
38. William Ferguson, *The Identity of the Scottish Nation* (Edinburgh: Edinburgh University Press, 1998), 303.
39. Colin Kidd, '*The Strange Death of Scottish History* revisited: Constructions of the Past in Scotland, c1790–1914', *Scottish Historical Review* (1997), 86–102 (93).

40. Cf. Clive Dewey, ' Celtic Agrarian Legislation and the Celtic Revival: Historicist Implications of Gladstone's Irish and Scottish Land Acts 1870–1886', *Past and Present* (August 1974), 30–70.

41. Peter Berresford Ellis and Seamus MacGhiobhainn, *The Scottish Insurrection of 1820* (London: Gollancz, 1967); Frank Andrew Sherry, *The Rising of 1820* (Glasgow: William Maclellan, n.d.); Colin Kidd, *Subverting Scotland's Past* (Cambridge: Cambridge University Press, 1993), 248–9.

42. Morton (1999), 191, 192.

43. Lynch (1991), 389.

44. Henry W. Meikle, *Scotland and the French Revolution* (Glasgow: James Maclehose, 1912), 67.

45. Lenman (1981), 102.

46. Keith Webb, *The Growth of Nationalism in Scotland* (Glasgow: Molendinar Press, 1977), 32.

47. Morton (1999), 176.

48. John Brims, 'The Scottish "Jacobins", Scottish Nationalism and the British Union', in Roger Mason (ed.), *Scotland and England 1286–1815* (Edinburgh: John Donald, 1987), 247–65 (247, 261).

49. Webb (1977), 33.

50. Brims in Mason (1987), 251, 253, 255.

51. James D. Young, *The Very Bastards of Creation: Scottish International Radicalism 1707–1995* (Glasgow: Clydeside Press, n.d. [1995]), 39.

52. G. Pratt Insh, 'Thomas Muir of Huntershill', National Library of Scotland Adv MS 23.3.30 (Eaglescarnie Papers), Deposit 344, Box 1, 61, 163, 166, 167; Peter Berresford Ellis, *The Celtic Revolution* (Talybont, Ceredigion: Y Lolfa, 1993 (1985)), 44.

53. Meikle (1912), 163, 164, 171.

54. E. W. McFarland, *Ireland and Scotland in the Age of Revolution* (Edinburgh: Edinburgh University Press, 1994), 233, 248 ff.

55. Ibid., 251, 253, 254, 255.

56. Morton (1999), 192.

57. McFarland (1994), 240.

58. Sherry (n.d.), 9, 15–19, 23, 26.

59. Peter Freshwater (ed.), *Sons of Scotia, Raise your Voice!* (Edinburgh: Edinburgh University Library, 1991), 8, 9, 15, 46.

60. Lenman (1981), 45–6.

61. William Gillies (ed.), *Ris A' Bhruthaich: Somhairle MacGill-eain* (Stornoway: Acair, 1985), 51.

62. Iain Fraser Grigor, *Mightier than a lord* (Stornoway: Acair, 1979), 14.

63. Malcolm MacLean and Christopher Carrell, *As an Fhearann* (Edinburgh: Mainstream, 1986), 21.

64. *Ibid.*, 39.

65. John Mercer, *Scotland: The Devolution of Power* (London: John Calder, 1978), 62.

66. Eric Richards, *A History of the Highland Clearances*, 2 vols (London: Croom Helm, 1985), II:239.

67. Withers (1998), 133, 141, 192.

68. Ibid., 133.

69. Colin Kidd, 'Sentiment, race and revival: Scottish identities in the aftermath of Enlightenment', in Laurence Brockliss and David Eastwood (eds), *A Union of Multiple Identities: The British Isles c1750–c.1850* (Manchester and New York: Manchester University Press, 1997), 110–26 (117).
70. *Ibid*.
71. Webb (1997), 34–5.
72. Morton (1999), 140.
73. Fry (1987), 206.
74. Morton (1999), 116, 135, 141; Kidd in Brockliss and Eastwood (1997), 122.
75. Morton (1999), 150; H. J. Hanham, *Scottish Nationalism* (London: Faber, 1969), 151.
76. Morton (1999), 140, 148, 149.
77. *Ibid.*, 152.
78. Hanham (1969), 77.
79. Morton (1999), 153.
80. Fry (1987), 206.
81. Morton (1999), 79, 80–1, 136, 138–9.
82. *Ibid.*, 180.
83. Hanham (1969), 79–80.
84. Murray G. H. Pittock, *The Invention of Scotland* (London and New York: Routledge, 1991), 116.
85. Morton (1999), 146.
86. Kidd in Brockliss and Eastwood (1997), 118.
87. Pittock (1999), 112; I am indebted to my research student, David McMenemy, who is working on national identity in the Irish comunity in Scotland, for the latter reference.
88. Morton (1999), 196; James Mitchell, *Strategies for Self-government: The Campaigns for a Scottish Parliament* (Edinburgh: Polygon, 1996), 303.
89. Webb (1977), 40.
90. Mitchell (1996), 44, 68–9; Fry (1987), 105, 106.
91. Mitchell (1996), 71–3, 303, 304.
92. Hanham (1969), 89; *Fiery Cross* 4 (1901), 5.
93. Hanham (1969), 121; *Fiery Cross* 17 (1905), 2.
94. Legitimist Jacobite League, balance sheet 1898–99, from League pamphlets donated by Theodore Napier, MacBean Collection, Aberdeen University Library; *Fiery Cross* 3 (1901), 5.
95. Pittock (1999), 125; Philip O'Leary, *The Prose Literature of the Gaelic Revival, 1881–1921* (University Park, PA: Penn State University Press, 1994), 67.
96. Pittock (1999), 125.
97. Mitchell (1996), 82.
98. Gordon Bryan (ed.), *Scottish Nationalism and Cultural Identity in the Twentieth Century* (Westport, CT: Greenwood Press, 1984), 10.
99. Hanham (1969), 123, 125; *Fiery Cross* 1 (1901), 3; 11 (1903), 2; 12 (1903), 8.
100. *Fiery Cross* 11 (1903), 6; Webb (1977), 41; Mitchell (1996), 72–3.
101. *Fiery Cross* 3 (1901), 3–4; 6 (1902), 8.
102. Hanham (1969), 95, 126–7.
103. O'Leary (1994), 164, 166.

104. Hanham (1969), 123, 133, 135.
105. *Fiery Cross* 12 (1903), 8.
106. *Fiery Cross* 1 (1901), 2; 4 (1901), 3; 6 (1902), 5; 10 (1903), 5; 12 (1903), 2.
107. *The Jacobite* I:5 (1920), 18.
108. Hanham (1969), 88.
109. *Ibid.*
110. *The Evergreen* (Spring 1895), 9, 131, 133.
111. Mitchell (1996), 26, 27–8.
112. *Ibid.*, 51, 69.
113. Webb (1977), 39.
114. *Glasgow Herald* 1 June 1908; cited Mitchell (1996), 304.
115. Graham Walker and David Officer, 'Scottish Unionism and the Ulster Question', in Catriona MacDonald (ed.), *Unionist Scotland 1800–1997* (Edinburgh: John Donald, 1998), 13–26 (15).
116. Elaine McFarland, *Protestants First* (Edinburgh: Edinburgh University Press, 1990), 213.
117. I. G. C. Hutchinson, *A Political History of Scotland 1832–1924* (Edinburgh: John Donald, 1986), 176.
118. Webb (1977), 40.
119. McFarland (1990), 104, 108–9, 132.
120. Walker and Officer in MacDonald (1998), 20.
121. Mitchell (1996), 73, 305.

Chapter 4

1. Christopher Harvie, *No Gods and Precious Few Heroes: Scotland 1914–80* (London: Edward Arnold, 1981), 24 (National War Memorial White Paper of 1920).
2. *Ibid.*, 17, 22.
3. *Ibid.*, vii, viii, 1.
4. James D. Young, *The Very Bastards of Creation: Scottish International Radicalism 1707–1995* (Glasgow: Clydeside Press, n.d. [1995]), 200–1.
5. H. J. Hanham, *Scottish Nationalism* (London: Faber, 1969), 133.
6. James Mitchell, *Strategies for Self-Government: The Campaigns for a Scottish Parliament* (Edinburgh: Polygon, 1996), 74–5, 82, 306.
7. Richard Finlay, *Independent and Free: Scottish Politics and the Origins of the Scottish National Party 1918–1945* (Edinburgh: John Donald, 1994), 30–1, 39.
8. Young (1995), 201–2.
9. Finlay (1994), 85.
10. Mitchell (1996), 83.
11. *Ibid.*, 79.
12. Douglas Young, *The Treaty of Union Between Scotland and England 1707*, 3rd edn (Glasgow: Scottish Secretariat, 1955), 27–8.
13. Keith Webb, *The Growth of Nationalism in Scotland* (Glasgow: Molendinar Press, 1977), 45.

14. Mitchell (1996), 307.
15. Harvie (1981), 94.
16. *Scots Independent* (herafter *SI*) I:1 (editorial).
17. Mitchell (1996), 83–4, 177.
18. Francis Russell Hart and J. B. Pick, *Neil M. Gunn: A Highland Life* (London: Murray, 1981), 108.
19. *SI* II:9, 129, 131–2; II:12, 169.
20. Mitchell (1996), 188, 307.
21. Hanham (1969), 157.
22. Mitchell (1996), 189.
23. Webb (1977), 50.
24. Harvie (1981), 99.
25. Webb (1977), 51.
26. Finlay (1994), 94.
27. Mitchell (1996), 181.
28. *SI* VI (1931), 17, 25.
29. Mitchell (1996), 115, 122, 182, 183, 184, 186, 187; Alan Bold, *MacDiarmid* (London: Murray, 1988), 228; *SI* IV, 100.
30. Hanham (1969), 175.
31. *SI* (18 January 1964), 1–2.
32. Joy Hendry, *The Way Forward*, pamphlet (Edinburgh, 1980), 15.
33. Mitchell (1996), 25.
34. Peter Berresford Ellis, *Celtic Dawn* (London: Constable, 1993), 164.
35. *SI* VIII (1933–4), 25; Michael Parnell, *Eric Linklater* (London: Murray, 1984), 113.
36. Parnell (1984), 123, 136.
37. *Ibid.*, 345.
38. Compton Mackenzie, *Prince Charlie* (London: Nelson, 1938 (1932)), 75.
39. *SI* IV (1930), 7, 85; VII (1932–3), 30.
40. Hanham (1969), 155.
41. *SI* III (c1929), 89–90; August 1945, 1.
42. Norman Allan, *Scotland: the Broken Image* (Ottawa: privately published, 1983), 28.
43. Hugh MacDiarmid, 'The Upsurge of Scottish Nationalism', in *Selected Essays of Hugh MacDiarmid*, ed. Duncan Glen (London: Jonathan Cape, 1969), 228–32 (228).
44. *SI* NS 4: 2 (1936), 3; III (1929), 1, 1.
45. *SI* VII (1932), 83.
46. Allan (1983), 29–30.
47. *SI* NS 7:12 (1940), 1.
48. Finlay (1994), 84, 96.
49. *SI* VII (1932), 172; VIII (1933), 12.
50. *SI* VII (1932), 124–5.
51. *SI* VI (1931), 151, 158.
52. Hart and Pick (1981), 95.
53. Richard Price, *Neil M. Gunn* (Edinburgh: Edinburgh University Press, 1991), 55, 57.
54. *SI* V (1930), 5, 77.
55. Finlay (1994), 84.

56. Cf. *SI* V (1930), 10, 151.
57. 'William Wallace and *This* War', National Library of Scotland Acc 9290 (Archie Lamont papers).
58. *SI* VII (1932), 188; VIII, 74, 122, 153.
59. Cf. L. M. G., 'The Elusive Gael – And the Highland Delusion', *SI* II:6 (1928), 94–5.
60. *SI* NS 3:2 (1936), 6–7.
61. Hart and Pick (1981), 78, 109–11.
62. *SI* NS 1:4 (1935), 1; 2:2 (1936), 12.
63. *SI* NS 8:3 (1938), 8.
64. Harvie (1981), 107.
65. Richard Finlay, 'Unionism and the Dependency Culture', in Catriona MacDonald (ed.), *Unionist Scotland 1800–1997* (Edinburgh: John Donald, 1998), 100–16 (105).
66. Mitchell (1996), 309.
67. *Ibid.*, 195.
68. SNP: Miscellaneous Pamphlets (Aberdeen University Library Per320 Sco).
69. Douglas Young, *An Appeal to Scots Honour* (n.p., 1944), 2.
70. Webb (1977), 63.
71. Peter Berresford Ellis, *The Celtic Revolution* (Talybont, Ceredigion: Y Lolfa, 1993 (1985)), 86.
72. Mitchell (1996), 44–5, 85, 309.
73. William L. Miller, *The End of British Politics?* (Oxford: Oxford University Press, 1981), 10.
74. *The Coronation Stone*, SNP Misc Pamphlets AUL Per 320 Sco.
75. Miller (1981), 2, 4, 25.
76. *SI* IV: 8, 100.
77. Mitchell (1996), 115, 122, 144, 148, 149, 152, 155.
78. Ibid., 155, 157, 288.
79. Hanham (1969), 162, 179.
80. Mitchell (1996), 268.
81. *Ibid.*, 309.
82. *SI* October 1947, 1; January 1948, 4.
83. Archie Lamont Papers, NLS Acc 9290.
84. Mitchell (1996), 311.
85. Miller (1981), 33.
86. Mitchell (1996), 199–200, 211.
87. *SI* 11 November 1967, 1.
88. *SI* 2 March 1968, 8; 1 June 1968, 4.
89. *SI* 27 January 1968.
90. Mitchell (1996), 315.
91. *Ibid.*, 312–16.
92. Harvie (1981), 82, 161.
93. Tom Nairn, 'Old Nationalism and New Nationalism', in Gordon Brown (ed.), *The Red Paper on Scotland* (Edinburgh: EUSPB, 1975), 22–57 (24).
94. Brown (1975), 18; Bob Tait, 'The Left, the SNP, and Oil', in *ibid.*, 125–33 (131).
95. Harvie (1981), 165.
96. Webb (1977), 75, 81, 86, 89, 95.
97. Harvie (1981), 148.

98. Miller (1981), 60.
99. Finlay in MacDonald (1998), 111, 112, 113.
100. Mitchell (1996), 51, 69.
101. George Rosie, 'Who's got their snouts in the trough', *Sunday Herald*, 12 March 2000.
102. Finlay in MacDonald (1998), 113.
103. James Mitchell, 'Contemporary Unionism', in MacDonald (1998), 117–39 (122, 136).
104. Mitchell (1996), 293, 295, 297, 298, 299.
105. Andrew Murray Scott and Ian Macleay, *Britain's Secret War: Tartan Terrorism and the Anglo-American State* (Edinburgh: Mainstream, 1990), 82, 90, 95, 127.
106. Minutes of the Patriot Group Meeting, 8 July 1979, on loan to the author.
107. Wood folder 26, Wendy Wood papers, National Library of Scotland.
108. Arnold Kemp, *The Hollow Drum* (Edinburgh: Mainstream, 1993), 118; New DNB article on Wood by the author, forthcoming.
109. Mitchell (1996), 320–1; *Hansard* 945 (2 March 1978), 705, 726.
110. Mitchell (1996), 321.
111. *Hansard* 957 (6 November 1978), 103, 499.
112. Mitchell (1996), 100–1, 321, 322.
113. *Ibid.*, 47.
114. *Ibid.*, 48.
115. Mitchell in MacDonald (1998), 128.
116. Scott and Mcleay (1990), 114–16, 124–5.
117. Mitchell (1996), 225–6, 245.
118. *Scottish Standard* (March 1935), 7–8; Gordon Bryan (ed.), *Scottish Nationalism and Cultural Identity in the Twentieth Century* (Westport, CT: Greenwood Press, 1984), 22.
119. *SI* VII (1932), 84.
120. *SI* II:12, 173 ff; NS 5:4, 6.
121. *Scottish Opinion* (November 1947), 11; Bryan (1984), 40.
122. Mitchell (1996), 193–4.
123. *SI* 18 May 1957, 4; 12 August 1961, 1, 4.
124. *The Economist* (6–12 November 1999), 'Undoing Britain?' survey, 4.
125. Mitchell (1996), 326.
126. Cf. new DNB article on Wendy Wood, forthcoming.
127. *Sunday Herald election 99*, 4 April 1999, 11.
128. *The Herald*, 15 April 1999, 6.
129. Mitchell (1996), 49, 61.
130. *SI* 13 April 1968, 5; *The Economist* (6–12 November 1999).
131. *The Herald*, 15 April 1999, 6.

Chapter 5

1. Murray G. H. Pittock, *The Invention of Scotland: the Stuart Myth and the Scottish Identity, 1638 to the Present* (London and New York: Routledge, 1991), 162.

2. For a detailed political picture of the 1970s, see James Mitchell, *Strategies for Self- Government* (Edinburgh: Polygon, 1996).

3. Joseph Bradley, *Sport, Culture, Politics and Scottish Society* (Edinburgh: John Donald, 1998), 155.

4. Joseph Bradley, *Ethnic and Religious Identity in Modern Scotland* (Aldershot: Avebury, 1995), xi, 37, 41.

5. Ibid., 47, 57, 58, 61–2.

6. Ibid., 69.

7. Ibid., 64–7, 124.

8. Cf. Bradley (1998).

9. Elaine MacFarland, *Protestants First* (Edinburgh: Edinburgh University Press, 1990), 213, 217.

10. *Herald*, 23 March 1992, 4.

11. Iain Paterson, 'Leakage from the faith', *The Herald*, 31 March 2000, 17.

12. Magnus Linklater and Robin Denniston (eds), *Anatomy of Scotland* (Edinburgh and New York: Chambers, 1992), 78, 91.

13. Jeremy Peat and Stephen Boyle, *An Illustrated Guide to the Scottish Economy* (London: Duckworth, 1999), 111.

14. *Herald*, 22 January 2000, 1.

15. Linklater and Denniston (1992), 122.

16. *Sunday Herald*, 30 January 2000, 25.

17. Linklater and Denniston (1992), 122, 131, 133, 134, 144.

18. George Rosie, 'Who's got their snouts in the trough?', *Sunday Herald: Seven Days*, 12 March 2000, 1.

19. Peat and Boyle (1999), 1.

20. Neil Hood in Peat and Boyle (1999), 38–53 (38).

21. Peat and Boyle (1999), 3, 4, 7, 12, 17, 82–3; Hood at 44, 49.

22. Ibid., 54–85, 76.

23. Ibid., 21, 23, 55–7, 76–7.

24. Charles Jedrej and Mark Nuttall, *White Settlers* (orig. pub. Australia; Luxembourg: Harwood Academic Press, 1996), 129, 168.

25. Christopher Harvie, *Scotland and Nationalism*, 3rd ed. (London: Routledge, 1998 (1977)).

26. *Sunday Herald*, 20 February 2000.

27. *The Economist* (6–12 November 1999), 'Undoing Britain?' supplement.

28. Jock Stein (ed.), *Scottish Self-Government: Some Christian Viewpoints* (Edinburgh: Handsel Press, 1989), 1.

29. Cf. Preface to Christopher Harvie, *Cultural Weapons* (Edinburgh: Polygon, 1982).

30. Tom Nairn, *After Britain* (London: Granta, 2000), 205, 207 for a concerned discussion of this kind of inflammatory journalism.

31. Norman Davies, *The Isles* (London: Macmillan Press – now Palgrave, 1999), xxxiii.

32. Stuart Trotter, 'A question of status', *Herald*, 10 March 2000, 7.

33. *The Times*, 28 March 1992, 12.

34. Michael Settle, 'Hague beats the drum for England', *Herald*, 31 March 2000, 6.

35. Ian Bell (ed.), *Peripheral Visions* (Cardiff: University of Wales Press, 1995), 24.

36. Rosie, 'Who's got their snouts in the trough?' (*Sunday Herald*, 12 March 2000).

37. Davies (1999), xxvii.

38. Cf. Angus Calder, 'Scott and Goethe: Romanticism and Classicism', in *Cencrastus* 13 (1983), 25–8, and the tendency of exhibitions up to and including '*O Caledonia!*' (Scottish National Portrait Gallery, 1999) to undermine Scottish history by a trivialization posing as an exposé of its 'myths'.

39. Murray G. H. Pittock, *The Myth of the Jacobite Clans* (Edinburgh: Edinburgh University Press, 1999 (1995)), 118.

40. SCCC report, *Scottish Culture and the Curriculum*, 1998.

41. *The Herald*, 4 May 1999, 19.

42. *The Times Education Supplement (Scotland)*, 26 June 1998.

43. Ian Bell, cited in Nairn (2000), 259.

44. *Ibid.*, 241.

45. *Ibid.*, 259.

46. James MacMillan, 'Desire for reconciliation', *The Herald*, 31 March 2000, 17.

SELECT BIBLIOGRAPHY

Anderson, Benedict. *Imagined Communities*. London: Verso, 1991 (1983).

Barrow, G. W. S. *Robert the Bruce and the Scottish Identity*. Tillicoultry: Saltire Society, 1984.

——. *Robert Bruce*. 3rd ed. Edinburgh: Edinburgh University Press, 1985.

Bradshaw, Brendan and Peter Roberts, eds. *British Consciousness and Identity*. Cambridge: Cambridge University Press, 1998.

Brockliss, Laurence and Eastwood, David, eds. *A Union of Multiple Identities: the British Isles c1750–c1850*. Manchester: Manchester University Press, 1997.

Broun, Dauvit. 'The Birth of Scottish History', *Scottish Historical Review* (1997), 4–22.

Brown, Alice *et al.* eds. *Politics and Society in Scotland*. Basingstoke: Macmillan Press – now Palgrave, 1996.

Checkland, Sydney and Olive. *Industry and Ethos: Scotland 1832–1914*. The New History of Scotland 7. London: Edward Arnold, 1984.

Chitnis, Anand. *The Social Origins of the Scottish Enlightenment*. Edinburgh: Edinburgh University Press, 1986.

Claydon, Tony and McBride, Ian, eds. *Protestantism and National Identity: Britain and Ireland c1650–c1850*. Cambridge: Cambridge University Press, 1998.

Davies, Norman. *The Isles*. London: Macmillan, 1999.

Devine, Tom. *Scotland 1700–2000*. London: Allen Lane, 1999.

Donaldson, Gordon. *Scottish Church History*. Edinburgh: Scottish Academic Press, 1985.

——. ed. *Scottish Historical Documents*. Edinburgh and London: Scottish Academic Press, 1974 (1970).

Donnachie, Ian and Whatley, Chris, eds. *The Manufacture of Scottish History*. Edinburgh: Polygon, 1992.

Duncan, A. A. M. *Scotland: The Making of the Kingdom*. The Edinburgh History of Scotland Volume 1. Edinburgh: Oliver & Boyd, 1978 (1975).

Ferguson, William. *The Identity of the Scottish Nation*. Edinburgh: Edinburgh University Press, 1998.

Finlay, Richard. *Independent and Free: Scottish Politics and the Origins of the Scottish National Party 1918–1945*. Edinburgh: John Donald, 1994.

Fletcher of Saltoun, Andrew, *Political Works*, ed. John Robertson. Cambridge: Cambridge University Press, 1997.

Fry, Michael. *Patronage and Principle*. Aberdeen: Aberdeen University Press, 1987.

Gibson, John. *Playing the Scottish Card: The Franco-Jacobite Invasion of 1708*. Edinburgh: Edinburgh University Press, 1988.

Harvie, Christopher. *No Gods and Precious Few Heroes: Scotland 1914–80*. New History of Scotland 8. London: Edward Arnold, 1981.

———. *Scotland and Nationalism*. 3rd ed. London: Allen & Unwin, 1998.

Hechter, Michael. *Internal Colonialism*. London: Routledge & Kegan Paul, 1975.

Hutchinson, John and Smith, Anthony D., eds. *Nationalism*. Oxford and New York: Oxford University Press, 1994.

Kidd, Colin. *Subverting Scotland's Past*. Cambridge: Cambridge University Press, 1993.

———. 'The canon of patriotic landmarks in Scottish history', *Scotlands* 1 (1994), 1–17 (12).

———. 'Antiquity and National Identity', *English Historical Review* (1994), 1197–1214 (1205).

———. '*The Strange Death of Scottish History* revisited: Constructions of the Past in Scotland, c1790–1914', *Scottish Historical Review* (1997), 86–102 (87).

Lenman, Bruce. *Integration, Enlightenment and Industrialization: Scotland 1746–1832*. The New History of Scotland 6. London: Edward Arnold, 1981.

'Scotland's Ruine': Lockhart of Carnwath's Memoirs of the Union. Ed. Daniel Szechi with an introduction by Paul Scott. Aberdeen: Association for Scottish Literary Studies, 1995.

Lynch, Michael. *Scotland: A New History*. London: Century, 1991.

McClure, Derrick. *Why Scots Matters*. Edinburgh: Saltire Society, 1988.

McCrone, David. *Understanding Scotland: The Sociology of a Stateless Nation*. London: Routledge, 1992.

MacDonald, Catriona, ed. *Unionist Scotland 1800–1997*. Edinburgh: John Donald, 1998.

McFarland, E. W. *Ireland and Scotland in the Age of Revolution*. Edinburgh: Edinburgh University Press, 1994.

Macinnes, Allan. *Clanship, Commerce and the House of Stuart*. East Linton: Tuckwell Press, 1996.

MacLean, Loraine, ed. *The Middle Ages in the Highlands*. Inverness: Inverness Field Club, 1981.

McNeill, Peter G. B. and MacQueen, Hector L., eds. *Atlas of Scottish History to 1707*. Edinburgh: University of Edinburgh, 1996.

Mason, Roger, ed. *Scotland and England 1286–1815*. Edinburgh: John Donald, 1987.

———, ed. *Scots and Britons*. Cambridge: Cambridge University Press, 1994.

Miller, William L. *The End of British Politics?* Oxford: Oxford University Press, 1981.

Mitchell, James, *Strategies for Self-government: The Campaigns for a Scottish Parliament*. Edinburgh: Polygon, 1996.

Morgan, Roger, ed. *Regionalism in European Politics*. London: Policy Studies Institute, 1986.

Morris, Angela and Morton, Graeme. *Locality, Community and Nation*. London: Hodder & Stoughton, 1998.

Morton, Graeme. *Unionist–Nationalism*. East Linton: Tuckwell Press, 1999.

Muir, Edwin. *Scottish Journey*. With an Introduction by T. C. Smout. Edinburgh: Mainstream, 1979 (1935).

Nairn, Tom. *The Break-Up of Britain*. London: NLB, 1977.

———. *After Britain*. London: Granta, 2000.

Osmond, John. *The Divided Kingdom*. London: Constable, 1988.

Paterson, Lindsay. *The Autonomy of Modern Scotland*. Edinburgh: Edinburgh University Press, 1994.

Peat, Jeremy and Boyle, Stephen. *An Illustrated Guide to the Scottish Economy*. London: Duckworth, 1999.

Pittock, Murray G. H. *Inventing and Revisiting Britain*. Basingstoke: Macmillan Press – now Palgrave, 1997.

———. *Celtic Identity and the British Image*. Manchester: Manchester University Press, 1999.

Pocock, J. G. A., 'The New British History in Atlantic Perspective: An Antipodean Commentary', *American Historical Review* (April 1999), 490–500.

Prebble, John. *The King's Jaunt*. London: Collins, 1988.

Riley, P. W. J. *The Union of England and Scotland*. Manchester: Manchester University Press, 1978.

CHRONOLOGY

84: Battle of Mons Graupius. Agricola defeats Caledonians under Calgacus, possibly at Bennachie.

142: Antonine Wall marks limit of Roman power on the Forth–Clyde line. After 200 it is in general only operational further south.

c.400: St Ninian converts the southern Picts.

before 500: the Scottish kingdom of Dal Ríata founded in Kintyre.

521–97: Life of St Columba.

c.550–600: *The Gododdin*, narrating an Edinburgh-based British war band's attack on the Angles at Catterick.

600: Anglian occupation of Lothian.

650: Anglians in southern Fife and Galloway.

681: Northumbrian bishop at Abercorn.

685: Battle of Nechtansmere or Dunnichen Moss. Brudei Mac Bili defeats Ecgfrith's Northumbrian army, thus halting Anglian intrusion beyond Forth.

729–61: Oengus MacFergus first to unite Scotland between the Great Glen and Forth.

731: Northumbrian bishopric set up at Whithorn in Galloway.

752: Northumbrians conquer the plain of Kyle.

794: First Norse raid.

800s: Heavy Scandinavian settlement in the north and west.

843–47: Kenneth MacAlpin unites the Picts and Scots.

c.860: Donald I promulgates the first laws of Scotland.

871: Dumbarton taken by the Vikings.

889: British nobility leave Strathclyde for Gwynedd after attack by Donald II.

900–43: Reign of Constantine II. Limited expansion south of Forth.

918: St Columba's staff carried at the Battle of Corbridge as 'apostle' of the 'men of Scotland'.

934: Athelstan raids Scotland by sea as far as Dunottar.

937: Battle of Brunanburgh. Constantine and his allies defeated by Athelstan.

945: King Edmund of England cedes 'Cumbria' to Malcolm I.

954: King Indulf gains Edinburgh from Northumbria.

973: King Edgar of England cedes Lothian to Kenneth II.

by 1000: Northumbria reoccupies Lothian.

1018: Battle of Carham. Victory by Malcolm II sets Scotland's border on the Tweed.

173

1031: Malcolm II submits to Cnut.

1058: Macbeth killed at Lumphanan.

1094: Duncan II established on the throne by William Rufus, only to be driven out by Donald Bán. First surviving Scottish royal charter.

1097: Edgar established on the throne by William Rufus.

1114: David maries Maud, daughter of the Earl of Northumbria.

1119: Callixtus II supports claim of Archbishop of York to jurisdiction over Scotland.

1124–53: Reign of David I. Significant Norman settlement in Scotland, which is territorially at its greatest extent: David controls Northumbria 50 miles south of Newcastle.

1138: Battle of the Standard: defeat of the Scottish forces at Northallerton.

1151: Last mainland Norse raid on Aberdeen.

1174: William the Lion accepts English overlordship by the terms of the Treaty of Falaise.

1176: Pope Alexander III accepts that the archdiocese of York has no established right over Scotland.

1189: Falaise cancelled by the Quitclaim of Canterbury.

1216: Alexander II's forces reach Dover as part of the rebellion against John's rule in England.

1218: The *Filia Specialis* Bull of Honorius III frees Scotland from subjection to any archbishop, being 'subject to the apostolic see as a special daughter, with no intermediary'.

1235: First sitting of a parliament in Scotland.

1237: Treaty of York: Alexander II resigns his claims to the northern counties of England.

1251: Papacy rejects an English petition requiring Henry III's consent for the coronation of a Scottish king.

1263: Battle of Largs: victory by Alexander III's forces over Norway.

1266: Treaty of Perth. Norway cedes the Western Isles and Man to Scotland.

1266–1308: Life of the Blessed Duns Scotus.

1270: Approximate date of birth of William Wallace.

1274: Birth of Robert I, the Bruce.

1278: Alexander III declines to give homage to Edward I for Scotland.

1286: St Andrew recorded as the patron saint of the Scottish nation.

1292: Following the failure of the succession, Edward I, having previously secured the submission of the claimants, appoints John Baliol king.

1295: Treaty between Scotland and France signed: beginning of the Auld Alliance.

1296: Edward I invades Scotland and deposes King John.

1296–1338: The Wars of Independence.

1297: Battle of Stirling Bridge, 11 September. Wallace and Andrew de Moray victorious over English army under the Earl of Surrey.

1298: Battle of Falkirk. Edward I defeats Wallace.

1305: William Wallace hanged and quartered in London.

1306: Robert I crowned.

1314: Battle of Bannockburn, 23 June. Edward II's army destroyed by Bruce.

1315: Edward Bruce lands at Larne.

1316: Edward Bruce High King of Ireland.

1318: Edward Bruce killed near Dundalk.

1320: Declaration of Arbroath.

1326: Representation of the Commons in the Scottish Estates.

1328: Treaty of Edinburgh–Northampton and recognition of Scottish sovereignty.

1329: Death of Robert I. Accession of David II.

1332: Battle of Dupplin. English victory leads to Edward Baliol being crowned at Scone and controlling southern Scotland with English support.

1335: Andrew de Moray (son of the victor of Stirling Bridge) defeats a Baliol army near Ballater, and by 1337 has recovered almost all Scotland.

1355: Galloway becomes the last Scottish diocese to be free of the metropolitan control of York.

1363: First proposals for Anglo-Scottish union retain Scottish political independence.

1375–77: Archdeacon John Barbour's *The Bruce* written.

1390: The Wolf of Badenoch sacks Elgin Cathedral.

1410: Foundation of the University of St Andrews.

1411: Battle of Harlaw.

1421: Battle of Baugé: Scottish army under the Earl of Buchan defeats English army under Duke of Clarence. Buchan made Constable of France.

1451: Foundation of the University of Glasgow.

1455: Mons Meg used at siege of Threave. Beginning of low-key arms race.

1462: Treaty of Westminster–Ardtornish: Lord of the Isles allies with England.

1468–72: Annexation of the earldom of Orkney and lordship of Shetland.

c.1470: Blin Hary's *Wallace*.

1472: St Andrews becomes an archbishopric.

1482: England captures Berwick.

1486–1568: Life of Robert Carver.

1492: Glasgow an archbishopric.

1495: Foundation of King's College, Aberdeen.

1496: 'Education Act': first attempt to develop universal education among the sons of freeholders.

1513: Battle of Flodden: Scotland's worst military defeat.

1532: Establishment of College of Justice by James V.

1543: Treaty of Greenwich agrees marriage of Mary to Edward, Prince of Wales, 1 July. Repudiated by the Scottish Parliament, 11 December.

1544: Earl of Hertford invades Scotland to try to force Mary to marry Edward, Prince of Wales.

1546: George Wishart burnt; Cardinal Beaton murdered.

1550: Scotland defended against further English aggression by French troops.

1558: Mary marries the Dauphin and subsequently becomes Queen of France.

1559: The Lords of the Congregation and their allies begin a militant campaign for reform in Scotland.

1560: The principal date of the Reformation in Scotland. Reformers make alliance with England under the terms of the Treaty of Berwick. Foundation of Marischal College, Aberdeen.

1561–67: Reign of Mary in Scotland. She flees to England in 1568.

1583: Foundation of the University of Edinburgh.

1592: Act of Parliament authorizing Presbyterian church government.

1603: James VI (1567–1625) becomes King of England.

1604–7: Attempts to promote Anglo-Scottish Union fail.

1606: Restoration of bishops.

1615: Martyrdom of St John Ogilvie, Glasgow.

1638–51: The National Covenant and the War of Three Kingdoms.

1643: Solemn League and Covenant. Possibility of 'a federal Britain'.

1644–5: The Marquess of Montrose briefly wins Scotland back for the king.

1650: Charles II crowned King of Scots at Scone.

1651: Following defeats at Dunbar, Hamilton (1650), Inverkeithing and Worcester (1651), Scotland incorporated into the Commonwealth.

1652–1713. Life of Andrew Fletcher of Saltoun

1660–62: Restoration of Scottish law, Parliament and Privy Council; re-establishment of Episcopacy.

1671–1729: Life of John Law.

1679: Murder of Archbishop Sharp on Magus Muir near St Andrews.

1679–82: James intermittently holds court at Holyrood as Duke of Albany and York.

1688–1766: Life of James VIII and III ('The Old Pretender').

1689: Scottish Convention's Claim of Right. Jacobite rising under Viscount Dundee. Bishops abolished in the established Church of Scotland.

1695: Establishment of Bank of Scotland and Company of Scotland.

1703–04: Act anent Peace and War; Act of Security.

1707: Union takes effect on 1 May.

1708: Scottish Privy Council abolished. Attempted Jacobite rising.

1710–96: Life of Thomas Reid.

1711–76: Life of David Hume.

1715: Jacobite rising under the Earl of Mar, aiming to break the Union and restore James VIII.

1719: Battle of Glenshiel: defeat of Jacobite rising supported by Spanish troops.

1720–88: Life of Prince Charles Edward Stuart ('The Young Pretender').

1723–90: Life of Adam Smith.

1723–1816: Life of Adam Fergusson.

1725: Malt Tax riots, Glasgow. First circulating library in UK at Edinburgh.

1728–99: Life of Joseph Black.

1736: Porteous Riots, Edinburgh.

1736–96: Life of James Macpherson.

1736–1819: Life of James Watt.

1739: MacDonald of Sleat and MacLeod of Dunvegan carry out experimental 'clearance' in Skye.

1745: Jacobite rising led by Prince Charles Edward Stuart. Its supporters aim to restore King James, end the Union and re-establish the Scottish Episcopal Church.

1746: Battle of Culloden: defeat of the Jacobite army.

1747: End of heritable jurisdictions and suspension of the Secretaryship of State for Scotland; widespread anti-Jacobite reforms.

1758: Public library in Montrose.

1759–96: Life of Robert Burns.

1765–98: Life of Thomas Muir, radical patriot.

1768: The *Encyclopaedia Britannica* published at Edinburgh.

1769: Glasgow surpasses 50 per cent of British tobacco trade.

1771–1832: Life of Sir Walter Scott.

1780: Foundation of Scottish Society of Antiquaries.

1780s: First modern Highland Games.

1783: Foundation of Royal Society of Edinburgh.

1791–1862: Life of Robert Knox, made famous by Burke and Hare.

1798: Rising in Ireland.

1805: General Sir John Moore dies at Corunna.

1814–20: Peak years of the Sutherland Clearances.

1815: Publication of *Waverley*.

1820: The 'Rising' or 'Radical Insurrection'.

1822: George IV's visit to Edinburgh.

1827: Scottish affairs entrusted to the Home Office.

1838–1914: Life of John Muir, founder of the National Parks movement.

1842: Queen Victoria's first visit to Scotland.

1843: The Disruption.

1847–1922: Life of Alexander Graham Bell.

1850–94: Life of Robert Louis Stevenson.

1850: Adoption of Balmoral as royal residence.

1853: Launch of the National Association for the Vindication of Scottish Rights.

1854–1941: Life of Sir James Frazer.

1857–8: Field Marshal Lord Clyde suppresses the Indian Mutiny.

1868–1928: Life of Charles Rennie Mackintosh.

1869: Wallace Monument completed at Stirling.

1884: Almost two million acres in Scotland given over to deer.

1885: Restoration of Scottish Secretaryship and establishment of Scottish Office. Establishment of the Napier Commission.

1886: Foundation of Scottish Home Rule Assocation.

1886–1946: Life of John Logie Baird.

1891: First Scottish League competition.

1892–1978: Life of Christopher Murray Grieve ('Hugh MacDiarmid').

1894: Establishment of Scottish Grand Committee.

1901: First Pan–Celtic Congress, Dublin.

1904–61: Life of John MacCormick.

1904: Foundation of Scottish National League.

1913: Scottish Home Rule Bill.

1919: 'Bolshevist rising' in Glasgow.

1926–28: Formation of the National Party of Scotland.

1931: Foundation of the National Trust for Scotland.

1932: Formation of the Scottish Party.

1934: National Party of Scotland and Scottish Party unite to form Scottish National Party (SNP).

1936: Foundation of the Saltire Society.

1937: Scottish Office moved to Edinburgh.

1941: Scottish Council of State; Scottish Grand Committee can meet in Scotland.

1945: Robert Macintyre wins Motherwell for the SNP at a by-election.

1946: Scottish Council for Development and Industry and Scottish Tourist Board set up.

1947: Scottish Claim of Right put to the United Nations.

1948: White Paper on Scottish Affairs suggests significant administrative devolution.

1949–52: MacCormick and others put forward a Scottish Covenant for Home Rule, which gains two million signatures.

1950: Ian Hamilton and others remove the Stone of Destiny from Westminster Abbey.

1959: Unionist Party (Conservatives) takes over 50 per cent of the vote in Scotland.

1967: Winnie Ewing wins Hamilton for the SNP.

1969: Royal Commission under Lord Crowther.

1970: SNP win 11 per cent of the vote at the General Election.

1972: Wendy Wood (1892–1981) threatens to fast to the death for Home Rule.

1973: Launch of 'It's Scotland's Oil' campaign. Kilbrandon Report published. Margo MacDonald wins Govan for the SNP.

1974: SNP wins 30 per cent of the vote and 11 seats in October general election.

1977–78: Scotland Bill passes with Cunningham amendment, requiring 40 per cent of the electorate to vote Yes.

1979: 52 per cent Yes vote for a Scottish Assembly on a 63 per cent turnout. SNP vote falls to 17 per cent in General Election and all but two seats are lost.

1983: SNP vote falls to 12 per cent in General Election.

1988: The SNP adopts the policy of 'Independence in Europe'. Jim Sillars wins Govan for the SNP.

1989: Scottish Constitutional Convention founded. The SNP gains 26 per cent of the vote in European elections.

1992: The SNP gains 21.5 per cent of the vote at the General Election on 9 April, but fails to win any seats despite much pre-election hype. In the May local elections, the SNP win control of West Lothian and Edinburgh gains its first Nationalist Lord Provost, Norman Irons.

1995: Scottish Convention's proposals for Home Rule launched on 30 November.

1996: Michael Forsyth returns the Stone of Destiny to Scotland.

1997: Scotland votes 74–26 in favour of a Parliament and 64–36 in favour of its having tax-varying powers.

1999: Scottish Parliamentary elections (May) result in a Lib-Lab administration. Parties favouring independence win 37 per cent of the vote and the SNP is the principal opposition party with 35 seats.

2000: The Scottish Executive's plan to describe itself as a 'government' meets with opposition in London.

INDEX